Consciousness

DETAIL FROM MICHELANGELO'S *CREATION OF ADAM* IN THE SISTINE CHAPEL. God is pictured on a background that bears more than a passing resemblance to a section of the human brain. A detailed comparison can be found in F. L. Meshberger, "An Interpretation of Michelangelo's *Creation of Adam* Based on Neuroanatomy," *Journal of the American Medical Association*, 264 (1990), 1837–41.

GERALD M. EDELMAN
and GIULIO TONONI

Consciousness

HOW MATTER BECOMES
IMAGINATION

ALLEN LANE
THE PENGUIN PRESS

ALLEN LANE
THE PENGUIN PRESS
Published by the Penguin Group
Penguin Books Ltd, 27 Wrights Lane, London W8 5TZ, England
Penguin Putnam Inc., 375 Hudson Street, New York, New York 10014, USA
Penguin Books Australia Ltd, Ringwood, Victoria, Australia
Penguin Books Canada Ltd, 10 Alcorn Avenue, Toronto, Ontario, Canada M4V 3B2
Penguin Books (NZ) Ltd, Private Bag 102902, NSMC, Auckland, New Zealand

Penguin Books Ltd, Registered Offices: Harmondsworth, Middlesex, England

First published in the USA as *A Universe of Consciousness* by Basic Books,
a member of the Perseus Books Group 2000
First published in Great Britain by Allen Lane The Penguin Press 2000
1 3 5 7 9 10 8 6 4 2

Printed and bound in Great Britain by The Bath Press, Bath
Cover repro and printing by Concise Cover Printers

A CIP catalogue record for this book is available from the British Library

ISBN 0-713-99308-1

Contents

Illustrations

Acknowledgments

We wish especially to thank our colleagues Ralph Greenspan, Olaf Sporns, and Chiara Cirelli for their useful suggestions and thought-provoking discussions during the writing of this book. We are also grateful to David Sington for his penetrating editorial suggestions and critical analysis. Jo Ann Miller, the executive editor of Basic Books, gave us valuable help in clarifying portions of the text. We, of course, take full responsibility for any inadvertent errors and deficiencies that may remain. Many of the ideas and most of the work described here occurred at the Neurosciences Institute, whose Fellows are dedicated to understanding how the brain gives rise to the mind.

Preface

Consciousness has been seen as both a mystery and a source of mystery. It is one of the main targets of philosophical inquiry, but only recently has it been accepted into the family of scientific objects that are worthy of experimental investigation. The reasons for this late acceptance are clear: Although all scientific theories assume consciousness and conscious sensation and perception are necessary for their application, the means to carry out scientific investigations of consciousness itself have only recently become available.

There is something special about consciousness: Conscious experience arises as a result of the workings of each individual brain. It cannot be shared under direct observation, as the physicist's objects can be shared. Thus, studying consciousness presents us with a curious dilemma: Introspection alone is not scientifically satisfactory, and though people's reports about their own consciousness are useful, they cannot reveal the workings of the brain underlying them. Yet, studies of the brain proper cannot, in themselves, convey what it is like to be conscious. These constraints suggest that one must take special approaches to bring consciousness into the house of science.

In this book, we do just that, and we develop ways to answer the following questions:

1. How does consciousness arise as a result of particular neural processes and of the interactions among the brain, the body, and the world?

2. How do these neural processes account for key properties of conscious experience? Each conscious state is unified and indivisible,

yet at the same time, each person can choose among an immense number of different conscious states.

3. How can we understand different subjective states—so-called qualia—in neural terms?

4. How can our understanding of consciousness help connect strictly scientific descriptions to the wider domain of human knowledge and experience?

To describe the neural mechanisms that give rise to consciousness, to show how the general properties of consciousness emerge as a result of the properties of the brain as a complex system, to analyze the origins of subjective states or qualia, and to show how the successful pursuit of all these efforts may change our views of the scientific observer and of long-held philosophical positions is, of course, a tall order, and in the short compass of this volume much of interest must be omitted. But the main outlines of a solution to the problem of consciousness can be sketched by paying close attention to our four basic questions. Our answers are based on the assumption that consciousness arises within the material order of certain organisms. However, we emphatically do not identify consciousness in its full range as arising solely in the brain, since we believe that higher brain functions require interactions both with the world and with other persons.

Once we establish this new understanding of how consciousness emerges, we touch on several interesting issues that derive from this perspective. We propose a new view of the scientific observer, and we explore how we can know what we know— the realm of epistemology. Finally, we discuss the question of which subjects are appropriate for scientific study. Exposing these matters to scrutiny is important because our position— that consciousness arises as a particular kind of brain process that is both highly unified (or integrated) and highly complex (or differentiated)—has wide-ranging implications.

To untangle the bases of consciousness and account for some of its properties, we consider a number of challenging subjects. Indeed, before we get to the central issue, the neural substrate of consciousness, we review structural and functional features of brain organization, as well as certain essential aspects of brain theory. To make the task easier for the reader, we have prefaced each major part of the book with a prologue and each chapter with a brief introduction. We suggest that to obtain a synoptic view, the reader peruse in order the six prologues and the introductions to the chapters. Doing so will help keep the whole picture in mind, especially in chapters that are necessary for analyzing consciousness but are not directly concerned with it. As for the later chapters, only two (chapters 10 and 11) have explicit mathematical content. The reader who is not inclined to follow the details may get a reasonable understanding of their meaning by perusing the figures and "humming the tune." For those who wish to pursue specific issues or references, we have placed notes at the back of the book. The notes are not, however, necessary for comprehending our argument. We hope that by the end of the journey through the text, readers will find themselves with a new view of how matter becomes imagination.

PART ONE

The World Knot

When I turn my gaze skyward I see the flattened dome of the sky and the sun's brilliant disc and a hundred other visible things underneath it. What are the steps which bring this about? A pencil of light from the sun enters the eye and is focussed there on the retina. It gives rise to a change, which in turn travels to the nerve layer at the top of the brain. The whole chain of these events, from the sun to the top of my brain, is physical. Each step is an electrical reaction. But now there succeeds a change wholly unlike any that led up to it, and wholly inexplicable by us. A visual scene presents itself to the mind: I *see* the dome of the sky and the sun in it, and a hundred other visual things beside. In fact, I perceive a picture of the world around me.[1]

With this simple example, in 1940, the great neurophysiologist Charles Sherrington illustrated the problem of consciousness and his belief that it was scientifically inexplicable.

A few years earlier, Bertrand Russell used a similar example to express his skepticism about the ability of philosophers to arrive at a solution:

We suppose that a physical process starts from a visible object, travels to the eye, there changes into another physical process, causes yet another physical process in the optic nerve, and finally produces some effects in the brain, simultaneously with which we see the object from which the process started, the seeing being something "mental," totally different in character from the physical processes, which precede and accompany it. This view is so queer that metaphysicians have invented all sorts of theories designed to substitute something less incredible.[2]

No matter how accurate the description of the physical processes underlying it, it is hard to conceive how the world of subjective experience—the seeing of blue and the feeling of warmth—springs out of mere physical events. And yet, in an age in which brain imaging, general anesthesia, and neurosurgery are becoming commonplace, we are aware that the world of conscious experience depends all too closely on the delicate workings of the brain. We are aware that consciousness, in all its glory, can be annihilated by a minuscule lesion or a slight chemical imbalance in certain parts of the brain. In fact, our conscious life is annihilated every time the mode of activity in our brain changes and we fall into dreamless sleep. We are also aware that our own private consciousness is, in a profound sense, all there is. The flattened dome of the sky and the hundred other visible things underneath, including the brain itself—in short, the entire world—exist, for each of us, only as part of our consciousness, and they perish with it. This enigma wrapped within a mystery of how subjective experience relates to certain objectively describable events is what Arthur Schopenhauer brilliantly called the "world knot."[3] Despite the appearance of mystery, the best hope of disentangling this knot will come from a scientific approach that combines testable theories and well-designed experiments. This book is dedicated to this end.

CHAPTER ONE

Consciousness: Philosophical Paradox or Scientific Object?

The subject of consciousness has not lacked for human attention. In the past, it was the exclusive domain of philosophers, but recently both psychologists and neuroscientists have begun to attack the so-called mind-body problem or, in Schopenhauer's suggestive phrase, "the world knot." In this chapter we briefly review classical and modern approaches to consciousness. We point out various positions taken by philosophers, psychologists, and neuroscientists, rejecting some of the more flagrant ones, such as dualism or extreme reductionism. We suggest that consciousness can be considered a scientific subject and that it is not the sole province of philosophers.

Everyone knows what consciousness is: It is what abandons you every evening when you fall asleep and reappears the next morning when you wake up. This deceptive simplicity reminds us of what William James said of attention at the turn of the century: "Everyone knows what attention is. It is the taking possession by the mind, in clear and vivid form, of one out of what seem several simultaneously possible objects or trains of thought."[1] More than one hundred years later, many think that neither attention nor consciousness is understood in any fundamental sense.

This lack of understanding is certainly not because of lack of attention in philosophical or scientific circles. Ever since René Descartes, few subjects have preoccupied philosophers so consistently as the riddle of consciousness. For Descartes, as for James more than two centuries later, to be conscious was synonymous with "to think": James's stream of thought, for example, was nothing but the stream of consciousness. The *cogito ergo sum*, "I think therefore I am," which Descartes posed as the foundation of his philosophy in his *Meditationes de Prima Philosophia*,[2] was a direct recognition of the centrality of consciousness with respect to both ontology (what is) and epistemology (what and how we know).

If taken too seriously, "I am conscious, therefore I exist" can lead to solipsism, the view that nothing exists but one's individual consciousness, evidently not a view that can appeal to two authors who are sharing the writing of a book. More realistically (pun intended), that starting point leads to idealistic positions that emphasize mind over matter—ideas; perception; thought; or, in one word, consciousness. By taking mind as a starting point, however, idealistic philosophies must take pains to explain matter—which is not necessarily a better predicament than starting from mere matter to derive mind.

Descartes argued that there is an absolute distinction between mental and material substance. The defining characteristic of matter, he thought, is to be extended, to occupy space, and thus be susceptible to physical explanation, whereas the defining characteristic of mind is to be conscious or, in a broad sense of the term, to think. In this view, mental substance exists in the form of individual minds. In this way, Descartes inaugurated dualism, a position that is unsatisfactory scientifically but appears intuitively simple and appealing until one attempts to explain the connection between the mind and the body (see figure 1.1). Since the days of Descartes, philosophers have suggested versions of dualism or related alternatives. For example, a related theory is epiphenomenalism, which agrees with other theories in holding that mental events and physical events are different but maintains that the only true causes of mental experiences are physical events, with mind as a causally inefficacious by-product. In the words of Thomas Huxley, "consciousness would appear to be related to the mechanism of [the] body simply as a collateral product of its working, and to be as completely without any power of modifying that working as the steam whistle that accompanies the working of a locomotive engine is without influence upon its machinery."[3]

In more recent times, philosophers have taken a materialistic stance, holding that the mind and consciousness are identical to the operations of the brain or, at least, to certain of these operations. Some materialistic positions go so far as to deny any ontological or epistemic validity to consciousness; they insist that there is literally nothing else beyond the functioning of brain circuits or, at least, that there is nothing else that needs to be explained. Several philosophers have suggested that once we understand the workings of the brain sufficiently well, the concept of consciousness will evaporate just as the concept of phlogiston (a hypothetical volatile constituent of all combustible substances that was thought to be released as a flame in combustion) evaporated when oxidation was understood. The mind-body problem is thus made to disappear by denying or explaining away the consciousness side of it. Other materialistic positions insist that although consciousness is generated by physical events in the brain, it is not reduced to them but, rather, emerges from them, just as the properties of water emerge from the chemical combination of two hydrogens and one oxygen but are not directly reducible to the properties of hydrogen or oxygen alone. Such positions come in various flavors, but, in general, they grant consciousness some residual status, at least from the point of view of explanation. Nevertheless, they insist that there is no "consciousness" substance separate from a "brain" substance.

The philosophical debate on the mind-body problem is by now extremely sophisticated and, in their variety, some current disputes rival those that flourished among post-Cartesian philosophers. As we had

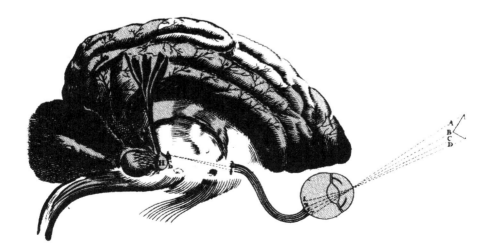

FIGURE 1.1   A diagram by Descartes illustrating his ideas about how the brain forms mental images of an object. The transaction between mental substance and physical substance was supposed to take place in the pineal gland (H).

Spinoza's dual-aspect theory, Malebranche's occasionalism, Leibniz's paral-
lelism and his doctrine of preestablished harmony, we now have the identity
theory, the central state theory, neutral monism, logical behaviorism, token
physicalism and type physicalism, token epiphenomenalism and type
epiphenomenalism, anomalous monism, emergent materialism, eliminative
materialism, various brands of functionalism, and many others.[4]

Despite the profusion of philosophical positions, it appears unlikely that
philosophical arguments alone will lead to a satisfactory solution to the
mind-body problem. In the words of Colin McGinn,[5] a philosopher who
takes an extreme position: "We have been trying for a long time to solve the
mind-body problem. It has stubbornly resisted our best efforts. The mystery
persists. I think the time has come to admit candidly that we cannot solve
the mystery. [We still have no idea of how] the water of the physical brain is
turned into the wine of consciousness."

There is indeed a fundamental limitation on philosophical efforts to discern the origins of consciousness that arises, in part, from the presumption
that the sources of conscious thought can be revealed by thinking alone.
This presumption is as patently inadequate as efforts in previous times to
understand cosmogony, the basis of life, and the fine structure of matter in
the absence of scientific observations and experiments. In fact, philosophers
have excelled not so much in proposing solutions to the problem but in
pointing out just how intractable the problem is. What many philosophers
are reiterating amounts to this: No matter what scientists do, the first-
person and third-person perspectives of conscious individuals will not be reconciled, the explanatory gap will not be bridged, and the "hard" problem—
the generation of sensations, of phenomenal or experiential states out of the
buzzing of neurons—will not be solved.[6]

How have scientists fared in explaining the mystery? If we look at psychology, we find that the "science of the mind" always had trouble in accom-
modating what should be its central topic—consciousness—within an
acceptable theoretical framework. The introspectionist tradition of
Titchener and Külpe[7] was the psychological counterpart of idealistic or phenomenological positions in philosophy; it attempted to describe consciousness viewed by the individual exclusively from the inside, hence the term
introspection. Many introspectionists were psychological atomists; not unlike
some present-day neurophysiologists, they postulated that consciousness
was made up of elementary parts that could be catalogued (never mind that
the American school came up with more than 40,000 sensations and the
German school with just 12,000). By contrast, behaviorists notoriously

attempted to eliminate consciousness completely from scientific discourse, a position not unlike that of some contemporary philosophers.

Present-day cognitive psychologists have reintroduced consciousness and mind as legitimate concepts. They conceive of consciousness as either a special module or a stage in the flowchart delineating an information-processing hierarchy. In fact, cognitive psychologists often consider consciousness in terms of a limited-capacity bottleneck in our mental functioning, possibly due to an unspecified limitation of our brains. Several such models of the functions associated with consciousness have been formulated, drawing their inspiration from cognitive psychology or artificial intelligence or using metaphors borrowed from computer science, such as that of a central executive system or an operating system. Psychologists have also used the metaphor of consciousness as a unified stage, scene, or theater in which information from multiple sources is integrated for the control of behavior.[8] Some of these intuitions may point in the right direction, while others may be as misleading as they are potentially appealing.

What is certain, however, is that such metaphors cannot substitute for a genuine scientific understanding of consciousness. Cognitive models usually have little to offer vis-à-vis the experiential, phenomenal side of conscious experience. Looked at from the perspective of these models, consciousness as a phenomenal experience (and often an emotional one) may as well not exist, as long as some of its presumed functions, such as control, coordination, and planning, can be carried out. Standard cognitive accounts offer no convincing explanation of why multiplication performed by a human is a slow and hesitant conscious process while the same multiplication quickly carried out by a pocket calculator is presumably not conscious at all. Nor do they explain why the complicated processes needed to balance your weight when you walk or to articulate words when you speak should remain unconscious, while the simple application of pressure to your finger produces a conscious experience. Finally, as many critics have pointed out, any information-processing, strictly functionalistic approach to consciousness has little to say about the fact that consciousness requires the activity of specific neural substrates. These substrates are actually the central concern of neuroscientists.

Except for fundamental observations about coma, anesthesia, and the like, neuroscientists used to be exceedingly careful in their approaches to consciousness. Most profess a convenient agnosticism about the subject and justify their caution by our present ignorance. Although many of them would probably subscribe to some kind of system-level explanation—if only they knew which one—for the present, they deem it more fruitful painstak-ingly to collect new facts and observations and to leave theorizing to the future. Over the past decade or so, however, something has definitely changed in the relationship between studies of consciousness and the neuro-sciences. Scientists seem less afraid of addressing the subject unabashedly, several books by neuroscientists have appeared, new journals have been launched, and studies have been conducted in which consciousness was actu-ally treated as an experimental parameter.[9]

Although certain recent "scientific" hypotheses do not cover as wide a spectrum as that offered by philosophers, they are in some ways even more exotic or extreme. For example, some neuroscientists have embraced dualis-tic positions according to which the conscious mind interfaces with the brain by virtue of "psychons" communicating with "dendrons" in certain areas of the left brain (Descartes suggested that the pineal gland was the site of the interaction because it is situated in the middle of the head).[10] Some scientists (who may or may not qualify as neuroscientists) have concluded that con-ventional physics is not enough of a basis for theorizing about conscious-ness—one has to invoke esoteric physical concepts, such as quantum gravity, to explain consciousness.[11]

Others have pursued what appears to be a more profitable strategy—focusing on the search for specific neural correlates of consciousness. Indeed, in this area definite progress has been made. For example, given the limited neurological knowledge of his times, James had to conclude that the neural basis for consciousness was nothing less than the whole brain.[12] Today, scientists are able to be more sophisticated and specific. Different authors believe that different brain structures support consciousness, structures with forbidding names, such as the intralaminar thalamic nuclei, reticular nucleus, mesencephalic reticular formation, tangential intracorti-cal network of layers I-II, and thalamocortical loops. Controversies rage over issues that were unthinkable at the time of James's writing: Does the pri-mary visual cortex contribute to conscious experience or not? Are areas of the brain that project directly to the prefrontal cortex more relevant than those that do not? Does only a particular subset of cortical neurons play a role? If so, are these neurons characterized by a special property or location? Do cortical neurons need to oscillate at 40 Hz or fire in bursts to contribute to conscious experience? Do different areas of the brain or groups of neurons generate different conscious fragments—a kind of microconsciousness?[13]

These questions are being debated more and more frequently, and new experimental data are fueling the debate. Yet, as this profusion of various questions and hypotheses indicates, something is definitely missing in attempts to identify the neural basis of consciousness with this or that set of neurons. Again, we confront the world knot. By what mysterious transformation would the firing of neurons located in a particular place in the brain or endowed with a particular biochemical property become subjective experience, while the firing of other neurons would not? It is not surprising that some philosophers view such attempts as prime examples of a category error—the error of ascribing to things properties that they cannot have.[14]

It is also not surprising that such errors are made, given how special consciousness is as a scientific object. In the next chapter we consider how the fundamental problem posed by this specialness may be confronted. We take the position that consciousness is not an object but a process and that, looked at from this point of view, it is indeed a fitting scientific subject.

CHAPTER TWO

The Special Problem of Consciousness

Science has always tried to eliminate the subjective from its description of the world. But what if subjectivity itself is its subject? In this chapter, we first explore the special status of consciousness and the assumptions necessary to study it from a scientific point of view. We then examine a fundamental problem posed by the existence of consciousness—one that needs to be explained by any scientific account. Consider this simple example: Why is it that when each of us performs certain discriminations, such as between light and dark, each of us is conscious, but a similar discrimination performed by a simple physical device is apparently not associated with conscious experience? This paradox suggests that attempts to understand consciousness that rely on the intrinsic properties of certain neurons or certain areas of the brain are doomed to failure. Next, we discuss the kinds of new approaches required if the bases of consciousness are to be understood. Finally, we delineate our strategy—to identify and characterize not just the neurons but the neural processes that can account for key properties of conscious experience.

We have looked at some of the obvious difficulties and uncertainties faced by both philosophers and scientists when dealing with consciousness. It is important to recognize the origin of these difficulties. Consciousness poses a special problem that is not encountered in other domains of science. In physics and chemistry, we are used to explaining certain entities in terms of other entities and laws. We can describe water with ordinary language, but we can also describe water, at least in principle, in terms of atoms and the laws of quantum mechanics. What we are really doing is connecting two levels of description of the same external entity—a commonplace one and a scientific one that is enormously powerful and predictive. Both levels of description—liquid water, or a particular arrangement of atoms behaving according to the laws of quantum mechanics—refer to an entity that is out there and that is assumed to exist independently of a conscious observer.

When we come to consciousness, however, we encounter an asymmetry. What we are trying to do is not just to understand how the behavior or cognitive operations of another human being can be explained in terms of the working of his or her brain, however daunting that task may be. We are not just trying to connect a description of something out there with a more sophisticated scientific description. Instead, we are trying to connect a description of something out there—the brain—with something in here—an experience, our own individual experience, that is occurring to us as conscious observers. We are trying to get inside—to know, as the philosopher Thomas Nagel felicitously phrased it—what it is like to be a bat.[1] We know what it is like to be us, but we would like to explain why we are conscious at all, why there is "something" it is like to be us—to explain how subjective, experiential qualities are generated. In short, we wish to explain the "I think therefore I am" that Descartes posited as the first, indisputable evidence upon which any philosophy should be built.

No amount of description will ever be able to account fully for a subjective experience, no matter how accurate that description may be. Many philosophers have used the example of color to make their point. No scientific description of the neural mechanisms of color discrimination, even if it is perfectly satisfactory, will make you understand *what it feels like* to perceive a particular color. No amount of description or theorizing, scientific or otherwise, will allow a color-blind person to experience color. In a famous philosophical thought experiment, Mary, a color-blind neuroscientist of the future, knows everything about the visual system and the brain, including the physiology of color discrimination. Yet, when she finally regains color vision, all her knowledge in no way substitutes for her genuine experience of color, for the way it feels like to see a color. John Locke clearly anticipated this problem long ago:[2]

A studious blind man, who had mightily beat his head about visible objects, and made use of the explication of his books and friends, to understand those names of light and colours which often came in his way, bragged one day, that he now understood what scarlet signified. Upon which his friend demanding, what scarlet was? the blind man answered, It was like the sound of a trumpet.

Locke also anticipated the so-called inverted spectrum argument, the idea that behavior may be identical, but subjective experience may be different, by wondering whether "the same object should produce in several men's minds different ideas at the same time; for example, the idea, that a violet produces in one man's mind by his eyes, were the same that a marigold produced in another man's, and vice versa."[3]

Philosophers have also imagined another conundrum, namely, the possibility of "zombies," creatures who look, act, and speak exactly like us, except for the fact that they are not conscious—that is, there is nothing it is like to be them. In fact, if one is a philosopher, one can easily imagine that everybody is a zombie (there would really be no way to find out) and that everybody's behavior could be described in terms of neurophysiology. But what about ourselves? We emphatically *are* conscious; we are not zombies. Yet no amount of description can account for the occurrence of first-person, phenomenal experience.

THE CONSCIOUS OBSERVER AND
SOME METHODOLOGICAL ASSUMPTIONS

Is a satisfactory scientific account of consciousness thus forever out of reach? Is there no way to untie the world knot? Or is there a way to break through both theoretically and experimentally to resolve the paradoxes of conscious awareness? The answer, we believe, lies in recognizing what scientific explanations in general can and cannot do. Scientific explanations can provide the conditions that are necessary and sufficient for a phenomenon to take place, can explain the phenomenon's properties, and can even explain why the phenomenon takes place only under those conditions. But no scientific description or explanation can substitute for the real thing. We all accept this fact when we consider, say, the scientific description of a hurricane: what kind of physical process it is, why it has the properties it has, and under what conditions it may form. But nobody expects that a scientific description of a hurricane will *be* or *cause* a hurricane.

Why, then, should we not apply exactly the same standards to consciousness? We should provide an adequate description of what kind of physical process it is, why it has the properties it has, and under what conditions it may occur. As we shall see, there is nothing about consciousness that precludes an adequate scientific description of the particular kind of neural process it corresponds to. What, then, is special about consciousness? What is special about consciousness is its relationship to the scientific observer. Unlike any other object of scientific description, the neural process we are attempting to characterize when we study the neural basis of consciousness actually refers to ourselves—it *is* ourselves—conscious observers (see figure 2.1). We cannot therefore tacitly remove ourselves as conscious observers as we do when we investigate other scientific domains.

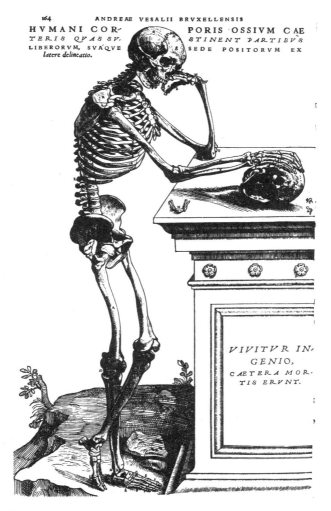

FIGURE 2.1   A skeleton observing a skull, from *De Fabrica Humani Corporis* (1543), one of the exquisite engravings from the work by Andreas Vesalius. The pose and the object tempt the title "The Thinker and the Thought."

Unlike any other entity, which we can describe in two different ways, commonsensically or scientifically as an outside object, with consciousness *we are what we describe* scientifically. This statement recognizes the special epistemic status of consciousness. If we accept it and devise new methods of description, we can avoid many paradoxes and, unencumbered by philosophical roadblocks, can still attempt to provide a satisfactory scientific account of consciousness as we do for any other scientific object: what kind of physical process it is, why it has the properties it has, and under what conditions it may occur. As we shall see, to do so, we have to develop a new view of how the observer may usefully investigate consciousness.

Before addressing this task, we adopt three related working assumptions as a methodological platform for the rest of this book: the physics assumption, the evolutionary assumption, and the qualia assumption.

The physics assumption states that only conventional physical processes are required for a satisfactory explanation of consciousness—no dualism is allowed. In particular, we assume that consciousness is a special kind of physical process that arises in the structure and dynamics of certain brains. The question is, of course, just what kind of physical process? In chapter 3 we note that conscious experience as a physical process can be characterized by certain general or fundamental properties. Two such properties are that conscious experience is integrated (conscious states cannot be subdivided into independent components) and, at the same time, is highly differentiated (one can experience billions of different conscious states). The scientific task, then, is to describe what particular kind of physical process can simultaneously account for these properties.

The evolutionary assumption states that consciousness evolved during natural selection in the animal kingdom. This assumption implies that consciousness is associated with biological structures, that it depends on dynamic processes generated by a certain morphology. Insofar as that morphology is the product of evolutionary selection, consciousness is not only such a product but it influences behaviors that are subject both to natural selection and to selective events within an individual animal's lifetime. Consciousness is efficacious. The evolutionary assumption also implies that because consciousness is a relatively recent development, not all animal species share it. This assumption about the evolutionary origin of consciousness helps us avoid fruitless efforts, such as attempting to characterize consciousness as a by-product of computation or applying exotic scientific notions like quantum gravity while ignoring neurology.

Finally, in accord with our view of the conscious observer, the qualia assumption states that the subjective, qualitative aspects of consciousness, being private, cannot be communicated directly through a scientific theory that, by its nature, is public and intersubjective. Accepting this assumption does not mean that the necessary and sufficient conditions for consciousness cannot be described, only that describing them is not the same as generating and experiencing them. As we shall see, qualia can be considered forms of multidimensional discrimination that are carried out by a complex brain. We can analyze them and give a prescription for how they emerge, but obviously we cannot give rise to them without first giving rise to appropriate brain structures and their dynamics within the body of an individual organism. This assumption helps us avoid the notion that a successful scientific theory of consciousness can act as a surrogate for conscious experience itself or allow one to grasp the *experience* of any quale simply on the basis of scientific descriptions and hypotheses, however pertinent they may be.

Exploring the philosophical implications of these assumptions in any depth would lead us into territories of ontology and epistemology that would distract us from our main task—a scientific explanation of consciousness and its properties. We therefore forgo the discussion of several interesting corollaries, which we consider only at the end of the book. Here, we simply mention useful points that will help us keep in mind the proper order of things. These points follow from our three methodological assumptions and, as we shall see, are important in understanding the special problems that must be addressed by a scientific analysis of consciousness. To avoid becoming mired too deeply in philosophical arguments, we should ponder the following:

Being and Describing. Being comes first, describing second. If consciousness is a physical process, albeit a special one, only embodied beings can experience consciousness as individuals, and formal descriptions cannot supplant or provide such experience. No description can take the place of the individual subjective experience of conscious qualia. The physicist Schrödinger once put it this way: No scientific theory itself contains sensations and perceptions. As the evolutionary assumption reminds us, not only is it impossible to generate being by mere describing, but, in the proper order of things, being precedes describing both ontologically and chronologically.

Doing and Understanding. A biological observation that is also connected to the evolutionary assumption is that during learning and in many matters of human comprehension, doing generally precedes understanding.[4] This is one of the great insights derived from studies of animal learning (animals can solve problems that they certainly do not understand logically); from psychophysiological studies of normal human subjects and those with certain kinds of frontal lesions (we choose the right strategy before we understand why);[5] from studies of artificial grammar (we use a rule before we understand what it is); and, finally, in innumerable studies of cognitive development (we learn how to speak before we know anything about syntax). Although this order can occasionally be inverted in linguistic animals such as ourselves, doing almost always comes first. This insight is important for the case we are making, since it helps avoid the difficulties encountered by formulations based on physics and artificial intelligence that do not take embodiment and action into account but instead assume that our perception and behavior are the result of a coded program.

Selectionism and Logic. The physics and evolutionary assumptions make explicit claims about what comes first and what follows. In other words, they force us to consider what is historically, pragmatically, and ontologically prior and what is derivative. Logic is, for example, a human activity of great power and subtlety. If the evolutionary assumption is correct, however, we can conclude that the workings of logic are not necessary for consciousness. Logic is not necessary for the emergence of animal bodies and brains, as it obviously is to the construction and operation of a computer. The emergence of higher brain functions depended instead on natural selection and other evolutionary mechanisms. Moreover, as we shall see, selectional principles akin to those of evolution apply to the actual workings of individual human brains well before they operate according to logic. This view has been called selectionism.[6] To encapsulate our position: Selectionism precedes logic. Later, we suggest that selectionist principles and logical principles each underlie powerful modes of thought. Now, however, it is essential to grasp that selectionist principles apply to brains and that logical ones are learned later by individuals with brains. Only with such notions in mind can one avoid the paradoxes that result from attempts to explain consciousness solely in terms of computation.

WHAT NEEDS TO BE EXPLAINED

The neuroscientist Charles Sherrington and the philosopher Bertrand Russell, in vividly illustrating the problem of consciousness, resorted to the same example: A pencil of light enters the eye, gives rise to a series of electrical and chemical steps, and finally produces effects at the top of the brain. But now, as Sherrington noted, "there succeeds a change . . . wholly inexplicable and unexpected": Each of us consciously *sees* the light. This seeing is something subjective, totally different from the objective physical processes that precede and accompany it. This, in a nutshell, is the special problem of consciousness—the world knot.

Sometimes the best way to solve a problem is simply to ask the right question. And sometimes the best way to ask the right question is to come up with an example that makes most explicit what the problem is about. Let us follow Sherrington's and Russell's leads and consider a simple physical device, such as a photodiode, that can differentiate between light and dark and provide an audible output.[7] Let us then consider a conscious human being performing the same task and then giving a verbal report. The problem of consciousness can now be posed in elementary terms: Why should the simple differentiation between light and dark performed by the human being be associated with and, indeed, require conscious experience, while that performed by the photodiode presumably does not? Or consider a thermistor that can differentiate between hot and cold. Why should the thermistor remain a simple, dull physical device, incapable of generating any subjective or phenomenal quality, while when we perform the same function we become conscious of cold, of hot, and possibly even of pain?

When considered in neural terms, this problem takes on an even more intriguing and paradoxical quality. Why should the activity of certain nerve cells, or neurons, in the brain correlate with the succession of private phenomenal states that we call conscious experience, while that of other neurons is deprived of such a remarkable property? For example, why is it that the activity of neurons in the retina that differentiate between light and dark is not directly associated with conscious experience, while that of certain neurons higher up in the visual system apparently is? Or why is it that we are conscious of whether we are hot or cold, but we are not directly conscious of whether our blood pressure is high or low? After all, there are intricate neural circuits that deal with the regulation of blood pressure just as there are neural circuits that deal with the regulation of body temperature. More generally, why would a mere location in the brain or the possession of a particular anatomical or biochemical feature make the activity of certain neurons so privileged that it suddenly imbues the possessor of that brain with the flavor of subjective experience, with those elusive properties that philosophers call qualia? This is the central problem of conscious experience.

Our strategy in attacking this problem is unusual. We do not attempt to explain everything—the many forms of perception, imagery, thought, emotion, mood, attention, will, and self-consciousness—and are not lured by the extraordinary variety of conscious phenomena. Instead, we concentrate on certain fundamental properties of consciousness, general properties that are shared by every conscious state. As we discuss in the next chapter, such properties include unity—the fact that each conscious state is experienced as a whole that cannot be subdivided into independent components—and informativeness—the fact that within a fraction of a second, each conscious state is selected from a repertoire of billions and billions of possible conscious states, each with different behavioral consequences. Rather than resort to vague metaphors, we consider what these properties mean in a fundamental theoretical sense and develop appropriate models, concepts, and measures to analyze them. This strategy expands on William James's prescient notion of consciousness as a *process*—one that is private, selective, and continuous yet continually changing.

FIGURE 2.2 William James, the great psychologist and philosopher, who gave the most wide-ranging account of the properties of conscious thought in his masterwork, *The Principles of Psychology.*

In the following chapters, we examine what kind of neural processes actually *explain* the fundamental properties of consciousness, rather than merely correlate with them. Many neuroscientists have emphasized particular neural structures whose activity correlates with conscious experience. It is not surprising that different neuroscientists end up favoring different structures. As we shall see in a number of cases, it is likely that the workings of each structure may contribute to consciousness, but it is a mistake to expect that pinpointing particular locations in the brain or understanding intrinsic properties of particular neurons will, in itself, explain why their activity does or does not contribute to conscious experience. Such an expectation is a prime example of a category error, in the specific sense of ascribing to things properties they cannot have.[8] We believe instead that what is crucial is to concentrate on the processes, not just the brain areas, that support consciousness and, more specifically, to focus on those neural processes that can actually account for the most fundamental properties of consciousness.

CHAPTER THREE

Everyman's Private Theater: Ongoing Unity, Endless Variety

Our strategy for explaining the neural basis of consciousness is to focus on the properties of conscious experience that are the most general, that is, that are shared by every conscious state. One of the most important of these properties is integration or unity. Integration refers to the fact that a conscious state cannot be subdivided at any one time into independent components by its experiencer. This property is related to our inability consciously to do more than two things at once, such as adding up a check while carrying on a heated argument. Another key, and apparently contrastive, property of conscious experience is its extraordinary differentiation or informativeness: At any moment, one out of billions of possible conscious states can be selected in a fraction of a second. We thus have the apparent paradox that unity embeds complexity—the brain must deal with plethora without losing its unity or coherence. Our task is to show how it does so.

The range and variety of conscious phenomenology stretch as widely as one's experience and as far as one's imagination can go; it is everyman's private theater. Books have been written about categorizing the realm of the conscious, and entire philosophical systems have been erected on the basis of attempts to decipher its structure. Consider some obvious characteristics of everyday conscious experience. Conscious states manifest themselves as sensory percepts; images; thoughts; inner speech; emotional feelings; and feelings of will, self, familiarity, and so on. These states can occur in any conceivable subdivision and combination. Sensory percepts—the paradigmatic constituents of conscious experience—come in many different modalities: sight, hearing, touch, smell, taste, proprioception (the feeling of our own body), kinesthesia (the sense of bodily positions), pleasure, and pain. Furthermore, each modality comprises many different submodalities. Visual experience, for example, includes color, form, movement, depth, and so on (see figure 3.1).

Though less vivid and less rich in detail than sensory percepts, thought, inner speech, and conscious imagery are all powerful reminders that a conscious scene can be constructed even in the absence of external inputs. Dreams are the most striking demonstration of this fact. Despite certain peculiarities, such as the dreamer's gullibility, singlemindedness, and loss of self-reflectiveness, dreaming and waking consciousness are remarkably alike: Visual objects and scenes are usually recognizable, language is intelligible, and even the stories that unfold in dreams are highly coherent and can be mistaken at times as true.[1]

FIGURE 3.1 Rousseau's painting *Virgin Forest with Setting Sun* (1910, Kunstmuseum, Basel), an apt emblem for the kinds of order and complexity within a working brain, provided that one removes the man and the jaguar.

Consciousness can be passive as well as active and effortful. When we let sensory input freely take possession of our conscious states, paying no attention to this or that in particular, consciousness is as receptive and broad as it is natural and effortless, as for example, when we stroll down the street and enjoy the sights of the town. On the other hand, when we specifically search for some item in the constant flow of sensory input to which we are exposed, perception becomes an action-oriented activity. The English language has incorporated the distinction between passive and active perception: seeing and watching, hearing and listening, feeling and touching. We are aware of when the more active side of consciousness is called for, since it usually requires an effort on our part. When we direct or focus attention or search for something in our consciousness; when we struggle to retrieve a memory; when we keep a number or an idea in working memory, perform a mental calculation or imagine a scene, or are deeply immersed in thought; when we plan, plot, or try to anticipate the consequences of our plans and plots; when we initiate an action or choose deliberately among multiple alternatives; when we impose our will; or when we struggle with a problem, consciousness is as active as it is effortful.

In most states of consciousness, there is an awareness of being situated or located in time and space and an awareness of our bodies, types of awareness that are clearly based on many different sources of information. There is also often a conscious fringe, which has to do with feelings of familiarity, of being right or wrong, of being satisfied or not. There can be, as well, all those refined discriminations that are the essence of culture and art.

Finally, conscious experience varies in its intensity; the global level of alertness can range from relaxed slumbering to the hypervigilant state of the fighter pilot in action, and sensory perception can be more or less vivid. There is the well-known ability, called attention, to select or differentially amplify certain conscious experiences to the exclusion of others. Furthermore, consciousness is inextricably linked to certain aspects of memory, as we emphasize in later chapters. Indeed, immediate memory, which lasts for fractions of a second, is often equated with consciousness itself. Working memory, the ability to "keep in mind" and manipulate conscious contents, such as phone numbers, sentences, and positions in space, for a few seconds is clearly closely related to consciousness.

This subdivision and analysis of different aspects of conscious experience could be extended ad libitum. One can spend a lifetime analyzing and refining one or another facet of one's conscious experience, from the appreciation of art to the discrimination of wines, from the exercise of will and concentration of thought to the attainment of blessed states of pure, unencumbered perception.

As interesting as the rich phenomenology of consciousness may be, we will not discuss its multitudinous aspects further. We simply acknowledge that the possible modalities and contents of conscious experience, although not arbitrary, are exceedingly numerous. Instead of analyzing the ever-changing situations played out in everyman's private theater, we concentrate on a few principles that, like the three unities of classical drama—time, place, and action—they all share. In this chapter, we therefore focus on those fundamental aspects of conscious experience that are common to all its phenomenological manifestations: privateness, unity, and informativeness.

THE IRREPRESSIBLE WHOLENESS OF BEING: PRIVATENESS, UNITY, AND COHERENCY OF CONSCIOUS EXPERIENCE

In the foreword to his classic, *The Integrative Action of the Nervous System*, Charles Sherrington expressed the personal and unitary character of consciousness with his usual eloquence: "Each waking day is a stage dominated for good or ill, in comedy, farce, or tragedy, by a *dramatis persona*, the 'self'. And so it will be until the curtain drops. . . . Although multiple aspects characterize [the conscious self], this self is a unity." William James also recognized that the unitary, private nature of consciousness is its foremost property. Notwithstanding the teachings of some Eastern religions, he concluded that each conscious event is a process that has a single "point of view" and has definite boundaries and cannot be shared:

> In this room—this lecture room, say—there are a multitude of thoughts, yours and mine, some of which cohere mutually, and some not. They are as little each-for-itself and reciprocally independent as they are all belonging together. They are neither: no one of them is separate, but each belongs with certain others and with none beside. My thought belongs with my other thoughts, and your thought with your other thoughts. . . . The only states of consciousness that we naturally deal with are found in personal consciousness, minds, selves, concrete particular I's and you's. . . . The universal conscious fact is not "feelings and thoughts exist," but "I think" and "I feel."[2]

In emphasizing the private character of conscious experience, both Sherrington and James referred to an individual self, endowed with autobiographical or episodic memories and with a notion of the past and the future. Inevitably, in an adult human being, the private becomes the personal, and the merely subjective becomes an actual subject. It is nearly impossible for us as humans to revert to or even contemplate a state of consciousness that is completely free of the self. In other words, we are agents, aware of being aware, and aware that we are making decisions that are based on our histories and plans.

As Sherrington recognized, the private nature of conscious events is closely coupled with their unity or their integration. Saying that a conscious state is unified and integrated simply means that the whole experienced conscious state is always more than the sum of its parts. Being in a particular conscious state, whether experiencing a pure sensation of warmth, a lively and multicolored view of a crowd in motion, the deepest intellectual ruminations, or the most improbable dreams, always constitutes information integrated into a unified coherent whole that is more than the sum of its parts.

Another way to say this is that a particular conscious state consists of a tightly interwoven set of relationships that cannot be fully broken down into independent components. Suppose you are presented for a fraction of a second with a visual stimulus comprising two adjacent digits, 1 and 7, as can be done with a tachistoscope. The conscious state that is triggered by this stimulus is not simply the sum of the state of seeing 1 and that of seeing 7; it is a unified picture, in this case of the number 17, which while it is happening cannot be decomposed into independent components.

An experiment on subjects with split brains offers a striking demonstration of this fact.[3] In this experiment, a sequence of spatial positions was displayed on the right side of a screen and presented to the left hemisphere, while an independent sequence of positions was displayed on the left side of the screen and presented to the right hemisphere. In these subjects, each hemisphere perceived a separate, simple visual problem, and the subjects were able to solve the double task well (the same thing would happen, of course, if the two different sequences were shown separately to two different individuals with normal brains). On the other hand, people with normal brains could not treat the two independent visual sequences as merely the sum of two independent, parallel tasks. They combined the visual information into a single conscious scene and thus into a single, large problem that they found difficult to solve. Although the purpose of this experiment was to demonstrate some peculiar consequences of the disconnection of the cerebral hemispheres, its results are equally interesting when viewed the other way around: They show that the connection of the cerebral hemispheres by a huge bundle of neural fibers—the corpus callosum—turns two simple, independent perceptual systems into a single, serial, unified perceptual system.

The unity of conscious experience is closely associated with the coherence of perceptual events. There are many demonstrations in psychology of so-called ambiguous figures—the Necker cube, the Rubin vase, the young lady–mother-in-law—that can be perceived only one way or the other (see figure 3.2). In these cases, we cannot be aware of two mutually incoherent scenes or objects at the same time because our conscious states are not only unified, but are internally coherent in the sense that the occurrence of a certain perceptual state precludes the simultaneous occurrence of another one.

This requirement that conscious states be coherent is also seen with ambiguous words. We know that the word *mean* can mean both average and lowly, yet at any given time we are conscious of only one of its meanings, depending on the context.

FIGURE 3.2 Tête à tête: an ambiguous figure.

The need to make a coherent, conscious scene out of seemingly disparate elements is seen at all levels and in all modalities of consciousness. A well-known case is binocular fusion. The images that the two eyes perceive are disparate, in the sense that they are slightly displaced horizontally one from the other. But the visual scene we perceive is a coherent synthesis of the two images, with the disparity cues added to provide a perception of depth. If the images presented to the two eyes are made artificially incongruous, for example, by showing one object to the right eye and a completely different object to the left eye, binocular fusion becomes impossible and it is replaced by binocular rivalry. Instead of perceiving an incongruent superposition of the two objects, a person alternately sees either one or the other of the two objects. Thus, perception chooses between fusion and suppression in the interest of coherence. Later, we discuss the usefulness of binocular rivalry in analyzing the neural correlates of conscious experience.

The unity and coherence of consciousness are strictly tied to consciousness's so-called *capacity limitation*—the fact that we cannot keep in mind more than a few things at a time. Try to juggle in your mind more than seven digits at a time or to keep more than four objects in the mind's eye at a given time. Or try to follow two movies simultaneously, and your perceptual and cognitive limitations will become obvious. In fact, the seeming richness of detail of many conscious scenes is more apparent than real. We believe that we can see at once all features of a landscape containing innumerable trees, houses, and people with different shapes, colors, movement, and depth or that we can perceive an extraordinary richness of detail in a single orchestral passage. However, if a visual scene is presented for a short period to avoid eye movements and if the elements of the scene are new and not predictably connected, psychologists have shown that out of this apparent richness we can accurately report just four to seven independent features or "chunks." For example, if we are shown twelve digits arranged in four rows of three for fewer than 150 milliseconds, we believe we see all the digits, and our retina certainly responds to them, but we can consciously report only four at a time (which four does not matter). As we shall see, this is a limit not on the information content of conscious states, but merely on how many nearly independent entities can be discriminated within a *single* conscious state *without interfering with the integration and coherence of that state*.[4]

When it comes to behavior, the limits imposed by conscious integration are even more severe. Consider how difficult it is to do two things at once. Try to add up a bill while arguing or rehearse a telephone number while giving directions or studying a map. Only if at least one of the two tasks is fairly automatic is the interference between the two tasks limited. Even more dramatically, we cannot make more than one decision—no matter how simple—within a few hundred milliseconds.[5] And, in fact, the duration of this interval—the so-called *psychological refractory period*—is comparable to the estimated duration of individual conscious states. Furthermore, regardless of how much we practice, we cannot learn, say, to discriminate simultaneously between two tones and two shapes; one discrimination must be completed, which takes at least 100-150 milliseconds, before the other one starts. This psychological refractory period cannot be eliminated. Evidently, almost everything can be automated but conscious choice itself. In other words, the limited capacity and serial succession of conscious states constitute the price that is paid for their integration—for the fact that they are not reducible to a simple sum of independent components.

Finally, we note that each conscious state is not only unified but more or less stable. Although conscious contents change continually (James called these changes "perches and flights"), to its possessor conscious experience remains continuous and even, some would say, seamless. Conscious states are stable and coherent enough to assure that we can recognize the world around us in terms of meaningful scenes, allowing us to make choices as well as plans.

Integration under Strain: Lessons from Neuropsychology

Some of the most striking indications of the inescapable unity of conscious experience come from the examination of certain pathological phenomena. Many neuropsychological disorders demonstrate that consciousness can bend or shrink and, at times, even split, but it does not tolerate breaks of coherence. For example, although a stroke in the right hemisphere leaves many people with their left sides paralyzed and affected with complete sensory loss, a number of them deny their paralysis, a phenomenon called *anosognosia*. If confronted with the evidence that their left arms and legs do not move, some of these people may even deny that these limbs belong to them, and they may treat them like extraneous objects. Some people with massive bilateral occipital damage cannot see anything, yet they do not recognize that they are blind (Anton's syndrome). People with split-brains provide another demonstration that consciousness abhors holes or discontinuities. After the surgery, the visual field of each hemisphere is split in two at the middle. However, people with split brains typically do not report any halving of their vision or any sharp boundary between vision and blindness on the midline. In fact, if the left hemisphere is shown only the right half of a face, the person reports seeing an entire face.[6]

People with *hemineglect*, a complex neuropsychological syndrome often seen when there are lesions of the right parietal lobe, are aware of only the left side of things, sometimes even of the entire left half of the world (see figure 3.3). For example, one man with this syndrome would only dress his right side; shave the right side of his face; read the right side of words, such as *cream* for *ice cream* and *ball* for *football*; ignore any visual or tactile stimuli presented to the left side; and draw only the right side of things.[7] With all this, he would deny that anything was wrong with him. Twenty-four hours before, his consciousness had suffered a terrible blow in the form of a stroke that had created a gaping hole in his right parietal brain and thereby in his ability to perceive the left side of things. Yet, his consciousness rapidly closed around this hole and sealed it off. What happened to this man's consciousness resembles, in a more abstract domain, what happens functionally to people who undergo a certain form of heart surgery: After a large wedge of heart is resected away and the margins are sutured together, the heart immediately goes on pumping in this reduced form.

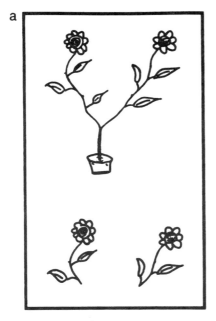 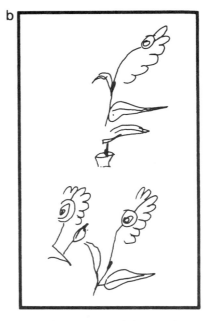

FIGURE 3.3 A drawing (a) was copied by a patient with a parietal defect leading to left hemineglect. The copy is shown in (b).

These and many other cases are often so counterintuitive that it is hard to imagine what it is like to be any of these patients. One is left with the impression that after a massive stroke or surgical resection, a conscious human being is rapidly "resynthesized" or reunified within the limits of a new, solipsistic universe that, to outside appearances, is warped and restricted. The network of relations that make up a conscious event is not left broken and discontinuous; rather, the loose ends tend rapidly to cohere again and bridge the rupture. The drive to integration is so strong that often no empty space is perceived where there is, in fact, a frightening gap. Apparently, the feeling of an absence is far less tolerable than the absence of a feeling. The detailed neural mechanisms underlying these syndromes are so far not well understood and are probably quite heterogeneous. Nevertheless, in most of these syndromes, the fact that consciousness may well shrink but always remain integrated and coherent suggests that the underlying perturbed neural processes behave in a similar way.[8]

THE INCOMPARABLE RICHNESS OF BEING: THE COMPLEXITY AND INFORMATIVENESS OF CONSCIOUS EXPERIENCE

If a fundamental property of conscious experience is that it is inherently private, unified, and coherent—in other words, integrated—an equally fundamental property is what we have called its extraordinary degree of differentiation or informativeness. What makes a conscious state informative is not how many "chunks" of information it appears to contain, but rather that its occurrence discriminates among billions of different states of affairs, each of which might lead to different behavioral outputs.[9] Think of the number of different people one has seen during a lifetime, the number of different paintings, or the number of different frames from different movies (see figure 3.4). The range of possible conscious states is such that there is no fear that experiences of life, art, poetry, and music will ever be exhausted. Yet, despite the enormous number of different conscious states that we can experience or imagine, we can easily discriminate among them, even if we cannot easily describe in words how they differ.

It is important to realize what this conclusion means. The ability to differentiate among a large repertoire of possibilities constitutes information, in the precise sense of "reduction of uncertainty."[10] Furthermore, conscious discrimination represents information *that makes a difference*, in the sense that the occurrence of a given conscious state can lead to consequences that are different, in terms of both thought and action, from those that might ensue from other conscious states.[11] Imagine paraphrasing a series of classic experiments,[12] in which different digits are flashed for, say, 100 milliseconds in front of a conscious person.[13] For instance, one could

FIGURE 3.4   EISENSTEIN REDIVIVUS. Shot sequence from the Odessa steps massacre in *Potemkin* hinting at the potentially endless number of conscious images one can experience.

flash the number 1, then flash the number 1,367, then the number 7,988, the number 3, and so on until all numbers between 1 and 9,999 have been presented in a random sequence. Each time, the person would experience a different, integrated conscious state, each of which could be easily discriminated. Furthermore, this discrimination could lead to demonstrable behavioral differences, such as speaking out a different number for each state.

Of course, instead of using numbers, we could repeat the experiment with words, and we would find that thousands and thousands of visually presented words could also be easily discriminated. Or we could use visual scenes. As shown in laboratory studies, our ability to discriminate and recognize photographs of scenes is exceptionally good, and we can rapidly differentiate among thousands of complex scenes within hundreds of milliseconds.[14] We could also present numbers and words through the ear, rather than through the eye. Furthermore, a little reflection suggests that this variety of discriminable situations would be only a small part of the tip of the iceberg. Consider again the occurrence of the conscious state corresponding to seeing the number 1. Its experienced occurrence contains far more information than is needed just to discriminate between the number 1 and 9,999 other numbers. For example, it conveys information about the fact that the person is in an experimental setting, that everything else is fine and quiet, that the person is supposed to sit through this boring task in the interest of science, and that there are no more pressing needs or issues. This additional information is typically not verbalized because it is part of a context that is constant and agreed upon, but it could certainly be verbalized, if necessary, and it is easy to reveal its presence. Consider what would happen if, while seeing the number 1, the person heard a fire alarm go off or felt hungry, bored, or anxious. Or if he were to see the same number 1 in a different setting, such as when waiting for his number in a line, when waiting for his placement in a sports event, or when choosing a television channel. Thus, the conscious state of seeing the number 1 in an experimental setting actually discriminates among a number of states that is as large as one cares to imagine, each of which can lead to different thoughts or actions.

Although we take for granted the enormous number of discriminable conscious experiences available to us, the enormity becomes strikingly apparent if this number is compared to the number of states presently discriminable by man-made gadgets. Consider, for instance, a digital camera faced with the same experiment as our conscious person. Each pixel of the camera would be able to discriminate between two states, that is, the states corresponding to the presence of a black or a white dot in its "visual field," respectively.[15] If we consider not just one pixel, but all the pixels of the camera, their joint state would be different for different stimuli, and there could be as many such states as there are images that can be displayed on a television screen. However, it is crucial to realize that these states cannot be discriminated by the camera itself: In no way does the occurrence of this or that state in any subset of the pixels make a difference to the state of the rest of the camera.[16]

Let us now imagine that the camera is connected to a gadget capable of "reading" strings of digits and converting them into a word-processing text. In this case, the occurrence of different intrinsic states of the scanner does make a difference, since it leads each time to a different outcome, such as the recognition of a different digit. This gadget can discriminate among a certain number of integrated states. However, over a fraction of a second, even a sophisticated scanner-software combination can discriminate among at most a few digits or a few letters and little more. It would never be able to discriminate among the different contexts that we previously mentioned. These contexts would make absolutely no difference to the gadget whether, for example, it were reading 1 with or without the fire alarm ringing. To attempt to compare the information integrated by such an artifact and that integrated by a conscious state, think of all the discriminable conscious states that each of us has experienced and will presumably go on experiencing. The enormous variety of discriminable states available to a conscious human being is clearly many orders of magnitude larger than those available to anything we have built. Whether we can verbally describe these states satisfactorily or not, billions of such states are easily discriminable by the same person, and each of them is capable of bringing about different consequences.

This perspective makes it easy to see where many of the paradoxes about conscious experience originate. Remember the example from chapter 2 of the photodiode that can differentiate between light and dark and provide an audible output, compared to a conscious human being performing the same task and giving a verbal report. Why should the simple differentiation between light and dark performed by the human being be associated with conscious experience, while that performed by the photodiode is not? The paradox disappears if one considers that to a photodiode, the discrimination between darkness and light is the only one available, and therefore it is only minimally informative. To a human being, in contrast, an experience of complete darkness and an experience of complete light are two special conscious experiences selected out of an enormous repertoire, and their selection thus implies a correspondingly large amount of information and discrimination among potential actions.

Although all these examples are based on the discrimination among conscious states referring to external stimuli, the information content of a conscious state has to do with the occurrence of a conscious state itself, and it does not necessarily need to be related directly to the external world. Dreams, for instance, can be as informative as waking conscious events, to such an extent that they can be used as sources of inspiration and insight. Indeed, under certain conditions, conscious states occurring in dreams may even determine immediate behavior. This possibility is strikingly demonstrated by a rare disorder, the REM (rapid eye movement) sleep behavior disorder, in which a lesion in the brainstem abolishes the behavioral paralysis that we normally experience during dreams.[17] People affected by such a disorder will act out their dreams, that is, they will produce a different behavioral act, depending on the particular conscious state they were experiencing in their dream. For example, it was reported that a man strangled his wife while in the midst of a dream.[18] Schizophrenic behavior provides an equally striking illustration. Anyone who has witnessed a schizophrenic person hallucinating knows that the information content of a conscious state can drive behavior in a specific way even if it does not originate in the external world.

It is important to note that the enormous information content of any given conscious state does not mean that conscious contents are arbitrary. Although each of us constantly moves among billions of discriminable conscious events, there are clear limits to what we can and cannot be conscious of. People who are blind from birth will never know what it feels like to have visual percepts. Before they learn to speak, children cannot be conscious of the meaning of a Shakespearean sonnet, not even in their dreams. Parts of our brain that regulate our blood pressure are constantly active, yet we have no conscious feeling of our blood pressure; to register it, we need an external device.

In the following chapters, we consider why certain activities of our brain and not others affect our consciousness. For the moment, however, we conclude that the occurrence of a given conscious state is immensely informative, in the sense that its occurrence rules out or discriminates among billions and billions of other conscious states, each of which may lead to different potential consequences. We have also concluded that the unity, coherence, and privateness of consciousness are among its most striking general phenomenological features and that the very unity of consciousness entails a bottleneck in choice and action, as well as an inevitable serial succession of conscious states. Can we relate these observations to actual brain events? We turn to the issue in the next part of the book.

PART TWO

Consciousness and the Brain

It is a reflection of human arrogance that entire philosophical systems have been constructed on the basis of subjective phenomenology—the conscious experience of a single, philosophically inclined individual. As Descartes recognized and took as his point of departure, such arrogance is partly justified, since our conscious experience is the only ontology of which we have direct evidence. As Schopenhauer noted,[1] this statement generates a curious paradox. The immense richness of the phenomenological world that we experience—conscious experience as such—appears to be dependent on what seems a mere trifle in the furniture of that world, a gelatinous piece of tissue contained in the skull. Our brain, presenting itself as a fleeting and minor actor on the stage of consciousness that most of us have never seen, seems to hold the key to the entire performance. As we are all too painfully aware when we enter a hospital, any insult to our brain may permanently modify our entire world. Indeed, we can be annihilated by a simple chemical, anesthetic, or toxin, acting on our brain.

In order to give readers a better understanding about this remarkable organ, we first provide some basic information on the structure and dynamics of the brain and of its cells or neurons. With this picture of the brain in place, we then consider a number of neurophysiological and neuropsycho-

logical facts that shed significant light on the neural mechanisms of consciousness. In organizing these facts, we present evidence that the neural processes
underlying conscious experience share common general characteristics.

Our analysis leads to several conclusions. First, conscious experience
appears to be associated with neural activity that is distributed simultaneously across neuronal groups in many different regions of the brain.
Consciousness is therefore not the prerogative of any one brain area;
instead, its neural substrates are widely dispersed throughout the so-called
thalamocortical system and associated regions. Second, to support conscious
experience, a large number of groups of neurons must interact rapidly and
reciprocally through the process called reentry. If these reentrant interactions are blocked, entire sectors of consciousness disappear, and consciousness itself may shrink or split. Finally, we show that the activity patterns of
the groups of neurons that support conscious experience must be constantly
changing and sufficiently differentiated from one other. If a large number of
neurons in the brain start firing in the same way, reducing the diversity of
the brain's neuronal repertoires, as is the case in deep sleep and epilepsy,
consciousness disappears.

CHAPTER FOUR

Building a Picture
of the Brain

To understand consciousness as a process, we must understand how the brain works; we must know about its architecture, its development, and its dynamic functions. This chapter presents a usable but by no means exhaustive picture of the brain, highlighting the brain's most important features: its anatomical organization and the remarkable dynamics that it generates. Although it is painted with a broad brush, this picture is necessary for understanding how consciousness emerges.

The brain is among the most complicated objects in the universe and is certainly one of the most remarkable structures to have emerged during evolution. Even before the advent of modern neuroscience, it was well known that the brain is necessary for perception, feelings, and thoughts. Less obvious is how consciousness is causally associated with certain brain processes and not others.

As an object and a system, the human brain is special—its connectivity, dynamics, mode of functioning, and relation to the body and the world is like nothing else science has yet encountered. This uniqueness makes building a picture of the brain an extraordinary challenge. Although we are far from a complete view of that picture, a partial view is better than none, especially if it gives us enough information to generate a successful theory of consciousness.

THE JUNGLE IN THE HEAD

The adult human brain (see figure 4.1) weighs about 3 pounds and contains about 100 billion nerve cells, or neurons. The most recently evolved outer corrugated mantle of the human brain, the cerebral cortex, contains about 30 billion neurons and 1 million billion connections, or synapses. If we counted one synapse per second, we would not finish counting for 32 million years. If we considered the number of possible neural circuits, we would be dealing with hyperastronomical numbers: 10 followed by at least a million zeros. (There are 10 followed by 79 zeros, give or take a few, of particles in the known universe.)

Neurons, which come in a variety of shapes, have treelike projections called dendrites that receive synaptic connections. They also have a single longer projection, called an axon, that makes synaptic connections either at the dendrites, or at the cell bodies, of other neurons. No one has made an exact count of different types of neurons in the brain, but a crude estimate of fifty would not be excessive. The lengths and branching patterns of dendrites and axons from a given type of neuron fall within certain ranges of variation, but even within a given type, no two cells are alike (see figure 4.2).

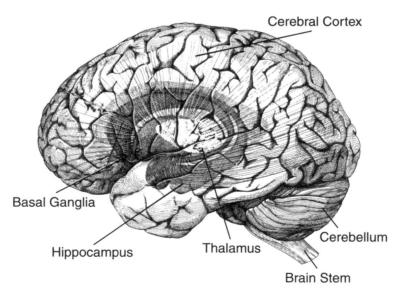

FIGURE 4.1 GROSS ANATOMY OF THE BRAIN. The figure shows: (1) the cerebral cortical mantle connected to the thalamus (the white oval in the middle), together constituting the thalamocortical system; (2) the three great cortical appendages (basal ganglia, cerebellum, and hippocampus); and (3) the brain stem, the oldest part of the brain, which contains the source of several diffusely projecting value systems.

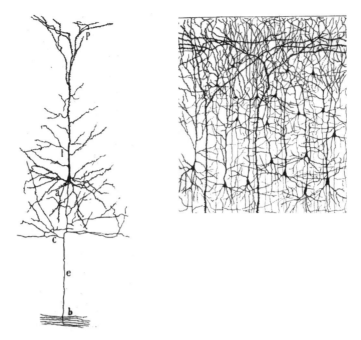

FIGURE 4.2 TWO ILLUSTRATIONS FROM THE GREATEST NEUROHISTOLOGIST OF MODERN TIMES, SANTIAGO RAMON Y CAJAL. The left-hand drawing shows a cortical neuron with an apical dendritic tree ascending and an axon descending from a small cell body. The right-hand drawing is a depiction of a meshwork of neurons in the cerebral cortex. The mesh that is stained with the so-called Golgi stain actually appears sparse because only a small proportion of the cells are impregnated by the stain.

A key characteristic of neuronal patterns at the microscopic level is their density and spread. The body of a single neuron measures up to about 50 microns (thousandths of a millimeter) in diameter, although its axon can range from microns to meters in length. In a tissue like the cerebral cortex, neurons are packed together at an extraordinary density; if all of them were stained with silver in the so-called Golgi stain used to visualize them in the microscope, the stained microscopic section would be pitch-black. (Actually, this classical stain is useful because it affects only a small fraction of cells in a given area, so the cells can be individually discerned, as figure 4.2 shows.) Interspersed among the neurons are nonneuronal cells, called glia, that support and nourish nerve cells without being directly involved in signaling. In some places, glia even outnumber neurons. Another important feature is the extraordinary blood supply that nourishes this jungle. Through large arteries emptying into a dense network of capillaries, the brain receives the oxygen and glucose it needs as the most metabolically active organ in the body. The regulation of blood flow is exquisite down almost to single neurons, and synaptic activity is tightly linked to blood flow and oxygenation. Indeed, modern techniques to image brain activity in living people rely on changes in blood flow and oxygenation.

In the dense networks of the brain, it is the spread and overlap of neuronal arbors—of dendritic trees and axonal projections—that are the most striking features. In some places, the spatial spread of an axon forming an arbor can be over a cubic millimeter. Overlapping that arbor, with all its intricate branchings, are arbors from countless other neurons. The overlap can be as great as 70 percent in three-dimensional space. (No self-respecting forest, made of trees and root structures, would permit such a large overlap.) Moreover, as the axonal arbors overlap, they can form an enormous variety of synapses, or connections (see figure 4.3), with cells in the paths of their branches, resulting in a pattern that is unique for each small volume of brain tissue. To this day, though we can trace the full arborization of a single nerve cell, we have no clear picture of the microanatomy of the interspersed arbors of the many neighboring cells at the scale of their synapses.

While the general cellular functions of neurons, such as respiration, genetic inheritance, and protein synthesis, are like those of other cells in the body, the special features of these cells related to the functioning of neurons mainly concern their ability to communicate through connections called synapses. Neurons come in two flavors, excitatory and inhibitory, and at the microscopic level, their synapses have different and characteristic structures. But, for each, the basic principles are similar and involve both electrical and chemical signaling. Although in certain species some synapses can be completely electrical, the vast majority of the synapses in human brains are chemical. In most cases, the so-called presynaptic neuron and postsynaptic neuron are separated by a cleft forming a single synapse (see figure 4.3). The inside of a neuron is negatively charged with respect to the outside. After a cell is stimulated as a result of the flow of ions, such as sodium and potassium, across a particular portion of the cell membrane, it becomes less negative. The resulting electrical signal, called an action potential, spreads down an axon, and when it reaches the region of the synapse, it causes the release of neurotransmitters from a series of vesicles in the presynaptic neuron. If the neuron is excitatory, the released neurotransmitters then cross the synaptic cleft, bind to specific receptors on the postsynaptic neuron, and cause the postsynaptic neuron to become less negative. These processes occur over periods of tens to hundreds of milliseconds. If the postsynaptic neuron becomes sufficiently less negative after several such events, it will fire, (generate an action potential of its own), relaying the signal, in turn, to other neurons to which it is connected. This is the action of an excitatory neuron. Inhibitory neurons act similarly but change the electrical charge of the postsynaptic neuron in such a fashion as to prevent firing.

As intricate as the microstructure of neuronal connections may be, this intricacy is magnified by the number of different interactions, in space and time, that can affect synaptic transmission. The brain contains a variety of chemicals called neurotransmitters and neuromodulators that bind to a variety of receptors and act on various biochemical pathways. The chemical identity of these neurotransmitters and of their receptors, the statistics of their release, and the time and place of electrical and biochemical interactions all govern the thresholds of response of neurons in an extraordinarily intricate and variable manner. Furthermore, as a result of the release of the neurotransmitters, electrical signaling not only takes place, but leads to changes in the biochemistry and even in gene expression of the target neurons. This molecular intricacy and the resulting dynamics superimpose several more layers of variability on that of the neuroanatomical picture,

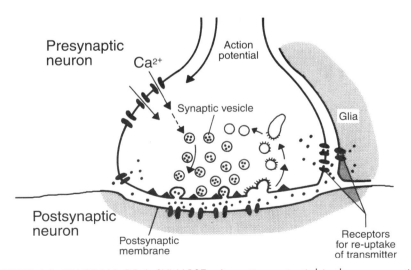

FIGURE 4.3 DIAGRAM OF A SYNAPSE. An action potential in the presynaptic neuron causes channels to open, and the influx of positively charged calcium ions leads to the release of a neurotransmitter into the synaptic cleft between the pre- and postsynaptic neurons. The transmitter molecules (dots) bind to receptors in the postsynaptic membrane and eventually cause the postsynaptic neuron to fire.

contributing to what may be called the historical uniqueness of each brain. Metaphorically, we can say that we house a jungle in our heads.

THE PRIMACY OF NEUROANATOMY

Despite the microanatomical variability of the brain, at the brain's higher levels of anatomical order, it is possible to distinguish important principles of organization. Indeed, if someone pointed a gun at us and threatened oblivion if we did not say the single word most significant for understanding the brain, we would say *neuroanatomy*. If we could only untangle its intricate connections fully, the brain would certainly qualify as the biological object with the most stunning morphology ever seen. And in biology, morphology is almost always the royal road to function.

Textbooks on neuroanatomy usually discuss one by one the various nuclei and regions of the brain, but for our purposes, we need to consider only three major topological arrangements in the brain that appear to be essential to understanding the brain's global functioning.

The first arrangement is a large, three-dimensional meshwork—the segregated yet integrated set of circuits constituting the so-called thalamo-cortical system (see figure 4.4A). This system is comprised of a structure located in the depths of the brain—the thalamus—which receives sensory and other inputs. The thalamus is reciprocally connected to the cerebral cortex, the convoluted sheet covering the surface of the brain. This sheet has six layers, each sending and receiving specific sets of outputs and inputs. The cortex and the thalamus are traditionally subdivided into a large number of areas that have different functions. This functional segregation is seen at many different spatial scales. For example, the back of the thalamocortical system is roughly devoted to perception, while the front is devoted to action and planning. Most of these cortical areas are assembled as maps: Neighboring neurons from one area connect with neighboring neurons in another. Different cerebral cortical areas and their associated thalamic nuclei are also specialized; some areas deal with visual stimuli, for instance, while others deal with acoustic stimuli and still others with tactile stimuli. Moreover, in the visual system, for example, different areas deal with different submodalities; some with visual form, others with color, still others with movement, and so on. Within each area, different groups of neurons deal preferentially with specific aspects of a stimulus; neighboring groups of neurons may deal with different orientations of a visual stimulus, for example.

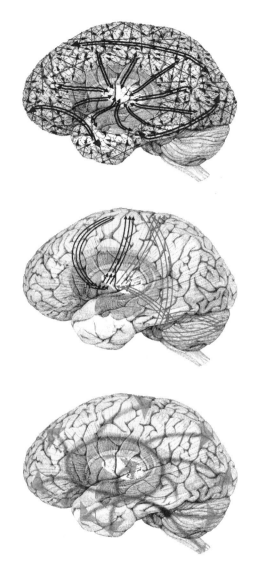

FIGURE 4.4 THREE MAIN TOPOLOGICAL ARRANGEMENTS OF FUNDAMENTAL NEUROANATOMY IN THE BRAIN. (A)The top diagram shows the thalamocortical system—a dense meshwork of reentrant connectivity between the thalamus and the cortex and between different cortical regions through so-called corticocortical fibers. (B)The middle diagram depicts long, polysynaptic loops that are arranged in parallel and that leave the cortex, enter the so-called cortical appendages (indicated here are the basal ganglia and the cerebellum), and return to the cortex. (C) The bottom diagram indicates one of the diffusely projecting value systems (the noradrenergic locus coeruleus), which distributes a "hairnet" of fibers all over the brain and can release the neuromodulator noradrenaline.

However, anatomical segregation is only half the story. The other half is anatomical integration: Most of these groups of neurons are reciprocally connected in certain patterns. Neurons within the same groups in a given location are tightly linked, so that many of them respond simultaneously when an appropriate stimulus is presented.[1] Neuronal groups with different locations but similar specificities are preferentially connected to each other; for example, neuronal groups that respond to vertical edges are linked by reciprocal connections much more tightly than neuronal groups that respond to edges in different orientations. Furthermore, neuronal groups that respond to nearby positions in the visual field are more strongly connected than those that respond to distant positions. In this way, when a long contour or line is presented to the eye, these linked groups fire simultaneously. Similar rules seem to apply to other areas of the cortex, whether these areas are devoted to perception or to action. At a still larger scale, cortical areas containing a large number of neuronal groups are themselves linked by reciprocal, convergent, and divergent connection paths—paths that connect disperse areas to a local area, and vice versa. Such paths from one area to another are sometimes called projections. There are, for example, at least three dozen visual areas in the visual system of the monkey (and probably more in humans). These areas are linked by more than 305 connection paths (some with millions of axonal fibers), over 80 percent of which have fibers running in both directions. In other words, the different functionally segregated areas are, for the most part, reciprocally connected. These reciprocal pathways are among the main means that allow for the integration of distributed brain functions. They provide a major structural basis for *reentry*, a process of signaling back and forth along reciprocal connections,[2] that, as we describe later, offers the key to resolving the problem of integrating the various functionally segregated properties of brain areas despite the lack of a central coordinative area.

With some effort of imagination, we can therefore form the following picture of the thalamocortical mode of organization. There are hundreds of functionally specialized thalamocortical areas, each containing tens of thousands of neuronal groups, some dealing with responses to stimuli and others with planning and execution of action, some dealing with visual and others with acoustic stimuli, some dealing with details of the input and others with its invariant or abstract properties. These millions of neuronal groups are linked by a huge set of convergent or divergent, reciprocally organized connections that make them all hang together in a single, tight meshwork while they still maintain their local functional specificity. The result is a three-dimensional tangle that appears to warrant at least the following statement: Any perturbation in one part of the meshwork may be felt rapidly everywhere else. Altogether, the organization of the thalamocortical meshwork seems remarkably suited to integrating a large number of specialists into a unified response.

The second topological arrangement is organized not at all like a meshwork but, rather, like a set of parallel, unidirectional chains that link the cortex to a set of its appendages, each with a special structure—the cerebellum, the basal ganglia, and the hippocampus. The cerebellum is a beautiful structure, appended to the back of the brain, that is organized in thin, parallel microzones, many of which receive connections from the cortex, and after a number of synaptic steps project back to the thalamus and through it back to the cortex. Traditionally, the cerebellum is considered to be concerned with the coordination and synchrony of motion, although its involvement in certain aspects of thought and language appears to be substantial. Another cortical appendage, called collectively the basal ganglia, consists of a set of large nuclei deep in the brain that receive connections from much of the cortex, go through a series of successive synaptic steps, and then project to the thalamus and from there back to the cortex. These nuclei are involved in the planning and execution of complex motor and cognitive acts and are dysfunctional in Parkinson's and Huntington's diseases.

Still another structural motif appears in a third cortical appendage, the hippocampus, an elongated structure that runs along the lower edge of the temporal cortex of the brain. Inputs from many different cortical areas are funneled into the hippocampus, which deals with these inputs in a series of synaptic steps and sends projections back to many of the same cortical areas. The hippocampus probably subserves many functions, but it certainly plays a major role in consolidating short-term memory into long-term memory in the cerebral cortex.

Although the specific ways in which these different cortical appendages interact with the cortex are of central importance, the appendages all seem to share a fundamental mode of organization (especially the cerebellum and basal ganglia): Long, parallel paths involving multiple synapses leave the cerebral cortex and reach successive synaptic stations within these cortical appendages and, eventually, whether they pass through the thalamus or not, they go back to the cortex (see figure

4.4B). This serial polysynaptic architecture differs radically from that of the thalamocortical system: The connections are generally unidirectional, rather than reciprocal, and form long loops, and there are relatively few horizontal interactions among different circuits except for, possibly, those locally responsible for reciprocal inhibition. In short, these systems seem admirably suited to the execution of a variety of complicated motor and cognitive routines, most of which are as functionally insulated as possible from each other, a feature that guarantees speed and precision in their execution.

The third kind of topological arrangement resembles neither a meshwork nor a set of parallel chains, but, rather, a diffuse set of connections resembling a large fan (see figure 4.4C). The origin of the fan is in a relatively small number of neurons that are concentrated in specific nuclei in the brainstem and hypothalamus that have beguiling and imposing technical names connected with the substance they release: the noradrenergic locus coeruleus, the serotonergic raphé nucleus, the dopaminergic nuclei, the cholinergic nuclei, and the histaminergic nuclei. All these nuclei project diffusely to huge portions of the brain, if not to all of it. The locus coeruleus, for example, consists of only thousands of neurons in the brainstem, but sends a diffuse sweeping "hairnet" of fibers to cover the entire cortex, hippocampus, basal ganglia, cerebellum, and spinal cord, and by this means, has the potential to influence up to billions of synapses. Neurons belonging to these nuclei appear to fire whenever something important or salient occurs, such as a loud noise, a flash of light, or a sudden pain. The firing of these neurons brings about the diffuse release in the brain of chemicals called neuromodulators that are capable of influencing not only neural activity but neural plasticity—a change in the strength of synapses in neural circuits yielding adaptive responses. Given their unique anatomical properties, their discharge characteristics, their effects on target neurons and synapses, and their evolutionary origins, we have designated them collectively as *value systems*.[3]

Although these systems have long captured the attention of neurobiologists and pharmacologists, there has been little historical agreement on their function. What is certain is their extreme importance as targets of pharmacological intervention in mental illness and dysfunction. The major sites of action of most of the modern drugs used to treat mental illness include cells from these groups. Small alterations in the pharmacology of these cells can have drastic effects on global mental function. As we discuss in chapter 7, such value systems appear perfectly suited to signaling the occurrence of salient events to the entire brain, leading to changes in the strength of billions of synapses.

THE BRAIN IS NOT A COMPUTER

Our quick review of neuroanatomy and neural dynamics indicates that the brain has special features of organization and functioning that do not seem consistent with the idea that it follows a set of precise instructions or performs computations. We know that the brain is interconnected in a fashion no man-made device yet equals. First, the billions and billions of connections that make up a brain's connections are *not exact:* If we ask whether the connections are identical in any two brains of the same size, as they would be in computers of the same make, the answer is no. At the finest scale, no two brains are identical, not even those of identical twins. Although the *overall* pattern of connections of a given brain area is describable in general terms, the microscopic variability of the brain at the finest ramifications of its neurons is enormous, and this variability makes each brain significantly unique. These observations present a fundamental challenge to models of the brain that are based on instruction or computation. As we shall see, the data provide strong grounds for so-called selectional theories of the brain—theories that actually *depend* upon variation to explain brain function.[4]

Another organizing principle that emerges from the picture we are building is that in each brain, the consequences of both a developmental history and an experiential history are uniquely marked. For example, from one day to the next, some synaptic connections in the same brain are likely not to remain exactly the same; certain cells will have retracted their processes, others will have extended new ones, and certain others will have died, all depending on the particular history of that brain. The individual variability that ensues is not just noise or error, but can affect the way we remember things and events. As we shall see, it is also an essential element governing the ability of the brain to respond to and match the countless unforeseeable scenes that may occur in the future. No present-day machine incorporates such individual diversity as a central feature of its design, although the day will certainly come when we shall build devices that are truly brainlike.

If we compare the signals a brain receives with those of computers, we uncover a number of other features that are special to brains. First, the world certainly is not presented to the brain like a piece of computer tape containing an unambiguous series of signals. Nonetheless, the brain enables an animal to sense the environment, categorize patterns out of a multiplicity of variable signals, and initiate movement. It mediates learning and memory and simultaneously regulates a host of bodily functions. The ability of the nervous system to carry out perceptual categorization of different signals for sight, sound, and so forth, dividing them into coherent classes without a pre-arranged code, is certainly special and is still unmatched by computers. We do not presently understand fully how this categorization is done but, as we discuss later, we believe it arises through the selection of certain distributed patterns of neural activity as the brain interacts with the body and the environment.

We have also shown that the brain contains a special set of nuclei with diffuse projections—the value systems—which signal to the entire nervous system the occurrence of a salient event and influence changes in the strength of synapses. Systems with these crucial properties are typically not found in man-made devices, yet their importance for learning and adaptive behavior is well documented. Together with the morphological peculiarities of the brain and its neural connections with a specific bodily phenotype, these systems provide an animal with a large set of constraints whose role in fostering species-specific perceptual categorization and adaptive learning cannot be underestimated.

Finally, if we consider neural dynamics (the way patterns of activity in the brain change with time), the most striking special feature of the brains of higher vertebrates is the occurrence of a process we have called reentry. Reentry, which we discuss in detail in chapters 9 and 10, depends on the possibility of cycles of signaling in the thalamocortical meshwork and other networks mentioned earlier. It is the ongoing, recursive interchange of parallel signals between reciprocally connected areas of the brain, an interchange that continually coordinates the activities of these areas' maps to each other in space and time. This interchange, unlike feedback, involves many parallel paths and has no specific instructive error function associated with it. Instead, it alters selective events and correlations of signals among areas and is essential for the synchronization and coordination of the areas' mutual functions.

One striking consequence of reentry is the widespread synchronization of the activity of different groups of active neurons distributed across many different functionally specialized areas of the brain. This synchronous firing of widely dispersed neurons that are connected by reentry is the basis for the integration of perceptual and motor processes. This integration ultimately gives rise to perceptual categorization, the ability to discriminate an object or event from a background for adaptive purposes. If the reentrant paths connecting cortical areas are disconnected, these integrative processes are disrupted. As we discuss in detail in chapter 10, reentry allows for a unity of perception and behavior that would otherwise be impossible, given the absence in the brain of a unique, computerlike central processor with detailed instructions or of algorithmic calculations for the coordination of functionally segregated areas.

Indeed, if we were asked to go beyond what is merely special and name the *unique* feature of higher brains, we would say it is reentry. There is no other object in the universe so completely distinguished by reentrant circuitry as the human brain. Although a brain has similarities to a large ecological entity like a jungle, nothing remotely like reentry appears in any jungle. Nor in human communication systems: Reentrant systems in the brain are massively parallel to a degree unheard of in our communication nets. In any event, communication nets are unlike brains, in that they deal with previously coded and, for the most part, unambiguous signals.

Because of the dynamic and parallel nature of reentry and because it is a process of higher-order selection, it is not easy to provide a metaphor that captures all the properties of reentry. Try this: Imagine a peculiar (and even weird) string quartet, in which each player responds by improvisation to ideas and cues of his or her own, as well as to all kinds of sensory cues in the environment. Since there is no score, each player would provide his or her own characteristic tunes, but initially these various tunes would not be coordinated with those of the other players. Now imagine that the bodies of the players are connected to each other by myriad fine threads so that their actions and movements are rapidly conveyed back and forth through signals of changing thread tensions that act simultaneously to time each player's actions. Signals that instantaneously connect the four players would lead to a correlation of their sounds; thus, new, more cohesive, and more integrated sounds would emerge out of the otherwise independent efforts of each player. This correlative process would also alter the next action of each player, and by these means the process would be repeated but with new emergent tunes that were even more correlated. Although no conductor would instruct or coordinate the group and each player would still maintain his or her style and role, the players' overall productions would tend to be more integrated and more coordinated, and such integration would lead to a kind of mutually coherent music that each one acting alone could not produce.

All these special features of the brain—connectivity, variability, plasticity, ability to categorize, dependence on value, and the dynamics of reentry—

operate heterogeneously to yield coordinated behavior. As we hinted earlier, the nonlinear aspects of the interaction among the brain, the body, and various parallel signals from the environment must be considered together to understand the processes of perceptual categorization, movement, and memory that underlie consciousness.

CHAPTER FIVE

Consciousness and Distributed Neural Activity

In this and the next chapter, we organize a wealth of old and new information on the relationship between neural activity and conscious states in health and disease. Our main goal is to highlight the overall characteristics of the neural processes underlying conscious experience. We touch on various observations, ranging from neurophysiology to neuropsychology, all of which provide fundamental evidence for how consciousness arises. We point out that the neural substrate of consciousness involves large populations of neurons—especially those of the thalamocortical system—that are widely distributed in the brain. Conversely, no single area of the brain is responsible for conscious experience. We also show that as a task to be learned is practiced, its performance becomes more and more automatic; as this occurs and it fades from consciousness, the number of brain regions involved in performing the task becomes smaller.

Our awareness that the brain is the organ of consciousness is a relatively recent achievement. Even among the Greeks, there were different schools of thought. While Plato was convinced that consciousness was probably connected to the brain, Aristotle cast his vote for the heart. In fact, the gradual realization that the brain is responsible for our conscious life should be considered at least as important as William Harvey's discovery that the heart is responsible for the circulation of the blood.

Today, of course, the privileged position of the brain is fully established, and certain general conclusions about areas of the brain that are important for consciousness can be safely drawn. In this chapter, we begin by briefly reviewing some conclusions about the role of certain brain *structures*, in preparation for a more thorough consideration of what is known about the neural *processes* underlying consciousness. Before we turn to this task, however, we should mention old and new techniques that allow us to image the activity of the brain in a living person. These techniques are of enormous value in looking at the neural correlates of consciousness in health and disease. They all work by sophisticated physical principles, reflected in their arcane names, but the principles need not concern us here. These techniques include electroencephalography (EEG) and magnetoencephalography (MEG), which measure, respectively, the minuscule electrical potentials and electrical currents generated by the synchronous activity of millions of neurons; we must also mention EEG- and MEG-evoked potentials, which record the electric responses of neurons to the repeated presentation of stimuli. These techniques have excellent temporal resolution, but they are not good for the precise localization of groups of neurons. Other techniques, such as positron emission tomography (PET) and functional magnetic resonance imaging (fMRI), though they offer lower temporal resolution, can assess relative changes in brain metabolism and blood flow with great spatial accuracy, and they provide us with invaluable images of the living brain at work. We refer to them frequently in our discussion of the various brain regions that are involved in conscious experience. Here, it is valuable to point out that response times are often indicated in thousandths of a second (milliseconds, abbreviated msec) and that 1 oscillation per second is denoted as 1 Hertz (Hz).

Attempts have been made to provide a detailed dissection of which brain structures are important for consciousness. Indeed, today's neuroscientists are hotly debating which regions of the cerebral cortex, or even which particular neurons, do and do not contribute to conscious experience.[1] However, as we already mentioned, the main intent of this book is to concentrate on the kinds of neural *processes* that can account for fundamental properties of conscious experience. By highlighting several observations, ranging from neurophysiology to neuropsychology, we argue that (1) neuronal processes underlying conscious experience involve groups of neurons that are widely distributed; (2) these distributed groups of neurons engage in strong and rapid reentrant interactions; and (3) for consciousness to appear, such rapidly interacting neuronal groups must be able to select among a sufficiently large number of differentiated activity patterns.

CONSCIOUS EXPERIENCE IS ASSOCIATED WITH THE ACTIVATION OR DEACTIVATION OF DISTRIBUTED POPULATIONS OF NEURONS

A statement often heard in casual conversations is how little of our brain we actually use: If only we could use it all! There is a grain of truth in these statements, but only a grain. Some people have had almost half their brains removed because of tumors or intractable epilepsy (in a so-called hemispherectomy), yet their cognitive abilities are only marginally affected.[2] There are even reports about people with severe hydrocephalus in whom only a thin stratum of cerebral cortex is preserved following the enormous enlargement of the fluid-filled ventricles of the brain, but whose IQs are surprisingly close to normal.[3] Leaving aside these special cases, the overwhelming majority of studies still indicate that every conscious task involves the activation or deactivation of large portions of the brain.[4]

Lessons from Neurology and Neurophysiology

It is generally agreed that the functioning of the cerebral cortex is responsible, to a large extent, for the *content* of consciousness. The results of lesioning experiments and of stimulation and recording studies indicate that the activity of specific cortical regions is closely tied to specific aspects of consciousness. This conclusion appears to be true whether a given conscious experience, say, the perception of color, is driven by external stimuli, by memory, or by imagery and dreams.[5] For example, if a certain area of the cortex, corresponding to the so-called fusiform and lingual gyri, is damaged, the perception of color is lost and the capacity to imagine color or remember color is also lost, and dreams become colorless. Moreover, it appears that, at least for short periods, consciousness can be generated by the activity of the thalamocortical system in relative autonomy from the rest of the body or the world. Conscious scenes experienced while dreaming may be, at times, almost indistinguishable from those of waking, yet we know that during dreaming, the thalamocortical system is functionally disconnected from the external world on both the input and the output sides.

A strong indication that consciousness may require the activity of distributed regions of the brain within the thalamocortical system comes from the examination of neurological lesions. Despite occasional claims to the contrary, it has never been conclusively shown that a lesion of a restricted portion of the cerebral cortex leads to unconsciousness.[6] Lesions of particular parts of the cerebral cortex may certainly lead to focal deficits in conscious experience—damage to one area may abolish the ability consciously to perceive color, while damage to another area may reduce the ability to perceive moving stimuli—but no single area seems to hold the key to consciousness as such.

The only localized brain lesions that result in loss of consciousness typically affect the so-called reticular activating system.[7] This highly heterogeneous system, which is located in the evolutionary older part of the brain—upper portions of the brainstem (upper pons and mesencephalon) and extends into the posterior hypothalamus, the so-called thalamic intralaminar and reticular nuclei, and the basal forebrain—projects diffusely to the thalamus and cortex. It is thought to "energize" or "activate" the thalamocortical system and facilitate the interactions among distant cortical regions. Indeed, it is now well established that the activity of the reticular activating system is essential for maintaining the *state* of consciousness.[8] For example, this system is important in determining whether we are awake or asleep.[9] During wakefulness, when this system is active, thalamocortical neurons are depolarized, fire in a tonic or continuous way, and respond well to incoming stimuli. During dreamless sleep, this system becomes less active or inactive; thalamocortical neurons become hyperpolarized, fire in repetitive bursts and pauses, and are hardly responsive to incoming stimuli. Moreover, if this system is lesioned, all consciousness is lost, and a person enters a state of coma.[10] On the basis of these observations, it has been suggested that the reticular activating system may have a privileged and direct connection to conscious experience.[11] However, although the functioning of this system is certainly a prerequisite for consciousness to occur, it is generally assumed that the role of this system is indirect and that the system does not, by itself, actually generate consciousness.[12] Rather, its unique anatomical and physiological characteristics make the reticular activating system a natural candidate for ensuring that distributed populations of neurons in the thalamocortical system fire in a way that is compatible with conscious experience.

The results of imaging studies strengthen the idea that distributed patterns of activity underlie conscious experience. Every year, hundreds of new imaging studies appear in the neurological literature comparing patterns of activity in the human brain when it performs one cognitive task versus another and pinpointing some particular region whose activity is powerfully modulated by the task. The frequent emphasis on what differs from one conscious task to another should not, however, obscure a common finding that is confirmed in all these studies: Every conscious task involves the activation or deactivation of widely distributed areas of the brain.[13]

To determine precisely which brain areas correlate with conscious experience *as such*, however, one would need an appropriate comparison or control state. A state of rest clearly will not do, since a person at rest is fully conscious. Deep sleep, which is marked by the appearance of high amplitude, slow waves in the EEG and is associated with a marked loss in conscious reports,[14] may represent a more appropriate reference state. According to a recent study, cerebral blood flow, which is an indirect measure of synaptic activity in the brain, is globally reduced during slow-wave sleep in comparison to both waking and rapid eye movement (REM) sleep, the stage of sleep during which we experience vivid dreams.[15] A comparison of the brain activity in a conscious subject versus that in a subject who is comatose or deeply anesthetized also reveals that unconsciousness is associated with a profound depression of neural activity in both the cerebral cortex and the thalamus,[16] although other areas may also be affected.

A more specific reference state would be the response to a simple sensory input when a subject is unaware of it versus when the subject is aware of it. In a recent study in our laboratory, we attempted to capture that difference and thus measure the neural correlates of consciousness. Our experiments were carried out under conditions of binocular rivalry. In binocular rivalry, a subject views two incongruent stimuli through each eye but consciously perceives only one stimulus at a time, with a switch in perceptual dominance every few seconds without specific voluntary attention. For example, a subject may see a red vertical grating with his left eye through a red lens and a blue horizontal grating with his right eye through a blue lens. Although both stimuli are presented, the subject will report alternately only one or the other. Somehow, while the visual system receives signals from both stimuli, only one at a time makes it to conscious experience.

We used MEG to measure electrical brain responses to rivalrous visual stimuli. A key to the success of this study was to have a way to know which brain responses corresponded to which stimulus: blue or red. This knowledge was obtained by causing each stimulus to flicker in intensity at a specific frequency. It turns out that the MEG potentials from the brain—the so-called steady-state evoked responses—show a sharp response to that frequency that can be used as a tag for that particular stimulus.

In this study, each stimulus was flickered at a different tag frequency in the range of 7 to 12 oscillations per second, for example, red vertical at 7.4 Hz and blue horizontal at 9.5 Hz. Steady-state evoked responses at either one or the other tag frequencies specific to each stimulus could be detected in many MEG channels. When we analyzed the data, a first important observation was that neural electrical responses to rivalrous visual stimuli occurred in a large number of cortical regions both when the subject consciously perceived the stimuli and when he did not. The second striking finding, however, was that the neuromagnetic responses evoked by a stimulus were stronger by 50–85 percent when the subjects were conscious of it than when they were not (see figure 5.1). These increased neural responses to a stimulus associated with its conscious perception were simultaneously distributed to a large subset of different brain regions, including the occipi-

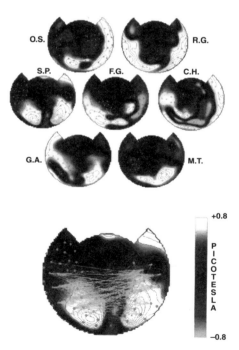

FIGURE 5.1 Distributed neural process underlying conscious experience, as revealed by MEG experiments on seven subjects during binocular rivalry. The plots show the changes in neuronal firing in a number of areas of the brain when the subjects are conscious of a stimulus. Note the remarkable differences from individual to individual.

tal, temporal, and frontal areas, although by no means to all the regions showing stimulus-related activity. Finally, a particularly striking finding was that the specific subset of different brain regions that showed such modulation by conscious perception varied significantly from subject to subject. Thus, the results of this study provide a clear indication that the set of brain regions whose activity correlates with conscious experience is widely distributed but locally specific and, equally important, that the distribution differs in different subjects.

A Lesson from Practice:
Conscious versus Automatic Performance

In addition to the evidence that the activity of widespread sets of cortical areas is increased or decreased even in the simplest conscious task, other findings suggest that if such a task is performed unconsciously or nearly so, a more limited portion of the brain may be involved.

We all know that when we first learn a new skill, we need consciously to control everything we do, but after some time our performance becomes automatic and soon fades from consciousness. Learning to switch gears with a stick shift, to ride a bicycle, or to play a musical instrument are good examples. In the initial stages of learning, conscious control has to be exerted at every step and about every detail, in a process that is slow, laborious, and prone to error. With practice, however, conscious control becomes superfluous and disappears. Performance becomes automatic, fast, easy, and accurate. An accomplished pianist knows well that he needs only to start the scale, and it will rattle itself off at great speed and with no need for conscious control. In fact, "If practice did not make perfect, nor habit economize the expense of nervous and muscular energy, man would be in a sorry plight."[17] Henry Maudsley put it like this: "If an act became no easier after being done several times, if the careful direction of consciousness were necessary to its accomplishments in each occasion, it is evident that the whole activity of a lifetime might be confined to one or two deeds."[18]

Much of our cognitive life may be the product of highly automated routines. When it comes to talking, listening, reading, writing, or remembering, we all are like accomplished pianists. When we read, all kinds of neural processes are going on that allow us to recognize letters irrespective of the font and size, to parse them into words, to enable lexical access, and to take care of syntactic structure. There was certainly a time in which we had consciously to learn about letters and words in a laborious way, but afterward these processes become effortless and automatic. How our brain performs these demanding tasks remains largely unknown to us. When we consciously add two numbers together, it seems that we simply pass a request to our brain, the brain carries it out, and the answer is delivered. When we search for an item in memory, we formulate the question in our consciousness. Unbeknownst to us, the brain seems to search for a while, and suddenly the response is made available to consciousness again. At times, our conscious self seems to act very much like the CEO of an organization. The CEO asks for a report, somebody in the organization produces that report (the CEO may not know who or where), and at some point the report is delivered to him or her.

This pervasive automatization in our adult lives suggests that conscious control is exerted only at critical junctures, when a definite choice or a plan has to be made. In between, unconscious routines are continuously triggered and executed, so that consciousness can float free of all those details and proceed to plan and make sense of the grand scheme of things. In action as well as in perception, it appears as if only the last levels of control or of analysis are available to consciousness, while everything else proceeds automatically. This feature has led many to conclude that we are conscious of the *results* of "computations" occurring in our brain, not of the computations themselves. It has also led to the conclusion that, by itself, consciousness like the CEO, has a limited capacity,[19] while the organization of the brain has almost unlimited resources,[20] More accurately, one should say that automatization is of help because in just one step, it allows us to select larger units of behavior. If only one selection occurs to carry out multiple actions, either in parallel or in sequence, the number of selections needed is reduced. This reduction considerably speeds up the action since, as we will see, it is the process of choosing among alternatives that is the real bottleneck.

The essence of the transformation between conscious control of performance and its automatization was aptly described by William James:[21]

[H]abit diminishes the conscious attention with which our acts are performed. One may state this abstractly thus: If an act requires for its execution a chain, A, B, C, D, E, F, G, etc., of successive nervous events, then in the first performance of the action the conscious will must choose each of these events from a number of wrong alternatives that tend to present themselves; but habit soon brings it about that each event calls up its own appropriate successor without any alternative offering itself, and without any reference to the conscious will, until at last the whole chain, A, B, C, D, E, F, G, rattles itself off as soon as A occurs. . . . A glance at the musical hieroglyphics, and the pianist's fingers have rippled through a cataract of notes.

Whatever the respective merits of conscious and unconscious modes of controlling actions, what is most instructive for our purposes is to consider the neural substrates associated with the transformation between these two modes. What changes in brain function accompany the transition between conscious and unconscious performance? In all the examples just mentioned, the action being performed before and after practice remains—if we make allowance for differences in speed and smoothness of execution—very much the same. The striking difference, however, is that at first, the action is performed consciously, but after some time, it is performed unconsciously. If we knew how the activity of the brain differs between these two modes of controlling actions, we might be able to have a clearer understanding of the neural processes underlying consciousness.

It has long been observed that the conscious performance of a motor act often involves the entire body, while with habit, only the necessary muscles are involved. As noted by James,[22] "the beginner at the piano not only moves his finger up and down in order to depress the key, he moves the whole hand, the forearm and even the entire body, especially the head, as if he would press down the key with that organ too." With practice, however, "an impulse which originally spread its effects over the whole body . . . is gradually determined to a single definite organ, in which it effects the contraction of a few limited muscles." It is not only the motor involvement that shrinks with practice. The number and range of sensory inputs that are initially "consulted" for conscious control and that can influence the performance are enormous, including many details and irrelevant stimuli. With practice, however, the inputs that affect the performance appear to be restricted just to the necessary ones.

The restriction of bodily inputs and outputs during the transition from controlled to automatic performance may have a fundamental parallel in terms of the dynamics of the brain. As long ago as the 1930s, it was observed that when a conditioned stimulus to which an animal had previously habituated is paired with an unconditioned stimulus, the electrical activity of the brain changes from so-called alpha activity (synchronized oscillations with a frequency around 10Hz) to a desynchronized pattern of higher frequencies in widespread regions of the brain.[23] However, as training proceeds and the conditioned response becomes fully established, the desynchronization is observed only in the regions of the cortex that are specifically involved in mediating the response (such as the visual and motor cortex if the conditioned stimulus involves perceiving light and the conditioned response is a motor response). Similar experiments were performed by exposing cats daily to periods of flickering visual stimulation (say at 6Hz). Early on, responses at the same frequency were observed in widespread areas of the brain. As the cats became accustomed to the flickering light, the response at 6 Hz greatly diminished and eventually disappeared. If the flickering stimulus was then coupled with foot-shock reinforcement, the response at 6 Hz again increased dramatically in many brain regions. In the fully trained animal, the responses decreased again in both amount and extent. But if the animal was trained to discriminate among new or more complex stimuli, the response stayed strong and spread to many regions of the brain.[24]

We can actually begin to see what is happening in the human brain by using modern imaging methods. For example, the cerebral glucose metabolic rate was measured using PET in young subjects who were playing the computer game Tetris, before and after practice.[25] After four to eight weeks of daily practice on Tetris, the glucose metabolic rate in cortical surface regions *decreased* despite a more than sevenfold *increase* in performance. Subjects whose performances improved the most after practice showed the largest glucose metabolic decreases in several areas. In another study, subjects were asked to say an appropriate verb for a visually presented noun (say, *pound* in response to a picture of a hammer).[26] Compared to responses triggered by simply repeating the visually presented nouns, several areas of the brain (the anterior cingulate cortex, left prefrontal and left posterior temporal cortices, and the right cerebellar hemisphere) showed sharply increased activity during naive performance. All these areas were significantly less active during practiced performance.[27] In effect, fewer than fifteen minutes of practice made the cortical circuitry used for selecting verbal responses indistinguishable from that seen when the subjects simply repeated the word. The introduction of a novel list of words, however, reversed these learning-related effects.

Another recent study examined the improvement in speed and accuracy of the performance of a rapid sequence of finger movements over several weeks (such improvement did not transfer to a second and different sequence of movements). fMRI, a technique that picks up relative changes in activity of areas of the living brain, was used to analyze a region centered on the primary motor cortex. The results showed that before training, a comparable extent of primary motor cortex was activated by both sequences. Within a short time, however, repeating a sequence resulted in a smaller area of activation.[28]

All these results suggest that after conscious practice, the spread of the cortical signals that influence the performance of a task involves a much more restricted set of areas. Presumably, the amount of information brought to bear on performing the task also becomes much more limited. On the other hand, since the only information brought to bear is what is sufficient and appropriate for the task, interference diminishes and performance improves. With further practice, new and specialized circuits may augment those already present in the specialized areas that are involved, and performance becomes fast, accurate, and largely unconscious. It is as if, at first, an initially distributed and large set of cortical specialists meets to try to address a task. Soon they reach a consensus about who among them is best qualified to deal with it, and a task force is chosen. Subsequently, the task force recruits the help of a local, smaller group to perform the task rapidly and flawlessly.

As we pointed out at the beginning of this section, the initial controlled performance is associated with conscious attention, while the later, more automatic performance is less attended to and less consciously vivid. These neurophysiological data, albeit still scant, provide a first indication that the cortical activity in the thalamocortical system, which is associated with conscious performance, is more widespread and distributed than brain activity associated with automatic performance. In chapter 14, we discuss some ideas about how the cortex and subcortical regions cooperate to connect conscious planning with unconscious routines. At this point, however, it is more relevant to focus on how neural activities underlying consciousness can be integrated as well as differentiated by means of reentrant interactions along the reciprocal fibers connecting the regions of the brain.

CHAPTER SIX

Neural Activity Integrated and Differentiated

The evidence we considered in the previous chapter suggests that conscious experience is associated not with a single area of the brain, but with changes of activity patterns occurring simultaneously in many regions of the brain. But is the occurrence of neural activity that is widely distributed in the thalamocortical system sufficient to generate consciousness? Is consciousness merely a matter of how many neurons are simultaneously active all over the brain? There are many indications that this is not the case. Something else is clearly required for conscious experience to emerge. According to our observations, what is required is that the distributed groups of neurons must engage in strong and rapid reentrant interactions. Furthermore, the activity patterns of such rapidly interacting neuronal groups must be constantly changing and sufficiently differentiated from each other. The evidence for these conclusions comes as much from the study of brain disease as from the study of people with normal brains.

We have shown that conscious experience is associated with the activation and inactivation of populations of neurons that are widely distributed in the thalamocortical system. In this chapter, we continue the exploration of the general properties of neural processes underlying conscious experience by turning to some fascinating aspects of neurological and psychiatric disease.

CONSCIOUS EXPERIENCE REQUIRES STRONG AND RAPID REENTRANT INTERACTIONS

Perhaps the most direct indications of how important rapid reentrant neural interactions are for generating a unified conscious experience are disconnection syndromes in neurology and dissociation disorders in psychiatry. These are syndromes in which one or more areas of the brain are anatomically or functionally disconnected from the rest of the brain owing to some pathological process, traumatic event, or surgery while the areas themselves are relatively undamaged.

Disconnection Syndromes[1]

The most dramatic and certainly the best studied form of disconnection is the split-brain syndrome, in which persons with intractable epilepsy undergo surgery that severs the large number of reciprocal connections between the two halves of the brain (see figure 6.1; these connections are made via the corpus callosum and, in a few cases, the anterior commissure).

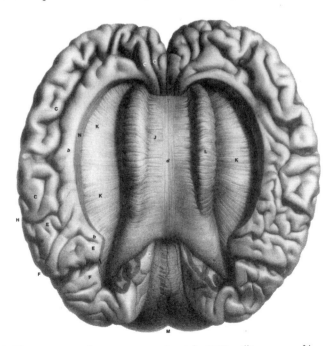

FIGURE 6.1 The corpus callosum, approximately 200 million nerve fibers reciprocally linking the two cerebral hemispheres. The brain was dissected from above; the fibers run horizontally, and their faint striations can be seen.

Outside the laboratory, these persons seem to behave quite normally. It is, in fact, remarkable that the world does not collapse for a person with a split brain. That it does not indicates that the dominant hemisphere, almost always the left, is sufficient to allow the person consciously to perceive the environment and control behavior well enough.[2]

The most obvious abnormality in people with split brains, confirmed by careful studies in animals, is a profound deficit in the interhemispheric integration of sensory and motor information. These persons are not able to integrate visual information presented to their two visual half-fields, nor is patterned somatosensory information presented to each hand available to the hemisphere on the same side as the hand (the "ipsilateral" hemisphere). Roger Sperry, a neuroscientist who made fundamental discoveries on splitbrains, summed up his impressions after decades of experiments by concluding that:

> the surgery has left these people with two separate minds, that is, two separate spheres of consciousness. What is experienced in the right hemisphere seems to be entirely outside the realm of awareness of the left hemisphere. This mental division has been demonstrated in regard to perception, cognition, volition, learning, and memory. One of the hemispheres, the left, dominant or major hemisphere, has speech and is normally talkative and conversant. The other, the minor hemisphere, however, is mute or dumb, being able to express itself only through nonverbal reactions.[3]

At times, however, the right, nondominant hemisphere may actively try to interfere with behavior controlled by the dominant one, as when the right hand attempts to dress the patient and the left hand to undress him or her. Such acts of rebellion by the nondominant left hand are also often found in people with anterior callosal lesions, and they have been called "the alien hand syndrome."[4]

The anatomical underpinnings of disconnection syndromes, such as the split brain, are clear-cut—millions of reentrant connections between the two hemispheres have been severed. However, the underlying neurophysiology has been more difficult to investigate. Despite the loss of direct cortico-cortical connections, the activity patterns of each hemisphere appear to be relatively conserved. What is lost, instead, may be the establishment of short-term temporal correlations between the activities of neuronal groups in the two hemispheres that are mediated by their reentrant interactions. This loss is reflected in a reduction of the correlation or coherence of neuronal firing between the two hemispheres in both humans[5] and animals.[6] In cats with callosal lesions, for example, some neurons in the primary visual cortex of both hemispheres respond normally to their preferred stimuli, such as elongated bars presented to the eye at a particular orientation. However, although the discharge patterns of these neurons are normally highly correlated when they are stimulated by an oriented bar that straddles the midline, these correlations are completely lost after callosal transection. This finding suggests that reciprocal connections between the two hemispheres are necessary to mediate the reentrant interactions by which their activities become correlated in time. It is highly likely that the loss of such reentrant interactions is responsible for the loss of conscious integration between the two hemispheres that is observed in humans.

Dissociative Disorders

Although the relationship between reentrant interactions and conscious integration may seem obvious with split brains and other neurological disconnections, this mechanism is often overlooked as a possible explanation for other dissociation phenomena. Cases of hysterical sensory symptoms, now called conversion or psychogenic symptoms, are perhaps not as frequent as they were among the female patients of Jean Charcot, Pierre Janet, and Sigmund Freud in the nineteenth century, but are nonetheless striking (see figure 6.2). A woman with full-blown hysterical blindness will flatly deny seeing anything, but most of the time she will be able to avoid obstacles as if she were seeing them. Thus, it would seem as if her ability to see has become unconscious or perhaps dissociated from her conscious self. Janet described several examples of dissociation at the turn of the twentieth century. For example, by focusing the attention of a patient elsewhere, Janet would place a pencil in the woman's hand and elicit automatic writing; the hand would write the correct answer to a question unbeknownst to her consciousness.[7] Freud analyzed many similar cases, elaborated on the unconscious origin of certain neurotic symptoms, and suggested a link between these disorders and everyday phenomena like slips of the tongue and selective amnesia.[8] In more recent times, attention has focused on pathologies, such as fugue states, in which a person commits acts that appear to be conscious states but of which he or she has no subsequent recall. Ernest Hilgard reexamined fugue states and other phenomena, including multiple personalities and hypnotic analgesia or amnesia, and categorized them as dissociated states of consciousness.[9] Dissociation is now defined as "a disruption in the usually integrated functions of consciousness, memory, identity, or perception of the environment."[10] The group of dissociative disorders includes an extraordinary set of conditions, such as dissociative amnesia, dissociative fugue, dissociative identity disorder (multiple personality disorder), and depersonalization disorder, in which what is normally a unified conscious experience undergoes all kinds of schisms and fractures.[11] Other psychiatric disorders, such as schizophrenia, may also share some traits with dissociative disorders qua disorders of neural integration.[12]

FIGURE 6.2 ANNA O. (BERTHA PAPPENHEIM). In 1880, Anna O., a young Viennese woman, developed a remarkable series of dissociative or hysterical symptoms, including paralysis and loss of sensation in her right extremities, occasional spells of deafnesss, and transitory loss of the ability to speak German but not English. She was assisted and cured by Sigmund Freud's friend and colleague Josef Breuer using the *cathartic* method—the systematic recollection of the events surrounding the emergence of a symptom. In 1895, Breuer and Freud examined the case of Anna O. and other similar cases in their *Studies on Hysteria*, one of the seminal works in the history of psychoanalysis. Bertha Pappenheim recovered and became a leading exponent of the women's movement.

The similarity between psychiatric dissociation syndromes and neurological disconnection syndromes is remarkable. The main difference is that the latter are defined in terms of physical disconnection between specialized brain regions, such as visual and motor areas, while the former are conceived as disconnection between psychic functions, such as seeing and acting. Nevertheless, both categories of disorders may be unified by considering them as disorders of integration, in the first case because of a neuroanatomical lesion and in the second, because of a "functional" or dynamic impairment of connectivity. According to this hypothesis, what is altered in both neurological disconnection syndromes and dissociative disorders is not so much the degree of *activity* of a brain area or a psychic function, but the degree of the *interactivity* between such areas or functions. Unfortunately, hardly any data exist about the neural basis of psychiatric dissociative disorders, and the hypothesis that they may be due to an impairment of reentrant interactions still remains to be tested.

PERCEPTION WITHOUT AWARENESS

Psychologists have long been aware that feeble, degraded, or short-lasting stimuli often fail to be perceived consciously, yet may lead to a behavioral response.[13] More than four decades ago, Vance Packard, in his best-seller, *The Hidden Persuaders*, popularized this "subliminal perception" with the famous story of the message "DRINK COKE" flashed briefly during a movie, intended to prime the thirst of the viewers without their consciously recognizing it.[14] For many years, the somewhat precarious scientific evidence for subliminal perception was regarded with considerable skepticism. But later studies have established the phenomenon in a well-controlled way.[15] In the laboratory, subliminal perception—now often called perception without awareness—is usually demonstrated by presenting stimuli that are too weak, too short, or too noisy to be consciously perceived but that are sufficient to prime or bias the subject's performance in lexical decision tasks or other similar tests.[16] For example, if the word *river* is flashed for a short time, a person will deny having seen anything. But if the person is then asked to choose a word that goes with *bank*, he or she is more likely to choose *boat* than *money*. Evidently, subliminal stimuli produce enough neural activation to trigger an appropriate behavioral response.[17] However, something in the neural activation produced by such stimuli is inadequate for conscious experience to arise. What is missing?

Some light on the issue is shed by a series of experiments started more than thirty years ago by Benjamin Libet. In one of these experiments, Libet delivered weak electrical stimuli, at 72 pulses per second, via electrodes chronically implanted in the thalamus of patients for the therapeutic control of intractable pain.[18] Stimulations of a certain part of the thalamus are known to activate neural pathways that deal with tactile stimuli and to produce an easily identifiable sensation of touch. The surprising finding was that such weak stimuli required a substantial duration of appropriate cerebral activity, about 500 msec (half a second), for the production of a conscious sensory experience. However, much shorter durations, less than 150 msec, were sufficient for sensory detection without awareness as determined by requiring the patients to guess whether a stimulus had been presented even if they had not perceived it. Libet concluded that simply increasing the duration of the same repetitive thalamic inputs to the cerebral cortex can convert detection without awareness to detection with awareness.

Libet knew, of course, that a single natural stimulus of short duration applied to the skin is sufficient to elicit conscious experience. Such a stimulus produces a primary electrical response in the cortex (called P1), which peaks *early* at about 25 milliseconds (msec). This response persists in sleep and anesthesia, that is, in the absence of conscious experience. However, stimuli to the skin also elicit *late* cortical evoked potentials (called N1) that begin at 100 msec and last for several hundred msec. Unlike the early P1 potentials, these N1 late potentials are modulated by attention and are absent in slow-wave sleep and anesthesia. Even with natural stimuli, therefore, the induction of long-lasting, late potentials seems to be necessary to elicit a conscious somatosensory sensation.

Potentials similar to the human P1 and N1 have recently been studied in monkeys who were trained to discriminate the intensity of tactile stimuli. The early response, P1, was correlated only with stimulus intensity, while the late response, N1, was correlated with the monkey's perceptual discrimination, as indicated by its behavioral response. Further studies have shown that N1 is generated by the excitation of neurons of the primary somatosensory cortex that have extensive distal dendrites in the most superficial layer of the cortex and that often have long corticocortical connections. What is most interesting is that this excitation appears to be mediated by reentry from other cortical areas.[19]

All these results suggest that ongoing reentrant interactions between multiple brain areas are required for a stimulus to be consciously perceived. However, at least under the conditions of these experiments, a stimulus can give rise to or maintain such interactions only if the neural response it causes persists for a few hundred milliseconds.

In another series of experiments focused on the motor side of consciousness, Libet showed that the conscious intention to act appears only after a delay of about 350 msec from the onset of specific cerebral activity that precedes a voluntary act.[20] Before a motor act, a specific event-related potential, called a readiness potential, can be recorded from the human scalp. Libet asked subjects to move a finger at arbitrary, self-determined times and to signal the earliest awareness of their intention to move by noticing the spatial clock position of a revolving spot. He found that the onset of the readiness potential invariably preceded such awareness by an average of about 350 milliseconds and by a minimum of about 150 milliseconds. He concluded that the cerebral initiation of a spontaneous, freely voluntary act can begin unconsciously, that is, before there is any recallable awareness that a decision to act has already been initiated cerebrally. Thus, it would seem that awareness of a motor intention, like that of a sensory stimulus, requires that the underlying neural activity persist for a substantial amount of time, on the order of 100–500 msec.

Evidence for a correlation between conscious experience and sustained neural activity also comes from tasks involving so-called visuospatial working memory—the ability to rehearse or "keep in mind" a spatial location. Working memory is used to bring or keep some item in consciousness or close to conscious access—whether the item is a spatial location, a telephone number, or a good idea.[21] In working-memory tasks, sustained neural activity is found in the prefrontal cortex of monkeys and is apparently maintained by reentrant interactions between frontal and parietal regions.[22] Such sustained neural activity facilitates the integration of the activity of spatially segregated brain regions. This integrated neural process is stable enough in time to permit us to carry out decision making and planning.[23]

Perhaps most important of all, recent investigations have shown that various kinds of cognitive tasks that require awareness are accompanied by short-term *temporal* correlations among distributed populations of neurons in the thalamocortical system.[24] When we examined binocular rivalry with MEG to look for signs of interactions among brain areas, for example, we found a remarkable result.[25] An index of how much the activity of distant brain regions is synchronized or in phase is provided by their so-called coherence. Coherence values between regions of the brain can be taken as a reflection of the strength of the reentrant interactions among them. In striking agreement with our predictions, coherence between distant brain regions responding to the stimulus was always higher when a subject was aware of the stimulus than when he was not (see figure 6.3).[26] These results provide strong evidence that the rapid integration of the activity of distributed brain regions through reentrant interactions is required for conscious experience to occur.

CONSCIOUS EXPERIENCE REQUIRES
PATTERNS OF NEURAL ACTIVITY
THAT ARE HIGHLY DIFFERENTIATED

Although the occurrence of effective, long-lasting distributed interactions among groups of neurons is necessary, it is still not sufficient for conscious experience to ensue. This conclusion is strikingly demonstrated by the fact that generalized epileptic seizures and slow-wave sleep meet these requirements even though consciousness is absent.

Epileptic Seizures

During an epileptic seizure, within a short time the discharge of neurons in much of the cerebral cortex and thalamus becomes hypersynchronous; that

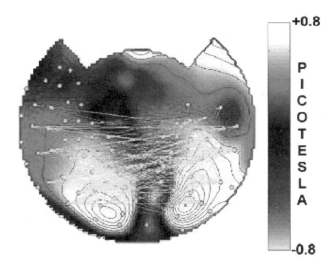

+0.8

P
I
C
O
T
E
S
L
A

-0.8

FIGURE 6.3. Coherence of neural processes underlying consciousness, measured using MEG during binocular rivalry; the straight lines indicate an increased synchronization between cortical regions when the subject is conscious of a stimulus. This result was derived from the same experiments illustrated in figure 12. See color plate on bookjacket.

is, most neurons discharge at high rates and almost simultaneously. In a form of generalized epilepsy that is common in children, for instance, the hypersynchronous discharge of neurons all over the cortex gives rise to characteristic spike-and–wave complexes at 3Hz on the EEG. Such "petit mal" seizures are invariably associated with the loss of consciousness, in this case in the form of short "absences." A child may stop talking in midsentence or cease walking, stare emptily in front of herself, and not respond to stimuli. One to several seconds later, the child is able to speak or move again. When the child awakens from such an unconscious spell, she has no memory of the episode. During these episodes of unconsciousness, the child's brain is by no means inactive; it is actually hyperactive. The repetitive spike-and-wave electroencephalographic activity during petit mal seizures indicates that cortical neurons are either all firing together or are all silent together and that these two neural states alternate every third of a second (see figure 6.4, top). The stereotyped alternation between a limited number of states, such as unison firing and unison silence, contrasts sharply with the continuous switching among the billions of different patterns of firing observed in normal waking. The loss of consciousness during a seizure is therefore associated with a dramatic reduction in the complexity of the diverse repertoire of neural states that are normally available.

SLEEP STATES

Sleep is divided into two main states: slow-wave sleep, during which consciousness is reduced, fragmentary, or lost, and REM sleep, during which conscious dreams are frequent and vivid. One may assume that when we fall into dreamless sleep, the activity of our neurons would also be reduced and that this may be the reason why consciousness is lost.[27] It was with great surprise, however, that neurophysiologists learned that the firing *rate* of individual neurons is not so different between sleep and waking.[28] In some cortical areas, in fact, firing rates may even increase during sleep. The observation of similar firing rates between waking and slow-wave sleep represents both the most common and the most striking dissociation between cortical activity and consciousness (see figure 6.4).[29] It indicates that the presence of "normal" firing *levels* in the cerebral cortex *is not* a sufficient criterion for consciousness. It was soon noticed, however, that what underwent a drastic change between waking and sleep was not so much the firing rate of neurons, but their firing *patterns*. As has been well known since the 1930s, during waking as well as during REM sleep, the EEG shows low voltage, fast-activity patterns over the entire scalp. During slow-wave sleep, in contrast, the EEG reveals a diffuse pattern of slow waves of high voltage. When the activity of individual neurons was recorded, it was found that in waking, their firing was continuous or tonic, while in slow-wave sleep, it followed a peculiar oscillatory pattern of high-frequency bursts followed by silent pauses.[30] The stereotyped "burst-pause" mode of activity during sleep affects a large number of neurons dispersed over the entire brain. Furthermore, the slow, oscillatory firing of such distributed populations of neurons is highly synchronized globally, in sharp contrast with waking, when groups of neurons dynamically assemble and reassemble into continuously changing patterns of firing (see figure 6.4, bottom). While the patterns of neural firing are

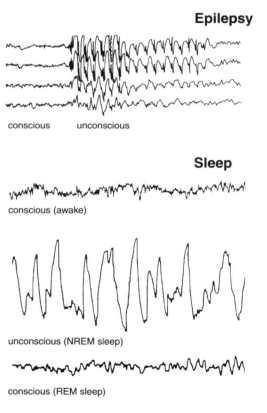

FIGURE 6.4 EEG PATTERNS DURING EPILEPSY AND SLEEP. Conscious experience requires a differentiated neural process reflected in the diverse patterns of low amplitude, fast activity in the EEG. The appearance of synchronous, high-amplitude waves in the EEG during an epileptic seizure or during NREM sleep is accompanied by unconsciousness.

remarkably diverse and the repertoire of available neural states is large during waking, the repertoire of available neural states is greatly reduced during slow-wave sleep. Corresponding to this dramatic reduction in the number of differentiated neural states, consciousness is diminished or lost, just as it is in generalized epileptic discharges. Thus, it appears that consciousness requires not just neural activity, but neural activity that changes continually and is thus spatially and temporally differentiated. If most groups of neurons in the cortex discharge synchronously, functional discriminations among

FIGURE 6.5 MICHELANGELO, *LA NOTTE* (*THE NIGHT*). In response to admiring verses from a young Florentine, Michelangelo wrote the following epigram for the statue:

Caro m'e' il sonno, e piu' l'esser di sasso,
mentre che 'l danno e la vergogna dura,
non veder, non sentir, m'e'gran ventura:
pero' non mi destar, deh! parla basso

Dearest is sleep to me, and more to be like stone,
While hurt and shame endure,
Not to see, not to feel, this is great solace:
But do not wake me at all! Low be thy speech

them are obliterated, brain states become extremely homogeneous, and with the shrinking of the repertoire of brain states that are available for selection, consciousness itself is lost.[31]

The requirement that brain activity must be sufficiently differentiated is also suggested by a set of observations that are hardly emphasized enough in discussions of consciousness: Neural activity must exhibit sufficient *variance in time* to support conscious perception. If images on the retina are stabilized by using a contact lens containing a stimulus pattern that moves with the eye, for example, conscious visual perception of those images fades rapidly. A similar effect is seen in so-called Ganzfeld stimulation, when the entire visual field is filled by a whitish, shapeless surface. Explorers of the arctic were the first to describe this effect. After gazing into a frosty field of snowy white, they reported experiencing a form of "snow-blindness." In the 1930s, psychologists discovered that when people gazed into a featureless field of vision (a Ganzfeld), all color would soon drain from the field of vision, after which visual experience itself would fade. It would appear that a sufficient number of variable and differentiated brain states must be continually available for conscious experience to arise and be sustained.[32]

Our brief review of the vast field of neurological and neurophysiological evidence in this and the previous chapter leads to the following conclusions. First, conscious processes are typically associated with distributed changes in activity in the thalamocortical system. Second, distributed changes in neural activity associated with conscious experience must be integrated through reentrant interactions that are both rapid and effective. Finally, these interactions are associated with conscious reports if they are highly differentiated but not if they are uniform or homogenous. These empirical observations suggest that underlying consciousness are distributed neural processes that, through reentrant interactions, are at once highly integrated but continually changing and thus are highly differentiated. This conclusion becomes particularly relevant when one realizes, as we discussed in chapter 3, that integration and differentiation are also general properties of conscious experience, irrespective of its specific content.

To understand how these phenomenological properties relate to the actual neural mechanisms that are responsible for consciousness cannot be just a matter of accumulating additional facts, It requires a robust theory— one that provides insights into the biological origins of pattern formation, perceptual categorization, memory, concepts, and values. What kind of brain theory is compatible with the distributed, integrated, but continuously changing patterns of neural activity that can give rise to the unitary yet immensely differentiated phenomenology of conscious experience? We turn to a brief description of one such theory, a theory that we believe provides the necessary basis for understanding the key principles underlying global brain function. Formulating such a theory required us to confront several challenging questions. What kind of system is the functioning brain? How can its properties lead to consciousness? How can we account for its function in the face of its enormous variability? In our effort to answer these questions, we take the position that the brain is a selective, or Darwinian, system, one whose rich functioning actually *requires* variability.

PART THREE

Mechanisms of Consciousness: The Darwinian Perspective

In his theory of natural selection, Charles Darwin provided the chief foundation of modern biology. After his return from the voyage of the *Beagle*, he made continuing efforts to understand how the functions performed by the brain arose during evolution. His notebooks reveal his struggle to explain how perception, memory, and language could have arisen by what he called descent. We now have a rich evolutionary theory graced by the Darwinian perspective, but the problem of understanding mental processes is still with us. It remains for neuroscience to complete Darwin's program.

In this part, we show how Darwinian principles embedded in a theory of brain function provide insights into the processes of perception, memory, and the assignment of value, all of which are critical to an understanding of consciousness. Once the reader grasps the nature of such processes, the stage will be set to consider the actual neural mechanisms by which consciousness arises during evolution and development. Our efforts here are focused on primary consciousness, the ability to construct an integrated mental scene in the present that does not require language or a true sense of self. We believe that this integrated mental scene depends not only on the perceptual categorization of incoming sensory stimuli—the present—but, most important, on their interaction with categorical memories—the past. In other words, this integrated mental scene is a "remembered present." The main means by which the scene is constructed is through reentrant interactions among groups of neurons distributed in the thalamocortical system. As we show, these are just the kinds of interactions responsible for the integration and differentiation that we discussed in chapter 6.

CHAPTER SEVEN

Selectionism

In considering the origin of species, Charles Darwin made a great contribution that centered on population thinking: the idea that variation or diversity among individuals in a population provides a basis for competition during natural selection. Natural selection is reflected in the differential reproduction of fitter individuals in a species. In principle, selective events require the continual generation of diversity in repertoires of individual variants, the polling by environmental signals of these diverse repertoires, and the differential amplification or reproduction of those repertoire elements or individuals that match such signals better than their competition. Could it be that the brain follows such principles? We believe it does, and in this chapter we briefly review some aspects of the theory of neuronal group selection, or Neural Darwinism. This theory embraces these selective principles and applies them to the functioning brain. Its main tenets are (1) the formation during brain development of a primary repertoire of highly variant neuronal groups that contribute to neuroanatomy (developmental selection), (2) the formation during experience of a secondary repertoire of facilitated neural circuits as a result of changes in the strength of connections or synapses (experiential selection), and (3) a process of reentrant signaling along reciprocal connections between and among distributed neuronal groups to assure the spatiotemporal correlation of selected neural events. Together, the three tenets of this global brain theory provide a powerful means for understanding the key neural interactions that contribute to consciousness.

In his later years, Darwin disagreed strongly with Alfred Russel Wallace, the codiscoverer of natural selection, who, as a spiritualist, insisted that the brain and mind of man could not have arisen by natural selection. Wallace reasoned that savages had brains roughly the size of the brains of civilized Englishmen yet lacked mathematics and had no obvious need for abstract thought, so it was difficult for him to see how natural selection would have led to similar brain sizes in both cases. He was too thoroughgoing a natural selectionist and failed to recognize that during natural selection, there is correlative variation: A primary trait can be selected for and bring along changes that are used later for other selective events. For example, the selection of enlarged brain structures for perception could be accompanied by enlargements of neighboring brain regions. At some later evolutionary

FIGURE 7.1 CHARLES DARWIN AS A YOUNG MAN.

epoch, these regions may become selectively advantageous for some other function, such as memory. In a letter to Wallace in the spring of 1869, Darwin said, "I hope that you have not murdered too completely your own and my child"—meaning, of course, natural selection (see figure 7.1).[1]

Aside from the faultiness of Wallace's reasoning, the accumulation of evidence since that time strongly supports Darwin's conclusions: Whatever the specialness of the human brain, there is no need to invoke spiritual forces to account for its functions. Darwinian principles of variation in populations and natural selection are sufficient, and the elements invoked by spiritualism are not required for our being conscious. Being human in mind and brain appears clearly to be the result of an evolutionary process. The anthropological evidence emerging for the evolutionary origin of consciousness in humans further substantiates the notion that Darwin's is the most ideologically significant of all grand scientific theories.

Darwinian principles turn out to be important even for a basic understanding of brain functions, especially given the enormous variation in the structure and function of individual vertebrate brains. As we have discussed, no two brains are alike, and each individual's brain is continually changing. Variations extend over all levels of brain organization, from biochemistry to gross morphology, and the strengths of myriad individual synapses are constantly altered by experience. The extent of this enormous variability argues strongly against the notion that the brain is organized like a computer with fixed codes and registers. Moreover, the environment or world from which signals are delivered to the brain is not organized to give an unambiguous message like a piece of computer tape. There is no judge in nature giving out specific pronouncements on the brain's potential or actual patterns and there is no homunculus inside the head deciding which pattern should be chosen and interpreted. These facts are incompatible with the notion that the brain operates according to an unambiguous set of algorithms or instructions, like a computer. Instructionism, the idea that the environment can reliably provide the kind of information required by a computer, fails as a principle of brain operation. Yet in a given species, individual animals show certain consistent behaviors within the broad spread of individual responses.

How does the brain give rise to such responses? What principles govern its global operations? To answer these questions, we need a global brain theory, one that sets out the principles governing the operation of vast and diverse neural networks. Of course, the principles of such a theory must be consistent with our observations of the neural processes necessary for consciousness.

THE THEORY OF NEURONAL GROUP SELECTION

We have repeatedly stressed that one of the most striking features of each brain is its individuality and variability. This variability occurs at all levels of brain organization, and it is so great that it cannot be dismissed as mere noise or ignored while pursuing a mechanical theory of brain action. As we shall see, this variability provides a key basis for the differentiation and diversity of conscious states. The existence of this enormous diversity and individuality, seen in the multilayered structures and dynamics of each brain, poses a major challenge to any theory that is proposed to account for global brain function. We believe that this challenge can be met by turning to population thinking, which Darwin invented. Population thinking centers on the idea that variations among individuals of a species provide the basis for natural selection in the struggle for existence that eventually leads to the origin of other species.

Although Darwin did not have a correct picture of genetics, he understood that different individuals inherit different traits. Certain individuals would have greater fitness as the environment changed or new environments were occupied. These individuals would, over several generations, leave more progeny than would be able to utilize resources in the competition for survival and reproduction. Natural selection would thus effectively lead to differential reproduction of those individuals who, on the average, had higher fitness. This population principle has deep ramifications: It not only provides the basis for the origin of species, but it governs processes of somatic selection occurring in individual lifetimes. When we say somatic selection, we mean what occurs in a single body in time frames ranging from fractions of seconds to years and, obviously, ending with an animal's death. Thus, selection and variation can also occur in the cellular systems of animals.

A well-analyzed example of somatic selection is provided by the immune system.[2] In animals with backbones, there is an extraordinary cellular system capable of distinguishing foreign molecules or bacteria, viruses, and even another person's skin from the molecules of an individual body (or soma). The recognition is carried out by a set of remarkable proteins, called antibodies, that are made by circulatory blood cells. Antibodies have special sites that match or bind portions of other molecules, almost the way a cookie cutter matches a cookie of a given shape. What is remarkable is that practically any foreign molecule or antigen injected into the body will elicit the production of a complementary antibody that is essential for subsequent immune defense.

The original theory to account for the complementary fit between the antigen and the antibody was an "instructive" one: The antibody folded around the antigen's shape and kept the appropriately shaped fold. This theory turned out to be incorrect. Instead, the immune system works by somatic selection. The basis for molecular recognition of an enormous number of different foreign molecules is somatic variation in the antibody genes of each individual that leads to the production of a vast repertoire of antibodies, each with a different binding site. Exposure of the enormous repertoire of different antibodies to a foreign molecule is followed by the selection and growth of the cells bearing just those antibodies that fit the foreign chemical structure of a given antigen sufficiently well, even a structure that never occurred before in the history of the Earth. Although the mechanisms and timing of selective events obviously differ in evolution and immunity, the principles are the same—the Darwinian processes of variation and selection.

Over two decades ago, one of us began to think about how the mind could arise in evolution and development.[3] It seemed that the mind must have arisen as result of *two* processes of selection: natural selection and somatic selection. The first process is hardly doubted except perhaps by some philosophers and theologians. Thinking about the second led to the proposal of a theory based on selective principles and concerned with the evolution, development, structure, and function of the brain. It is worth reviewing here not only because one of its main tenets (reentry) is central to the origin of consciousness, but because its way of dealing with variability in the brain is essential to understanding the complexity of conscious processes.

This theory of neuronal group selection (TNGS), or Neural Darwinism, has three main tenets that are illustrated in figure 7.2:

1. *Developmental selection.* During the early development of individuals in a species, formation of the initial anatomy of the brain is certainly constrained by genes and inheritance. But from early embryonic stages onward, the connectivity at the level of synapses is established, to a large extent, by somatic selection during each individual's ongoing development. For example, during development, neurons extend myriads of branching processes in many directions. This branching generates extensive variability in the connection patterns of that individual and creates an immense and diverse repertoire of neural circuits. Then, neurons strengthen and weaken their connections according to their individual patterns of electrical activity: Neurons that fire together, wire together. As a result, neurons in a group are more closely connected to each other than to neurons in other groups.

2. Experiential selection. Overlapping this early period and extending
throughout life, a process of synaptic selection occurs within the repertoires
of neuronal groups as a result of behavioral experience. It is known, for
example, that maps of the brain corresponding to tactile inputs from the fingers can change their boundaries, depending on how much different fingers
are used. These changes occur because certain synapses within and between
groups of locally coupled neurons are strengthened and others are weakened
without changes in the anatomy. This selectional process is constrained by
brain signals that arise as a result of the activity of diffusely projecting value
systems, a constraint that is continually modified by successful output.

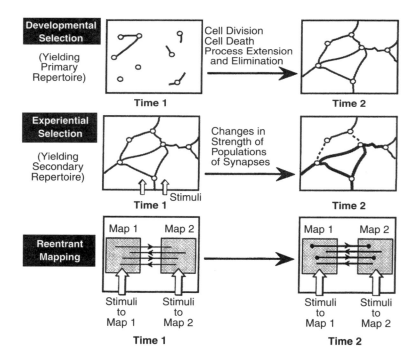

FIGURE 7.2 DIAGRAM OF THE THREE MAIN TENETS OF THE THEORY OF NEU-
RONAL GROUP SELECTION. (1) Developmental selection leads to a highly diverse set
of circuits, one of which is shown. (2) Experiential selection leads to changes in the
connection strengths of synapses favoring some pathways over others (see the black
lines). (3) Reentrant mapping. Brain maps are coordinated in space and time through
ongoing signaling across reciprocal connections. The black dots in the maps indicate
strengthened synapses.

3. Reentry. The correlation of selective events across the various maps of the brain occurs as a result of the dynamic process of reentry. Reentry allows an animal with a variable and uniquely individual nervous system to partition an unlabeled world into objects and events in the absence of a homunculus or computer program. As we have already discussed, reentry leads to the synchronization of the activity of neuronal groups in different brain maps, binding them into circuits capable of temporally coherent output. Reentry is thus the central mechanism by which the spatiotemporal coordination of diverse sensory and motor events takes place.

The first two tenets, developmental and experiential selection, provide the bases for the great variability and differentiation of distributed neural states that accompany consciousness. The third tenet, reentry, allows for the integration of those states. It is particularly important to understand the central role played by reentry in our efforts to build a consciousness model, and it therefore requires some further elaboration. A key anatomical precondition for reentry is the remarkable massively parallel reciprocal connectivity of brain areas. Although reciprocity between two different maps across multiple parallel fibers is common (think, for example, of the corpus callosum—the huge bundle of reciprocal fibers linking the two cortical hemispheres; see figure 6.1), many more complicated arrangements exist. The number of possible geometric and topological patterns possible in such a system is enormous. If we consider the combinatorial possibilities for reentrant selection across such patterns, even after allowing a number of neuroanatomical constraints to operate, we begin to glimpse the remarkable power of neuroanatomy in a selectional system. A jungle or food web, like the brain, has many levels and routes for the passage of signals but has nothing corresponding to reentrant neuroanatomy. Indeed, if asked, What characteristic uniquely differentiates higher brains from all other known objects or systems, we would say "reentrant organization." Note that while complex wide-area computer networks are beginning to share some properties with reentrant systems, such networks rely fundamentally on codes and, unlike brain networks, they are instructional, not selectional.

It is important to emphasize that reentry is not feedback. Feedback occurs along a *single* fixed loop made of reciprocal connections using previous *instructionally* derived information for control and correction, such as an error signal. In contrast, reentry occurs in selectional systems across *multiple* parallel paths where information is not prespecified. Like feedback, however, reentry can be local (within a map) or global (among maps and whole regions).

Reentry carries out several major functions.[4] For example, it can account for our ability to discern a shape in a display of moving dots, based on interactions between brain areas for visual movement and shape.[5] Thus, reentry can lead to the construction of new response properties. It can also mediate the synthesis of brain functions by connecting one submodality, such as color, to another, such as motion. It can also resolve conflicts among competing neural signals.[6] Reentry also ensures that changes in the efficacy of synapses in one area are affected by the activation patterns of distant areas, thereby making local synaptic changes context-dependent. Finally, by assuring the spatiotemporal correlation of neuronal firing, reentry is the main mechanism of neural integration.

Since the initial formulation of the TNGS, considerable evidence to support the theory has accumulated. Moreover, certain aspects of the theory have been greatly expanded. One of these aspects relates to the issue of degeneracy—the ability of structurally different variants of brain elements to produce the same function. Another important aspect of the theory is related to the notion of value, which we touched on briefly in chapter 4 in our discussion of diffusely projecting value systems. We consider each of these aspects in turn.

DEGENERACY

All selectional systems share a remarkable property that is as unique as it is essential to their functioning: In such systems, there are typically many different ways, *not necessarily structurally identical*, by which a particular output occurs. We call this property degeneracy.[7] Degeneracy is seen in quantum mechanics in certain solutions of the Schrödinger equation and in the genetic code, where, because of the degenerate third position in triplet code words, many different DNA sequences can specify the same protein.

Put briefly, degeneracy is reflected in the capacity of structurally different components to yield similar outputs or results. In a selectional nervous system, with its enormous repertoire of variant neural circuits even within one brain area, degeneracy is inevitable. Without it, a selectional system, no matter how rich its diversity, would rapidly fail—in a species, almost all mutations would be lethal; in an immune system, too few antibody variants would work; and in the brain, if only one network path was available, signal traffic would fail. Degeneracy can operate at one level of organization or across many. It is seen in gene networks, in the immune system, in the brain, and in evolution itself. For example, combinations of different genes can lead to the same structure, antibodies with different structures can recognize the same foreign molecule equally well, and different living forms can evolve to be equally well adapted to a specific environment.

There are countless examples of degeneracy in the brain. The complex meshwork of connections in the thalamocortical system assures that a large number of different neuronal groups can similarly affect, in one way or another, the output of a given subset of neurons. For example, a large number of different brain circuits can lead to the same motor output or action. Localized brain lesions often reveal alternative pathways that are capable of generating similar behaviors. Therefore, a manifest consequence of degeneracy in the nervous system is that certain neurological lesions may often appear to have little effect, at least within a familiar environment. Degeneracy also appears at the cellular level. Neural signaling mechanisms utilize a great variety of transmitters, receptors, enzymes, and so-called second messengers. The *same* changes in gene expression can be brought about by *different* combinations of these biochemical elements.

Degeneracy is not just a useful feature of selectional systems; it is also an unavoidable consequence of selectional mechanisms. Evolutionary selective pressure is typically applied to individuals at the end of a long series of complex events. These events involve many interacting elements at multiple temporal and spatial scales, and it is unlikely that well-defined functions can be neatly assigned to independent subsets of elements or processes in biological networks. For example, if selection occurs for our ability to walk in a particular way, connections within and among many different brain structures and to the muscoloskeletal apparatus are all likely to be modified over time. While locomotion will be affected, many other functions, including our ability to stand or jump, will also be influenced as a result of the degeneracy of neural circuits. The ability of natural selection to give rise to a large number of nonidentical structures yielding similar functions increases both the robustness of biological networks and their adaptability to unforeseen environments.

VALUE

As powerful as it is in providing alternative pathways for a given function, degeneracy cannot provide constraints for a selectional system; indeed, it is a relaxation of constraints. Given that this is so, how can a selectional system achieve its goals without specific instructions? It turns out that the necessary constraints or values are provided by a series of diverse phenotypic structures and neural circuits that have been selected during evolutionary time. We define values as phenotypic aspects of an organism that were selected during evolution and constrain somatic selective events, such as the synaptic changes that occur during brain development and experience. For example, the mere fact of having a hand with a certain shape and a certain propensity to grasp in one way and not in another enormously enhances the selection of synapses and of neural patterns of activity that lead to appropriate actions. The same actions would be almost impossible to synthesize or program from scratch, as experts in robotics know all too well. Another example is seen in the many reflexes with which newborn babies are endowed. These are not the only contributors to value, however. The diverse morphological characteristics (such as those of sensory organs and the motor apparatus) that link the parts and organs of the body to various brain functions are further examples. Hormonal loops can be prime contributors, but so can the way limbs are jointed in different vertebrate species. Values thus provide a basis for the development and refinement of brain-based categorization and action within a species.

It is important to stress that value is not identical to category. Value is only a *precondition* for arriving at a perceptual or behavioral response. Such a categorical response depends on the actual occurrence of selection. Perceptual categorization usually emerges as a result of selection during actual behavior in the real world. In general, although value shapes categorization in accord with evolution, it cannot convey or preserve the details of a real-world event. For example, value may be necessary for orienting the eyes of a baby toward a light source, but may not be sufficient for the recognition of different objects.

There are two limits to the concept of value as so far described. First, even a conglomerate of morphologically based values handed down in the phenotype (such as opposed thumbs and different kinds of joints) may not be specific enough to guide neural behavior (perceptual categorization, for example). The second limit is that evolutionarily defined, fixed value parameters may, by themselves, be too rigid to guide sufficiently rich behavior when an animal is confronted with unforeseen demands of the environment.

The first limit appears to have been transcended by the evolution of the special brain centers that we mentioned in chapter 4 when discussing the anatomy of the brain. In higher vertebrates, a series of diffusely projecting neural *value systems* appear to have evolved that are capable of continually signaling to neurons and synapses all over the brain. Such signals carry information about the ongoing behavioral state of the organism (sleep, waking, exploration, grooming, and the like), as well as the sudden occurrence of events that are salient for the entire organism (including, for example, novel stimuli, painful stimuli, and rewards).[8] These systems, whose importance vastly outweighs the proportion of brain space they occupy, include the noradrenergic, serotoninergic, cholinergic, dopaminergic, and histaminergic cell nuclei (see figure 4.4C). These are all small, compact cell groups, each of which sends diffuse projections to a substantial portion of the brain. The locus coeruleus, for example, consists of only a few thousand neurons in the brainstem. These neurons give rise to a vast meshwork of axons that blanket the cortex, hippocampus, basal ganglia, cerebellum, and spinal cord, potentially influencing transmission at billions of synapses over all levels of the central nervous system (see figure 7.3).

Neurons within some of the nuclei of value systems fire in a continuous or tonic manner when an animal is awake and stop firing when the animal falls asleep. Moreover, neurons belonging to value systems often produce a sudden burst of firing whenever something important or salient occurs to

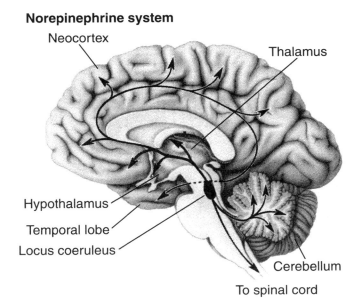

FIGURE 7.3 DIAGRAM OF A VALUE SYSTEM. The noradrenergic system originating in the locus coeruleus projects diffusely to the entire brain and releases the neuromodulator noradrenaline.

the animal. For example, neurons in the locus coeruleus fire whenever an animal enters a novel environment or something unexpected happens. When they fire, they release a neuromodulator—in this case, noradrenaline—over most, if not all, brain regions. Noradrenaline and neuromodulators that are released by different value systems can thus modify the activity of a large number of target neurons. They can also alter the probability that the strengthening or weakening of synapses will occur in response to neural activity.[9] In this way, value systems are perfectly poised to signal the occurrence of important events to the entire brain.

The importance of value systems for the functioning of a selectional brain has been demonstrated in a set of synthetically modeled artifacts that are capable of real-world behavior.[10] For example, in one such artifact, Darwin IV, a value system was required to allow a system controlling eye movements to track randomly moving targets (see figure 7.4). This value system reflected the inherited bias that "light is better than darkness" by firing whenever a spot of light hit the center of the eye, at which point a simu-

FIGURE 7.4 DARWIN IV TRACKING COLORED CUBES. The brain of this artifact is simulated in a powerful computer, but the artifact itself is not controlled by a conventional computer program.

lated modulating substance was released. This substance decayed over time, but, at sufficiently high levels, it led to the selective strengthening of synapses. With this value system in place, the simulated eye came to track objects after a certain number of trials. Of course, the system would also have responded as well in low light conditions if the value, "darkness is better than light" was used instead. In the appropriate nighttime environment, bats, with their sonarlike system, are as effective as eagles are in daylight or more so. In both cases, value systems are essential.

The second potential limit to the concept of value—too rigid a set of evolutionarily derived value constraints, leading to a pinched repertoire of stereotyped responses in a selectional system—can be met by evolving *modifiable* value systems. We predict, for example, that connections will be found that allow the responses of the ascending value systems themselves to be modified during learning experiences. A recent computer simulation that contrasts fixed and modifiable value systems has been used to test the effects of altering value constraints by learning. The introduction of a modifiable value system in this model led to rich behavior and allowed higher-order conditioning of that behavior that was not possible under a rigid inherited value constraint.[11]

An intriguing possibility is that the various value systems of the brain work together to affect brain action by interacting combinatorially, releasing various proportions of their different neuromodulators at the same time. For example, it is well known that during active waking, the noradrenergic, serotoninergic, and cholinergic systems are firing together. During slow-wave sleep, these three systems reduce their discharge, while during REM sleep, the noradrenergic and serotoninergic systems shut off completely, as the cholinergic system resumes its firing. Different combinations of the corresponding neuromodulators in vast areas of the brain are certainly responsible for many differences among behavioral states in the responses to external stimuli, learning and memory, emotion, and cognition. The possibilities are numerous but have so far not been explored.

It is but a small step to realize that much more sophisticated interactions among value systems related to pleasure, pain, bodily states, and various emotions are possible and are likely to govern cortical responses. The effects of value-dependent learning can range from alignment of auditory and visual maps in the brain stem of the barn owl[12] to the exquisite distinctions made by a connoisseur of wine or the emotional responses of a guilty person. Value and emotions, pleasant and unpleasant, are obviously tightly coupled and are central to conscious experience.[13]

Value is a sign of *nested* selective systems—a result of *natural selection* that yields alterations of the phenotype that can then serve as constraints on the *somatic selection* occurring in an individual's nervous system. Unlike evolution, somatic selection can deal with the contingencies of immediate environments that are rich and unpredictable—even ones that have never occurred before—by enabling an individual animal to categorize critical features of these environments during short periods. But we again emphasize that neuronal group selection can consistently accomplish this categorization only under the constraint of inherited values determined by evolution. The nest of systems is a beautiful one, guaranteeing survival for each species in terms of what may be called its necessary prejudice—one required for survival under behavioral control by a selectional brain. As we shall see, the existence of such arrangements is essential for the operation of various forms of memory found in selectional systems—forms that are essential for the evolution of consciousness. When we complete our discussion of memory, we will show how a conscious scene may be built by interactions of memory systems constrained by value with systems carrying out perceptual categorization.

CHAPTER EIGHT

Nonrepresentational Memory

Memory is a central component of the brain mechanisms that lead to consciousness. It is commonly assumed that memory involves the inscription and storage of information, but what is stored? Is it a coded message? When it is "read out" or recovered, is it unchanged? These questions point to the widespread assumption that what is stored is some kind of representation. This chapter takes the opposite viewpoint, consistent with a selectionist approach, that memory is nonrepresentational. We see memory as the ability of a dynamic system that is molded by selection and exhibits degeneracy to repeat or suppress a mental or physical act. This novel view of memory is illustrated with a geological comparison; memory is more like the melting and refreezing of a glacier than it is like an inscription on a rock.

We have argued that the brain is not organized like a computer, that its functioning rests instead on such properties as variability, differential amplification, degeneracy, and value. But if the brain is not like a computer, how does memory work? There is a widespread assumption that, at least in its cognitive functions, the brain is fundamentally concerned with representations and that what is stored in memory is also some sort of representation. In this view, memory is the more or less permanent laying down of changes that, when appropriately addressed, can recapture a representation and, if necessary, act on it. In this view, learned acts are themselves the consequences of representations that store definite procedures or codes.

The idea that representational memory occurs in the brain carries with it a huge burden. Although it allows an easy analogy to informational transac-

tions embedded in computers by humans, that analogy presents more problems than it solves. In the case of humans working with computers, semantic
operations occurring in the human operator's brain, not in the computer, are
necessary to make sense of the coded syntactical strings that are stored phys-
ically in the computer. Coherence must be maintained in the code (or, if not,
error correction is required), and the memory capacity of the system is natu-
rally expressed in terms of storage limits. Above all, the input to a computer
must itself be coded in an unambiguous fashion.

The problem the brain confronts is that signals from the world do not
generally represent a coded input. Instead, they are potentially ambiguous,
are context-dependent, and are not necessarily adorned by prior judgments
of their significance.[1] The signals entering the eye of an animal in the jungle—patches of green and overlapping browns and of movements in the
wind—can be combined in countless ways. An animal must nevertheless categorize these signals for its own adaptive purposes, whether in perception or
in memory, and somehow it must associate this categorization with previous
experiences of the same kinds of signals. In the case of humans, we would
most likely report seeing "trees." Because of the enormous number of
changeable combinations, to do so with a coded or replicative storage system would require endless error correction and a precision at least as great
or greater than that of computers. There is no evidence, however, that the
structure of the brain could support such capabilities directly; neurons do
not do precise floating-point arithmetic. Such mathematical capabilities are
not directly represented in brains but have arisen in human culture as a consequence of linguistic interactions and the application of logic, all, of course,
because we have brains.

Representation implies symbolic activity, an activity that is certainly at
the center of our semantic and syntactical language skills. It is no wonder
that in thinking about how the brain can repeat a performance—that it can,
for example, call up what may appear to be an image already experienced—
we are tempted to say that the brain represents. The flaws in yielding to this
temptation, however, are obvious: There is no precoded message in the signal, no structures capable of the high-precision storage of a code, no judge
in nature to provide decisions on alternative patterns, and no homunculus in
the head to read a message. For these reasons, memory in the brain cannot
be representational in the same way as it is in our devices.

How, then, can one conceive of a nonrepresentational memory? An analogy will help. Consider the immune system. An antibody is not a representation of a foreign antigen, yet through the system of immunological memory,

it and other antibodies can recognize that antigen. An animal can be well adapted to an environment but is not a representation of that environment. Similarly, a memory is not a representation; it is a reflection of how the brain has changed its dynamics in a way that allows the repetition of a performance.

In a complex brain, memory results from the selective matching that occurs between ongoing, distributed neural activity and various signals coming from the world, the body, and the brain itself. The synaptic alterations that ensue affect the future responses of the individual brain to similar or different signals. These changes are reflected in the ability to repeat a mental or physical act after some time despite a changing context, for example, in "recalling" an image. It is important to indicate that by the word *act*, we mean any ordered sequence of brain activities in a domain of perception, movement, or speech that, in time, leads to a particular neural output. We stress repetition after some time in this definition because it is the ability to re-create an act separated by a certain duration from the original signal set that is characteristic of memory. And in mentioning a changing context, we pay heed to a key property of memory in the brain: that it is, in some sense, a form of constructive *recategorization* during ongoing experience, rather than a precise replication of a previous sequence of events.

GLOBAL MAPPINGS

The cerebral cortex alone is not sufficient to bear the burden of perceptual categorization and control of movement. That burden is carried out, according to the theory of neuronal group selection (TNGS), by a structure called a global mapping (see figure 8.1). A global mapping relates an animal's movement and changing sensory input to the action of the hippocampus, basal ganglia, and cerebellum as they connect to the cerebral cortex. It links the first two topological arrangements of anatomy, the thalamocortical system and the subcortical appendages that we considered in chapter 4. A global mapping is thus a dynamic structure containing multiple reentrant local maps (both motor and sensory) that interact with nonmapped regions, such as those of the brain stem, basal ganglia, hippocampus, and parts of the cerebellum. The activity of a global mapping reflects the fact that perception generally depends on and leads to action. When one moves one's head to follow a moving target, the motor and sensory portions of a global mapping continually readjust. In other words, categorization does not occur solely in a cortical sensory area that then executes a program to activate a motor output. Instead, the results of continual motor activity are considered to be an essential part of perceptual categorization. This consideration implies that the global mappings carrying out such categorization must contain both sensory and motor elements. Neuronal group selection in global mappings occurs in a dynamic loop that continually matches gesture and posture to several kinds of sensory signals. In other words, the dynamic structure of a global mapping is maintained, refreshed, and altered by continual motor activity and rehearsal.

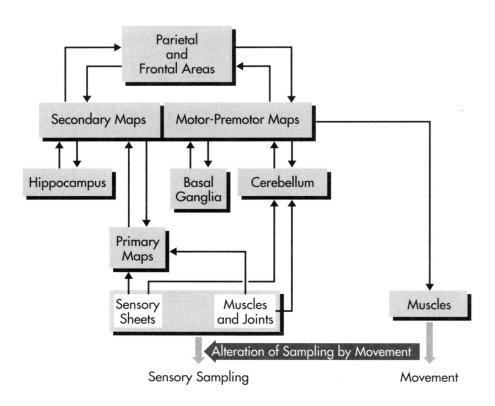

FIGURE 8.1 DIAGRAM OF A GLOBAL MAPPING. This structure is made up of multiple brain maps. These maps are connected to subcortical appendages, such as the hippocampus, basal ganglia, and cerebellum. Note that signals from the outside world enter into this mapping and that outputs lead to movement. This movement, in turn, alters how sensory signals are picked up. A global mapping is thus a dynamic structure, one that changes with time and behavior. Its reentrant local maps, which correlate features and movement, make perceptual categorization possible.

Global mappings provide a necessary substrate for relating categorization to memory. This relationship cannot generally be accounted for by the activity of any one small neural region, for, by their nature, global mappings must include large portions of the nervous system. Within a global mapping, long-term changes in synaptic strengths tend to favor the mutual reentrant activity of those groups whose activity has been correlated across different maps during past behavior. When we prepare to grasp a glass and drink, for example, a whole set of different circuits, modified by previous synaptic changes, are called up. Such synaptic changes over large portions of a global mapping provide the basis for memory, but memory in global mappings is not a store of fixed or coded attributes to be called up and assembled in a replicative fashion as in a computer. Instead, memory results from a process of continual recategorization, which, by its nature, must be procedural and involves continual motor activity leading to the ability to repeat a performance—in our example, grasping a glass. The ongoing synaptic changes in global mappings that occur as a result of such rehearsals favor degenerate sets of pathways *with similar outputs*. The contribution of global mappings to memory also carries the major burden of unconscious performance in the brain. In chapter 14 we discuss how such unconscious activity can be linked to the processes responsible for consciousness.

MEMORY AND SELECTION

What characteristics of the brain give rise to a dynamic memory without coded representation? We believe the answer is just those characteristics that one would find in a selectional system. These characteristics are a set of degenerate neural circuits making up a diverse repertoire, a means of changing the synaptic populations upon receiving various input signals, and a set of value constraints that increase the likelihood of repetition of an adaptive or rewarding output regardless of which degenerate circuit is used. Given these constraints, signals from the world or from other parts of the brain act to select certain circuits from the enormously various combinatorial possibilities available. Selection occurs at the level of synapses through alteration of their efficacy or strengths. Which particular synapses are altered depends on previous experience, as well as on the combined activities of the ascending value systems that we mentioned before (the locus coeruleus, raphé nucleus, cholinergic nuclei, and so forth).

Thus, the triggering of *any* set of circuits that results in a set of output responses sufficiently similar to those that were previously adaptive provides the basis for a repeated mental act or physical performance. In this view, a memory is dynamically *generated* from the activity of certain selected subsets of circuits. These subsets are degenerate: A comparison would indicate that different subsets contain circuits that are not the same; nevertheless, activation of any of them can result in a repetition of some particular output. Under these conditions, a given memory cannot be identified uniquely with any single specific set of synaptic changes because the particular synaptic changes associated with a given output and eventually with an entire performance are subject to further change during that performance. So what is called forth when an act is repeated must be any one or more of the neural *response patterns* adequate to that performance, not some singular sequence or specific detail.

We see that synaptic change is fundamental and essential for memory but is not identical to it. There is no code, only a changing set of circuits corresponding to a given output. The more or less equally effective members of that set of circuits can have widely varying structures. It is this property of degeneracy in neural circuits that allows for changes in particular memories as new experiences and changes in context occur. Memory in a degenerate selectional system is recategorical, not strictly replicative. There is no prior set of determinant codes governing the categories of memory, only the previous population structure of the network, the state of the value systems, and the physical acts carried out at a given moment. The dynamic changes linking one set of circuits to another within the enormously varied neuroanatomical repertoires of the brain allow it to *create* a memory. The probability of creating a memory is enhanced by the activity of value systems.

In our example of reaching for a glass, the satisfaction of thirst will activate value systems and lead to the selection of a number of circuits appropriate for performing that action. By these means, structurally different circuits within the degenerate repertoires are each able to produce a similar output, leading to repetition or variation of the act of reaching. Their activity gives rise to the associative properties of memory; for example, an act can trigger another act, a word can trigger other words, or an image can provoke a narrative. These associative properties arise materially from the fact that each different member of the degenerate set of circuits used at different times has different alternative network connections.

In this view, there are hundreds, if not thousands, of separate memory systems in the brain. These systems range from all the perceptual systems in different modalities—sight, smell, touch, and so on—to the systems that govern intended or actual movement, to the language systems that organize speech sounds. This view is compatible with various types of memory described and tested by experimentalists in the field—so-called procedural, semantic, episodic memories, and the like—but it does not restrict itself to these types, which are defined mainly by operational criteria and, to some degree, by biochemical criteria.

Although such individual memory systems differ, the key conclusion is that whatever its form, memory itself is a system property. It cannot be equated exclusively with circuitry, with synaptic changes, with biochemistry, with value constraints, or with behavioral dynamics. Instead, it is the dynamic result of the interactions of *all* these factors acting together, serving to select an output that repeats a performance or an act. The overall characteristics of a particular performance may be similar to a previous performance, but the ensembles of neurons underlying any two similar performances at different times can be and usually are different. This property ensures that one can repeat the same act, despite remarkable changes in background and context, with ongoing experience.

Besides guaranteeing association, the property of degeneracy also gives rise to the remarkable stability of memorial performance. In a degenerate system, there are large numbers of ways of assuring a given output. As long as a sufficient population of subsets of circuits remains to give an output, neither cell death nor changes in a particular circuit or two nor switches in the contextual aspects of input signals will generally be sufficient to extirpate a memory. Thus, nonrepresentational memory is extraordinarily robust.[2]

AN ALPINE METAPHOR

We can better understand the operation of a nonrepresentational memory by means of an analogy. Consider a mountain, with a glacier at its top, under changing climatic conditions leading to melting and refreezing (see figure 8.2). Under one set of warming conditions, certain rivulets will run and merge downhill to a stream that feeds a pond in the valley below. Let that pond formation stand for the output leading to a repeated performance, that is, the feed to the pond has occurred before with similar consequences. Now change the sequence of weather conditions, resulting in the freezing of some rivulets, followed by a warming period leading to melting and merger with some other rivulets as well as the creation of new ones. Even though the structure on the heights is now changed, the same output stream may be fed exactly as before. But given even a small further change in temperature, wind, or rain, a new stream may result, feeding or creating another pond

FIGURE 8.2 KNIK GLACIER, ALASKA.

associated with the first. With further changes, the two systems may merge their rivulets, which simultaneously may then feed both ponds. These ponds may, in turn, become connected in the valley.

In this analogy, consider the value constraints to be gravity and the texture of the valley terrain, the input signals to be the changes induced by the weather, the synaptic change to involve freezing and melting, and the detailed rocky pattern down the hill to be the neuroanatomy, and you have a way of seeing how a performance can be repeated dynamically without a code. Now we must switch the scene and imagine the vast set of graphs constituted by the neuroanatomy of the brain. If we consider all the different kinds of connections that can operate simultaneously in the brain, we must go to a space of higher dimension than the one we used in our example, which has only three dimensions. By extending the process to any number of dimensions, one can, at least figuratively, see how a dynamic nonrepresentational memory may work.

Such a memory has properties that allow perception to alter recall and recall to alter perception. It has no fixed capacity limit, since it actually generates "information" by construction. It is robust, dynamic, associative, and adaptive. If our view of memory is correct, in higher organisms every act of perception is, to some degree, an act of creation, and every act of memory is, to some degree, an act of imagination. Biological memory is thus creative and not strictly replicative. It is one of the essential bases of consciousness, to the mechanisms of which we now turn.

CHAPTER NINE

Perception into Memory: The Remembered Present

To uncover the neural mechanisms of consciousness, it is useful to keep in mind the distinction between primary consciousness and higher-order consciousness. Primary consciousness is seen in animals with certain brain structures similar to ours. These animals appear to be able to construct a mental scene but have limited semantic or symbolic capabilities and no true language. Higher-order consciousness (which flourishes in humans and presupposes the coexistence of primary consciousness) is accompanied by a sense of self and the ability in the waking state explicitly to construct past and future scenes. It requires, at the minimum, a semantic capability and, in its most developed form, a linguistic capability.

In this chapter, we present a model that accounts for the appearance of primary consciousness in the course of evolution that is consistent with a selectionist view of the brain. We briefly consider the neural requirements to be incorporated in such a model. The first requirement is perceptual categorization, the ability to carve up the world of signals into categories adaptive for a given animal species. The second requirement is the development of concepts. We propose that concepts arise from the mapping by the brain itself of the activity of the brain's own areas and regions. Two more requirements for conscious experience are the appearance of a categorical memory responsive to value and the activity of reentry, which is the fundamental integrative mechanism in higher brains. We propose that primary consciousness emerged in evolution when, through the appearance of new circuits mediating reen-

try, posterior areas of the brain that are involved in perceptual categorization were dynamically linked to anterior areas that are responsible for a value-based memory. With such means in place, an animal would be able to build a remembered present—a scene that adaptively links immediate or imagined contingencies to that animal's previous history of value-driven behavior.

The greatest challenge to modern neuroscience is to provide an adequate analysis of the brain mechanisms that give rise to consciousness. In this chapter, we consider a proposal for the neural mechanisms of consciousness that is based on the selectional brain theory we presented in chapter 7. To understand the neural processes that underlie consciousness, one must first understand a number of other brain processes at a variety of organizational levels. These processes include perceptual categorization; concepts; value; memory; and, at the neural level, special dynamic processes of corticothalamic organization. Without such an understanding, it is no wonder that the apparently simultaneous and complex experiences of various sensations, moods, scenes, situatedness, thoughts, feelings, and emotions, all occurring in parallel or in serial causal sequences, can appear hopelessly disconnected in their complexity from any brain-based mechanisms proffered to explain them. And since, unlike the procedures of physics, the phenomenal experience itself is part of the object of scrutiny, it is no wonder that some students of the subject have pointed out that conscious experience and its purported underlying brain mechanisms are printed in noninterchangeable currencies. We believe, on the contrary, that the currencies can be related, but that the exchange demands some prerequisite understanding.

PREREQUISITES FOR A MODEL OF PRIMARY CONSCIOUSNESS

In analyzing consciousness, we deliberately avoid addressing too many difficult problems at once or being distracted by its rich phenomenology. In line with this restraint, we emphasize the useful distinction between primary consciousness and higher-order consciousness.[1] Primary consciousness—the ability to generate a mental scene in which a large amount of diverse information is integrated for the purpose of directing present or immediate behavior—occurs in animals with brain structures similar to ours. Such animals appear able to construct a mental scene but, unlike us, have limited semantic or symbolic capabilities and no true language. Higher-order consciousness is built on the foundations provided by primary consciousness and is accompanied by a sense of self and the ability in the waking state explicitly to construct and connect past and future scenes. In its most developed form, it requires a semantic capability and a linguistic capability. By necessity, only individuals who are endowed with higher-order consciousness can report conscious states and speak about consciousness; they are conscious of being conscious. In what follows, we concern ourselves mainly with primary consciousness but bring in higher-order consciousness when it affords experimental insights. In the last part of the book, we deal in detail with some of the more intriguing aspects of higher-order consciousness, including thought, language, the notion of the self, and self-reference.

Before we consider a mechanistic model for the appearance of primary consciousness during the course of evolution, we must rapidly review certain essential neural processes. What we need to consider are the structures and mechanisms that must be described to account for the consciousness that we ascribe to dogs and to ourselves when, in certain subjective states, we are least in bondage to language. Here we must face a number of complex processes and their interactions, all of which we have touched on before. There are four. The first is a property shared by all animals—*perceptual categorization*, the ability to carve up the world of signals into categories useful for a given species in an environment that follows physical laws but itself contains no such categories. Along with the control of movement, perceptual categorization is the most fundamental process of the vertebrate nervous system. We have described how it occurs in higher vertebrates as a result of reentrant signaling among the various areas of the brain that are present within global mappings. It occurs, usually simultaneously, in a number of modalities (including sight, hearing, joint sense, or kinesthesia) and in a variety of submodalities (within the visual modality, for example, color, orientation, and motion).

The next process required for understanding primary consciousness is the development of *concepts*. By *concept*, we do not mean a sentence or proposition that is subject to the tests of the philosopher's or logician's truth table. Instead, we mean the ability to combine different perceptual categorizations related to a scene or an object and to construct a "universal" reflecting the abstraction of some common feature across a variety of such percepts. For example, different faces have many different details, but the brain somehow manages to recognize that they all have similar general features. It has been proposed that concepts arise as a result of the mapping by the brain itself of the activity of the brain's different areas and regions. By these means, various common features of responses to different signals can be abstracted—for example, general features of a given form of object motion may be abstractly obtained when the brain, say of a cat, can register a particular state (described here verbally for explanatory purposes) as "cerebellum and basal ganglia active in pattern *a*, neuronal groups in premotor and motor regions engaged in pattern *b*, and visual submodalities x, *y*, and *z* simultaneously interactive." Higher-order maps register these activities and yield an output corresponding to the notion that an object is moving forward in reference to the cat's body. Forward motion is a concept. Of course, no words are involved. No simple combination of the maps that are reentrantly interactive to yield perceptual categorizations can lead to this abstractive capability. What is required is higher-order mapping by the brain itself of the categories of brain activity in these various regions.

Two more processes, related respectively to memory and value, must be understood before we describe a mechanism for primary consciousness. As we have seen, according to the theory of neuronal group selection (TNGS), *memory* is the capacity specifically to repeat or suppress a mental or physical act. That capacity arises from combinations of synaptic alterations in reentrant circuits. Furthermore, because a selectional nervous system is not preprogrammed, it requires *value* constraints to develop categorical responses that are adaptive. The diffuse ascending value systems of the brain are known to be richly connected to the concept-forming regions of the brain, notably the frontal and temporal cortex, but also to the so-called limbic system, a set of brain regions located on the medial (internal) side of the brain that form a circle around the brainstem. These regions affect the dynamics of individual memories, which, in turn, are established or not, depending on positive or negative value responses. The rich psychological literature on learning suggests that value, emotional responses, and salience provide strong constraints on the establishment of a conceptual, category-based memory. The death of President John F. Kennedy, for example, carried rich emotional freight, and many people report that they remember exactly what they were doing and where they were when they first heard of it. The synaptic alterations that combine to develop various individual memories, collectively constituting a "value-category memory," are essential to a model of primary consciousness.

THE CRITICAL ROLE OF REENTRY

We have one final process to consider before we turn to a description of the mechanisms of consciousness. This process, reentry, is the third main tenet of the TNGS. As we previously discussed, reentry is a process of ongoing parallel and recursive signaling between separate brain maps along massively parallel anatomical connections, most of which are reciprocal. It alters and is altered by the activity of the target areas it interconnects. Reentry is not only the most important integrative mechanism in higher brains, but is conceptually the most challenging of the principles proposed in the TNGS. It is critical to a variety of processes, ranging from perceptual categorization and motor coordination to consciousness itself. In chapter 4, we gave the example of a string quartet in which the players were linked by myriad fine threads that gave ongoing signals shared among the otherwise independent instrumentalists and thus coordinated their individual performances. In our brains, the "threads" are actually parallel, reciprocal fibers connecting separate maps; the neural firings among these fibers go from one map to another and then come back or reenter in a constant dynamic interchange. This interchange synchronizes and coordinates the functions of the various maps.

Reentry plays the central role in our consciousness model, for it is reentry that assures the integration that is essential to the creation of a scene in primary consciousness. Integration can best be illustrated by considering exactly how functionally segregated maps in the cerebral cortex may operate coherently together even though there is no superordinate map or logically determined program. As we mentioned in chapter 4, the organization of the cerebral cortex is such that even within a single modality, for example, vision, there is a multitude of specialized or functionally segregated maps devoted to different submodalities—color, movement, and form. Despite this diversity, we are aware of a coherent perceptual scene. When we see such a scene, we are not aware of colors, movements, and forms separately and independently, but bind the color with the shape and the movement into recognizable objects. Our ability to act coherently in the presence of diverse, often conflicting, sensory stimuli requires a process of neural interaction across many levels of organization without any superordinate map to guide the process. This is the so-called binding problem: How can a set of diverse and functionally segregated maps cohere without a higher-order controller? Within a single area, *linking* must occur among various neuronal groups in the same feature domain or submodality. Examples are perceptual groupings within a map in sensing color or in another map sensing movement. At a higher level, *binding* must take place among *different* distributed maps, each of which is functionally segregated or specialized. Binding, for example, assures the integration of the neuronal responses to a particular object contour with its color, position, and direction of movement.

Since there is no superordinate map that coordinates the binding of the participating maps, the question arises: How does binding actually take place? A set of models and computer simulations, discussed in chapter 10, has shown that binding can occur as a result of reentry across brain maps that establishes short-term temporal correlations and synchrony among the activities of widely spaced neuronal groups in different maps. As a result, neurons in these groups fire at the same time. Thus, reentry correlates a large number of dynamic circuits in space and time. The selection of those circuits that are temporally correlated under constraints of value leads to a coherent output. This binding principle, made possible by reentry, is repeated across many levels of brain organization and plays a central role in mechanisms leading to consciousness.

PRIMARY CONSCIOUSNESS: THE REMEMBERED PRESENT

With a grasp of the mechanisms of reentry and the notions of perceptual categorization, concept formation, and value-category memory in hand, we can now formulate a model of how primary consciousness arose in the course of evolution. The model assumes that during evolution, the cortical systems leading to perceptual categorization were already in place before primary consciousness appeared. With the further development of secondary cortical areas and the various cortical appendages, such as the basal ganglia, conceptual memory systems emerged. At a point in evolutionary time corresponding roughly to the transitions between reptiles and birds and reptiles and mammals, a critical new anatomical connectivity appeared. Massively reentrant connectivity arose between the multimodal cortical areas carrying out perceptual categorization and the areas responsible for value-category memory. This evolutionarily derived reentrant connectivity is implemented by several grand systems of corticocortical fibers linking one part of the cortex to the rest and by a large number of reciprocal connections between the cortex and the thalamus (see figure 4.4A). The thalamocortical circuits mediating these reentrant interactions originate in the major subdivisions of the thalamus: structures known as the specific thalamic nuclei, the reticular nucleus, and the intralaminar nuclei. The specific nuclei of the thalamus are the ones that are reentrantly connected with the cerebral cortex; they do not communicate directly with each other, but the reticular nucleus has inhibitory connections with those nuclei and can act to select or gate various combinations of their activity. The intralaminar nuclei send diffuse projections to most areas of the cerebral cortex and help to synchronize its overall level of activity. All these thalamocortical structures and their reciprocal connections acting together via reentry lead to the creation of a conscious scene (see figure 9.1).

The dynamic reentrant interactions that occur via the connections between memory systems and systems for perceptual categorization take place within periods ranging from hundreds of milliseconds to seconds—the "specious present" of William James. Strongly interacting neuronal groups that change and are differentiated from each other can be integrated by these means. These groups are distributed in the thalamocortical system in

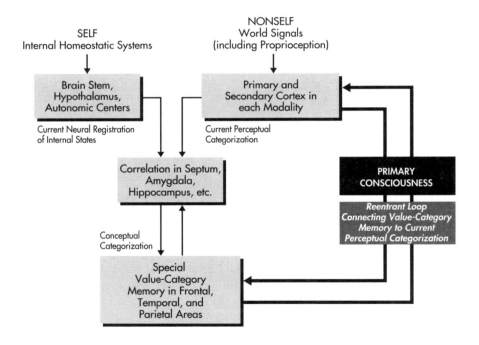

FIGURE 9.1 MECHANISMS OF PRIMARY CONSCIOUSNESS. Signals related to value and categorized signals from the outside world are correlated and lead to memory in conceptual areas. This memory, which is capable of conceptual categorization, is linked by reentrant paths (the heavy lines) to *current* perceptual categorization of world signals. This reentrant linkage results in primary consciousness. When it occurs through many modalities (sight, touch, and so forth), primary consciousness is of a "scene" made up of objects and events, some of which are not causally connected to each other. An animal with primary consciousness can nonetheless connect these objects and events through memory via its previous value-laden experience.

ways that we described in chapters 5 and 6. What emerges from their inter-actions is an ability to construct a scene. The ongoing parallel input of sig-nals from many different sensory modalities in a moving animal results in reentrant correlations among complexes of perceptual categories that are related to objects and events. Their salience is governed in that particular animal by the activity of its value systems. This activity is influenced, in turn, by memories conditioned by that animal's history of reward and punishment acquired during its past behavior. The ability of an animal to connect events and signals in the world, whether they are causally related or merely con-temporaneous, and, then, through reentry with its value-category memory system, to construct a scene that is related to its own learned history is the basis for the emergence of primary consciousness.

The short-term memory that is fundamental to primary consciousness reflects previous categorical and conceptual experiences. The interaction of the memory system with current perception occurs over periods of fractions of a second in a kind of bootstrapping: What is new perceptually can be incorporated in short order into memory that arose from previous catego-rizations. The ability to construct a conscious scene is the ability to construct, within fractions of seconds, a remembered present. Consider an animal in a jungle, who senses a shift in the wind and a change in jungle sounds at the beginning of twilight. Such an animal may flee, even though no obvious danger exists. The changes in wind and sound have occurred independently before, but the last time they occurred together, a jaguar appeared; a con-nection, though not provably causal, exists in the memory of that conscious individual.

An animal without such a system could still behave and respond to partic-ular stimuli and, within certain environments, even survive. But it could not link events or signals into a complex scene, constructing relationships *based on its own unique history of value-dependent responses*. It could not imagine scenes and would often fail to evade certain complex dangers. It is the emer-gence of this ability that leads to consciousness and underlies the evolution-ary selective advantage of consciousness. With such a process in place, an animal would be able, at least in the remembered present, to plan and link contingencies constructively and adaptively in terms of its own previous his-tory of value-driven behavior. Unlike its preconscious evolutionary ancestor, it would have greater selectivity in choosing its responses to a complex envi-ronment. As we have emphasized, if there is one central structural principle that underlies the appearance of consciousness, it is the emergence during evolution of new anatomically based reentrant systems. Under the constraint of values, these systems serve to relate new forms of memory to perceptual and conceptual activities in the brain.

Following the appearance of primary consciousness and after the evolutionary emergence of higher-order consciousness with language in humans, one of the most important global values related to survival was the continuity and coherence of the self. Reentry, continually operating in a degenerate system to allow recategorical memory, provides a fundamental mechanism by which this continuity can be achieved despite ongoing internal and external change. The paradox that concerned James—how momentary conscious states could be reconciled with various previous states, creating a stable sense of present unity or personal identity—is dissolved when one understands the dynamic nature of the functional integration imposed by reentry between perceptual and memorial systems. Of course, such a self appears in humans who are capable of higher-order consciousness, which emerged later in evolution when a new set of reentrant connections were established between language centers and conceptual centers. We consider the implications of this second transcendent evolutionary event involving reentry in the last part of this book.

The model we have proposed here is, of course, bare bones. Nevertheless, it provides a firm neuroanatomical and neurophysiological foundation for understanding the neural mechanisms underlying consciousness. It also provides a unitary framework that allows us to pursue the goal we stated at the beginning of this book: to formulate a specific hypothesis about the kinds of neural processes that can account for the fundamental integrative and informative properties of conscious experience.

PART FOUR

Dealing with Plethora: The Dynamic Core Hypothesis

At the beginning of this book, we proposed that a scientific analysis of consciousness should account for the fundamental properties of conscious experience—those shared by every conscious state. Among such fundamental properties are the following two: first, consciousness is highly integrated or unified—every conscious state constitutes a unified whole that cannot effectively be subdivided into independent components—and second, at the same time, it is highly differentiated or informative—there is an enormous number of different conscious states, each of which can lead to different behavioral consequences.

As we have already seen, the distributed neural processes underlying conscious experience also share these properties: They are highly integrated and, at the same time, highly differentiated. We believe that this convergence between neurobiology and phenomenology is not mere coincidence.

On the contrary, it can yield valuable insights into the kinds of neural processes that can account for the corresponding properties of conscious experience.

In this part of the book, we attempt to account for the unity and informativeness of conscious experience and further develop our ideas on the neural bases of conscious experience by providing a solid theoretical framework for the notions of integration and differentiation. First, we have to be clear about what we mean by integration and differentiation. Then we need to deal in a more precise fashion with how integration and differentiation are actually realized in the brain. We develop a quantitative measure of the functional clustering of neural activity, which is related to integration, as well as a quantitative measure of neural complexity, which is related to differentiation. Dealing clearly with these issues calls for some mathematics, although most of the technical aspects can be conveniently ignored as long as the concepts remain. The results of these analyses allow us to propose a hypothesis, called the dynamic core hypothesis, which provides a concise operational statement of what is special about the activity of groups of neurons that underlies conscious experience. On the basis of the dynamic core hypothesis, we revisit the key properties of consciousness that we described before and provide a set of clear-cut empirical criteria for distinguishing the neural processes that contribute to consciousness from those that do not.

CHAPTER TEN

Integration and Reentry

In this chapter we intend to achieve a more complete scientific understanding of the neural processes that explain the unity or integration of conscious experience. Toward this end, we define precisely what we mean by integration, how integration can be measured, and how an integrated neural process can be identified. We do so by introducing a new concept: the "functional cluster." We also discuss the means by which the integration or binding of the activity of distributed brain areas can be brought about in less than a second. This is a famous problem in today's neuroscience—often called the "binding problem." Using the results of large-scale computer simulations, we show that reentry is the key neural mechanism by which integration can be achieved within the thalamocortical system and indicate how such integration can lead to a unified behavioral output. These results provide a parsimonious solution to the binding problem.

When we drive, the visual scene in front of us is full of objects—cars, trucks, bikes, pedestrians, lanes, trees, houses, sky—each of which has a specific shape, a specific color, and a specific position in the visual field. Some objects may move and emit specific sounds or smells. Furthermore, these objects may be related to each other in specific and meaningful ways, and we could provide a concept and a name for each of them . Yet, with all this remarkable richness and diversity, what we experience at any one moment is a single, unified conscious scene, a scene that is meaningful only as a whole and that, while it is being experienced, cannot be subdivided into independent components. Moment by moment, the scene nevertheless changes continuously as we drive along.

Given the remarkable unity or integration of each conscious state, the neural processes that sustain conscious experience must certainly be integrated as well. Indeed, in chapter 6, we described several studies that demonstrated that coherent patterns of firing among distributed groups of neurons do occur, providing a clear sign of integration. By themselves, however, the results of such experiments are not sufficient for an understanding of the *mechanisms* underlying the rapid integration of neural activity in the brain. To dissect such mechanisms, we have constructed a number of large-scale models that embody the anatomical and physiological arrangement of the thalamocortical system. These models provide a clear-cut solution to the binding problem and show how an integrated neural process that includes many distributed elements can emerge in the central nervous system.

REENTRY AND NEURAL INTEGRATION: SOLVING THE BINDING PROBLEM

Studying the mechanisms by which different signals from a large number of neurons are integrated in the central nervous system is a daunting task. Only over the past few years has it become experimentally feasible to record electrical activity simultaneously from multiple neurons in awake, behaving animals. Despite the importance of this approach, the number of neurons that can be sampled is still severely limited. In contrast, neuroimaging techniques, such as PET and fMRI, can probe the activity of millions of synapses and brain areas at once, but their spatial and temporal resolution is insufficient to follow the fate of individual neural signals. To examine the behaviors of such large populations of interacting cells we must turn to neural modeling.

Large-scale computer simulations have allowed us not only to follow the activity of individual neural units in intricately connected systems, but to examine the spatiotemporal patterns of firing of tens of thousands of neurons as these patterns develop after the presentation of, for example, certain visual stimuli. Such simulations offer the opportunity to carry out various perturbations and manipulations that would otherwise be experimentally difficult.[1]

The notion of reentry has been explored in a large-scale simulation of the visual system, which provides a solution to the problem of integrating, or "binding," the activity of functionally segregated brain areas (see figure 10.1).[2] Inasmuch as they reflect general properties of cortical organization, many of the principles embodied in this model appear to be applicable not just to the visual system, but to other sensory or motor modalities.[3]

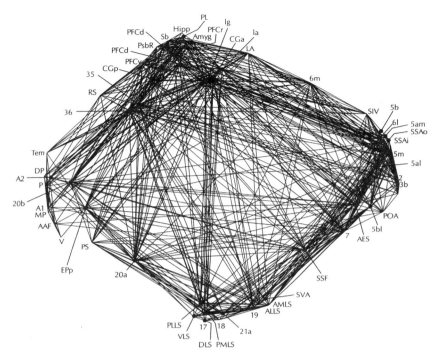

FIGURE 10.1 WHAT IS CONNECTED TO WHAT. The diagram represents 64 areas from the cerebral cortex of the cat with 1,134 connection paths between them (the abbreviations referring to the technical names of different brain areas do not need to concern us here). Most connection paths are reciprocal. Areas are depicted close to each other if they are connected and far away if they are not connected. The resulting topological organization reflects their connections, not their locations in the brain.

In the model (figure 10.2), reentry occurs among nine visual cortical areas, divided into three anatomical streams mediating responses to form, color, and motion, respectively. No superordinate area coordinates the responses of the model. Consistent with functional segregation in the visual cortex, neural units within each separate area of the model respond to different properties of the stimuli, and the firing of each has different functional consequences within the network. For example, groups of neurons in model area V1, corresponding to the primary visual cortex, respond to elementary features of objects, such as the orientation of edges in a particular position of the visual field. Groups of neurons in higher visual areas, such as area IT, corresponding to the inferotemporal cortex, respond to classes of objects that have a certain shape irrespective of their position in the visual field.

Other groups of neurons, such as those in area V4, respond to the color of objects, not to their shape or direction of movement, while neurons in model area V5 respond to their direction of movement but not to their shape or color.

The model was tested with several tasks that required the integration of signals produced by the activity of multiple functionally segregated areas.

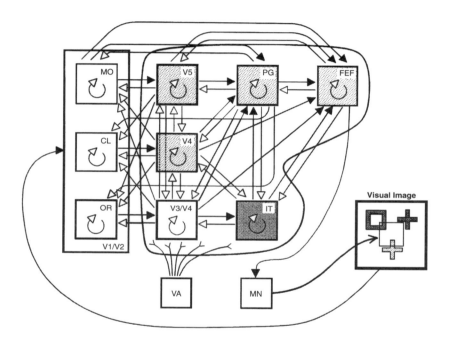

FIGURE 10.2 SCHEMATIC DIAGRAM OF A LARGE-SCALE COMPUTER MODEL OF CORTICAL INTEGRATION. Functionally specialized visual areas are indicated as boxes; pathways (composed of many thousands of individual connections) are indicated as arrows. The model comprises three parallel streams involved in the analysis of visual motion (top row), color (middle row), and form (bottom row). Areas are finely topographic (no shading), coarsely topographic (light shading), or nontopographic (heavy shading). The visual image (sampled by a color camera) is indicated at the extreme right. The output of the system (simulated eye movements under the control of eye motoneurons MN) is indicated at the bottom. Filled arrows indicate voltage-independent pathways; unfilled arrows indicate voltage-dependent pathways. Curved arrows within boxes indicate intra-areal connections. The box labeled VA refers to the diffusely projecting value system used in the behavioral paradigm; the general area of projection is outlined. The complete system contains a total of about 10,000 neuronal units and one million connections.

For example, one task required the discrimination of a red cross from a green cross and a red square, all of which were presented simultaneously in the visual field (see figure 10.3). A correct discriminatory response implied the conjunction of several properties of the individual stimuli—their color, shape, and position. Training was achieved by activating a simulated "value system" with diffuse projections that released neuromodulators whenever the model moved its "eye" toward the correct object; this activation corre-

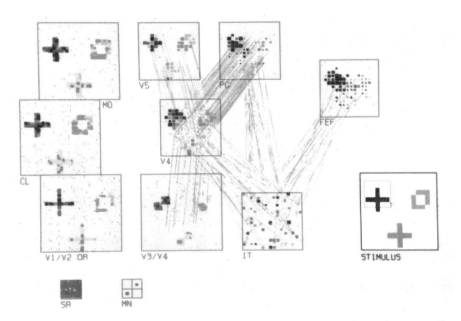

FIGURE 10.3 SOLVING THE BINDING PROBLEM. Activity and synchrony in the model ~150 milliseconds after the presentation of a visual image consisting of a red cross, a red square, and a green cross. The model was conditioned to pick the red cross by triggering the diffusely projecting value system whenever its simulated eye happened to move toward that object, independent of the object's position. Note that neural units responding to the same object are correlated (indicated by the color they share) both within and between (topographic or nontopographic) areas. About 5 percent of the connections that have been strengthened during conditioning due to the firing of value systems are shown superimposed in shades of red. Note that strengthened connections appear between multiple areas. Notice also that units at the position corresponding to the red cross in areas FEF, PG, and V4 show sharply increased activity. This activity produces an eye movement toward that position (the square window with white borders representing the center of the eye has moved to the upper left).

sponds to rewarding an experimental animal with some juice whenever it makes the correct response. Activation of the value system globally signaled the occurrence of a salient event and permitted changes in the strength of the connections among the distributed groups of neurons (indicated by the faint red lines in figure 10.3). After some training, the model was able to achieve the correct discrimination with 95 percent accuracy.

As is shown in figure 10.3, a still frame of the model after what would correspond in the real world to 200 msec of activity following the presentation of the stimuli indicates that many groups of neurons in different functionally segregated areas of the brain were jointly activated by the visual scene. Furthermore, the activity of neurons responding to different attributes of the *same* object was *synchronous* at the time scale of tens of milliseconds. This synchronous firing was observed not only in parallel across different streams, such as those for form, color, and motion, but hierarchically between lower and higher visual areas.[4] However, the activity of neurons responding to *different* objects was asynchronous. Thus, the objects were differentiated from each other at this time scale. Despite these fine temporal differences, all these neurons were active together at the longer time scale (hundreds of milliseconds) required for "behavioral" output. By these means, the model was able to achieve unified, coherent responses to the visually presented scene, as well as to make use of this integration to lead to a given discriminatory response.

The short-term correlations of neuronal activity observed in the simulations were indicative of rapid, reciprocal interactions mediated by reentry. Their occurrence depended on the presence of intact reciprocal connections within and between areas. They also required the functioning of voltage-dependent connections mediating rapid changes in the strength of synapses. Such connections are called voltage dependent because they can be activated only if the voltage of the receiving neuron has been increased by some other excitatory input. (In an actual brain, NMDA receptors for the neurotransmitter glutamate have this property.)

The most important point is that in this model, the conjunction or integration of the appropriate attributes of an object to yield a correct output was not achieved in any one particular simulated cortical area or by just one particular group of neurons. The model contained no units that were directly selective for arbitrary conjunctions of object properties, such as a "red cross located in the upper left quadrant." Thus, integration was achieved not in any place, but by a coherent *process*. This process was the result of reentrant interactions among neuronal groups distributed over many areas. Furthermore, integration occurred rapidly, within 100–250 msec after the presentation of the stimulus. These simulations revealed how reentry can solve the binding problem by coupling neuronal responses of distributed cortical areas to achieve synchronization and global coherence.

In addition to this remarkable ability to integrate the activity of distributed populations of neurons, the model showed an unanticipated feature that reminds one of a property encountered when we examine our own conscious experience: limited capacity. When human subjects are presented with more than a few objects characterized by multiple attributes, they often confuse which object has which attribute. Such conjunction errors have been extensively documented in human perception.[5] For example, when we briefly see a display containing multiple letters in different positions that are printed in different colors and different sizes, conjunction errors become frequent: we may report seeing a green letter *A*, when actually there was a green letter *b*. When our model was tested with one to three objects, it performed with great accuracy, and the correct binding between the various properties of different objects was maintained. With four or more objects, however, false conjunctions, in which units that responded to two different objects were spuriously synchronized, became more frequent. The frequency of such false conjunctions depended not only on the number of objects, but on several other variables, such as their particular features and size. On the basis of these findings, we predict that conjunction errors in living subjects will be found to be due to inconsistencies in the patterns of short-term temporal correlations among different brain areas.[6] Although this prediction has not yet been confirmed, new experimental means, such as MEG, may be adequate to test it.

In a different and much more detailed model of cortical areas, which included interconnected thalamic regions, we further examined the dynamics of reentrant interactions within the thalamocortical system.[7] The results obtained from these simulations indicate that reentrant signaling within the cortex and between the cortex and the thalamus, bolstered by fast changes in synaptic efficacy and spontaneous activity within the network, can rapidly establish a transient, globally coherent process. This process is characterized by strong and rapid interactions among the participating neuronal groups in the cortex and the thalamus and it emerges at a well-defined threshold of activity. [8] What is remarkable is that this coherent process is quite stable, being capable of sustaining itself continuously while changing its precise composition. This stability means that although there is always a large pool of synchronously firing neurons, the neurons that are actually engaged in this pool change from moment to moment. This process includes a large number of neurons both in the cortex and in the thalamus, although it does not include all of them nor even all those that are active at a given time. That such a self-perpetuating dynamic process, characterized by the strength and speed of reentrant neural interactions, can originate from the connectivity of the thalamocortical system is of considerable significance for understanding the actual neural events that underlie the unity of consciousness.

IDENTIFYING AN INTEGRATED PROCESS: MEASURES OF FUNCTIONAL CLUSTERING

The experiments described in chapter 6 and the large-scale simulations just reviewed provide essential insights into the mechanisms by which integration is rapidly achieved in the thalamocortical system. If we want to understand the unity of consciousness, however, we need to provide a more general theoretical framework to connect neural and conscious integration. What does it mean when we say that a neural process is integrated? How can integration be measured, and how can one determine the extent and boundaries of an integrated neural process? To answer these questions, we must develop a formal analysis of the behavior of the neural system.

A useful intuitive criterion for integration is this: A subset of elements within a system will constitute an integrated process if, on a given time scale, these elements interact much more strongly among themselves than with the rest of the system. Consider, for example, a tightly knit, old-fashioned family: Each member has occasional interactions with various acquaintances, but nothing compared to either the frequency or the intensity of the bonding within the family. Such a subset of strongly interacting elements that is functionally demarcated from the rest of a system can be called a "functional cluster."[9] It is important to be able to make this criterion explicit and to have an actual measure of functional clustering that is theoretically satisfactory and empirically useful. Unfortunately, no universally accepted definition of *cluster* exists in the statistical literature,[10] although it is generally agreed that a cluster should be defined in terms of internal cohesion and external isolation. With this in mind, we recently developed a measure of functional clustering that is designed to evaluate whether there are subsets of elements within a neural system that strongly interact among themselves but interact much less strongly with the rest of the system.[11]

Consider, for simplicity, an *isolated* neural system—a system that does not receive any input from the external environment—which is spontaneously active. Let us assume that the elements of the system correspond to neuronal groups. Now imagine that these neuronal groups are completely discon-nected among themselves and thus do not interact in any way. Under these conditions, the elements of the system would be statistically independent— there would be *no* correlation between the time-varying activity of any one element and that of any other elements. On the other hand, if the elements of the system were connected, they would be able to interact and influence each other's activity. Any interaction among the elements of the system would result in a deviation from statistical independence in their firing patterns.

What is needed is a way to evaluate this deviation from independence simultaneously among all elements of a system in the most general fashion. Toward this end, one can resort to measures of statistical variability, such as statistical entropy. If we assume that a system can take a number of discrete states or patterns of activity, the entropy of that system can be considered as a (logarithmic) function reflecting the number of possible patterns of activ-ity that the system can take, weighted by their probability of occurrence.[12]

For example, consider a system X composed of n units that can be either on or off with equal probability (2 equiprobable states, corresponding to $\log_2(2) = 1$ bit of entropy per unit). If these units are independent, the num-ber of states that the system can occupy will be 2^n: Every possible system state can occur, and each occurs with equal probability (corresponding to a system entropy of $\log_2(2^n) = n$ bits). In this case, the entropy of the system, designated as $H(X)$, is simply the sum of the entropies of its individual ele-ments, designated as $H(x_i)$. On the other hand, if there are any interactions within the system, the number of states that the system can take will be *less* than would be expected from the number of states that its separate elements can take, and at least some system states will be more or less probable than when all elements were independent. In this case, the entropy of the entire system will be less than the sum of the entropies of its individual elements.

The difference between the sum of the entropies of all individual compo-nents (x_i) considered independently and the entropy of the system X consid-ered as a whole is called[13] the integration $I(X)$ of system X:

$$I(X) = \sum_{i=1}^{n} H(x_i) - H(X)$$

Thus, integration measures the loss of entropy that is due to the interac-tions among its elements. The stronger the interactions among the elements of an isolated system, the greater their overall statistical dependence and the higher their integration. Note that the integration can be calculated not just for the entire system, but for any of its subsets. If we consider any subset $_j$ constituted of k elements of the isolated neural system X, the integration $I(X^k_j)$ measures the total statistical dependence *within* that subset.

As we can measure the statistical dependence *within* a subset, we can also measure the statistical dependence *between* the subset (X^k_j) and the rest of the system $(X - X^k_j)$. This dependence can be usefully expressed in terms of mutual information *(MI)*. Mutual information is given by:

$$MI(X^k_j; X - X^k_j) = H(X^k_j) + H(X - X^k_j) - H(X)$$

and it measures the extent to which the entropy of X^k_j is accounted for by the entropy of its complement $X - X^k_j$ (and vice versa, *MI* being a symmetrical quantity).[14] Thus, mutual information measures the total amount of statistical dependence between any chosen subset of elements and the rest of a system, as indicated in figure 10.4.

Having in hand the integration of the subset and its mutual information with the rest of the system, a functional *cluster index* (CI) can then be calculated for each subset i of the system according to:

$$CI(X^k_j) = I(X^k_j) / MI(X^k_j; X - X^k_j)$$

where $I(X^k_j)$ and $MI(X^k_j; X - X^k_j)$ are appropriately normalized to discount the effect of subset size.[15] This index of functional clustering offers precisely

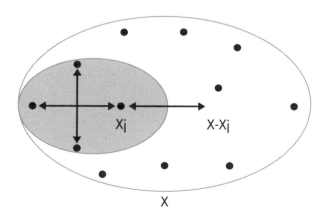

FIGURE 10.4 DIAGRAM OF FUNCTIONAL CLUSTERING. The small ellipse represents a subset of brain regions (dots) that are strongly interactive with each other (crossed black arrows) and only weakly interactive with the rest of the brain (horizontal light arrow).

what we are looking for. For an isolated system, it reflects the relative strength of the interactions within a subset of elements compared to the interactions between that subset and the rest of the system. Thus, a cluster index near 1 indicates a subset of elements that are as interactive with the rest of the system as they are among themselves. On the other hand, a cluster index much higher than 1 indicates the presence of a functional cluster— a subset of elements that are strongly interactive among themselves but only weakly interactive with the rest of the system.[16] By evaluating this cluster index for all possible subsets of elements of a given system (or for a representative number of them), one can determine whether that system contains one or more functional clusters. A functional cluster will correspond to the subset of elements having a high cluster index that does not contain within itself any smaller subset with a higher cluster index.

In summary, the cluster index provides a theoretically sound way of defining and identifying a functional cluster—a subset of elements strongly interacting among themselves and weakly interacting with the rest of the system and that cannot be decomposed into independent or nearly independent components.

This measure of functional clustering has been successfully applied both to simulated data sets and to a PET imaging data set obtained from schizophrenic and normal subjects who were performing cognitive tasks.[17] By using the cluster index, we were able to find evidence of particular brain regions belonging to a functional cluster that were separated by a functional boundary from other regions. Suggestive differences in functional clustering were found between controls and schizophrenics. Although it is too early to interpret fully the diagnostic usefulness of these results because of the relatively limited number of brain regions sampled, there is the possibility that such an approach may provide an objective means for diagnosing schizophrenia.

Clearly, the search for functional clustering during cognitive activity has just begun, and it needs to be expanded by imaging methods that offer better spatial and temporal resolution. The only functional relationships that can be captured on the basis of multiple PET or fMRI scans are those occurring over time scales of seconds or longer, while the functional relationships that are crucial for conscious experience must be realized within a second or less. Can one find evidence for subsets of integrated brain regions that are functionally insulated as clusters at a time scale of hundreds of milliseconds and that vary with a cognitive task? Some evidence already exists, although theoretically sound measures of functional clustering may be more difficult to obtain for this kind of data. It is a reasonable conjecture that the existence of synchronous activity among distant brain areas is often an indication of rapid functional clustering. Various studies using EEG, MEG, and local field potentials have revealed that the activity of large populations of neurons can be highly synchronized over a short period.[18] Experiments using electrodes to record directly from neural cells in animals have demonstrated that short-term temporal correlations can be found within single areas of the brain, as well as between different areas.[19] In some cases, it has even been demonstrated that short-term temporal correlations between the two cerebral hemispheres are due to direct reentrant interactions:[20] If the millions of reentrant fibers connecting the hemispheres are cut, these short-term correlations vanish. We take these findings as direct evidence that integration and rapid functional clustering occur in the thalamocortical system and that reentry is the major mechanism by which integration is achieved.

With the notion of functional clustering introduced in this chapter, we now have a measure of integration that can be applied to neurophysiological data to characterize the neural processes underlying consciousness. Establishing that a neural process constitutes a functional cluster means that, over a given time interval, it is functionally integrated—it cannot fully be decomposed into independent or nearly independent components. But to account for the fundamental properties of conscious experience, we still must find a way to characterize a neural process in terms of how differentiated or informative it is—how many different patterns of activity it may take. We do so in the next chapter by considering a measure of neural complexity. After that, we will be in a position to build a general hypothesis about the fashion in which certain neural processes can give rise to the fundamental properties of conscious experience.

CHAPTER ELEVEN

Consciousness and Complexity

Consciousness is extraordinarily differentiated. At any given time, we experience a particular conscious state selected out of billions of possible states, each of which can lead to different behavioral consequences. The occurrence of a particular conscious state is therefore highly informative in the specific sense that information is the reduction of uncertainty among a number of alternatives. If this is the case, the neural processes underlying conscious experience must also be highly differentiated and informative. In this chapter, we examine how the information content of a neural process can actually be evaluated. To do so, it is crucial to take the point of view of the neural system itself and of its constitutive subsets of elements. As we show, the information content of such a system can be expressed by a statistical measure that we call "neural complexity." This measure of complexity provides an estimate of the degree to which a unified neural process is differentiated. A major task of this chapter is to show that consciousness and complexity are intimately linked and to illustrate how complexity is realized in the brain. The analysis not only resolves a number of vexing problems, it adds something new to our ideas of how a scientific observer should examine a conscious system.

In chapter 10 we discussed what is meant by integration. A high degree of differentiation is an equally fundamental property of conscious experience. By differentiation, we simply mean that billions of different conscious states can be experienced, each of which may lead to different behavioral outputs. For example, think of a word. Before you actually thought of one, you were uncertain about which particular word would come to mind out of the tens of thousands you know. But after a word pops to mind, say, the word *irrelevant*, the uncertainty is reduced and information is generated. Then speak the word, and see what reactions you elicit. It is information that has actually led to different behavioral outputs. Now consider any word or phrase you have read in this book or in any other book you read before. Or imagine all the different possible scenes from a movie and from all movies you have previously seen or all the faces that you can conjure up from your past experience and all the combinations of feelings that you can have with each face. There are literally billions of possible conscious states. The ability to differentiate among all these different states constitutes information, which is the reduction of uncertainty among a number of alternatives.[1] This argument implies that the selection within a short time of any particular integrated state out of such a large repertoire of different possible states is enormously informative.

Given that we can determine that a neural process is integrated, can we also determine to what degree it is differentiated? To the extent that the constitutive elements of such a process can take on many different activity patterns, can we decide whether these different patterns make a difference to the system itself and are therefore informative?

In this chapter, we answer this question in the affirmative and show that the degree to which a neural system is differentiated can be assessed precisely by a measure called neural complexity.[2]

MEASURING DIFFERENCES THAT MAKE A DIFFERENCE

To measure the information generated by an integrated neural process, it is useful to rely on the statistical foundations of information theory, which provide a general means of assessing the reduction of uncertainty.[3] We should note, however, that a number of applications of information theory in biology have been fraught with problems and have had a notoriously controversial history. This is the case largely because at the heart of information theory as originally formulated lies the sensible notion of an external, intelligent observer who encodes messages using an alphabet of symbols. So-called information-processing views of the brain, however, have been severely criticized because they typically assume the existence in the world of previously *defined* information (begging the question of what information is) and often assume the existence of precise neural codes for which there is no evidence.

The statistical foundations of information theory can nevertheless be profitably used to characterize objective properties of any system, including the brain.[4] By using the statistical aspects of information theory, it is possible to conceptualize and measure how differentiated or informative a neural process is without any reference to symbols, codes, or an external observer.[5] In this chapter, we use such statistical measures to identify differences that make a difference to the brain as a system that is simultaneously integrated and differentiated.

Mutual Information

Consider again, as we did in chapter 10, an isolated neural system composed of a number of elements. Imagine, for example, an isolated cortical area comprising a number of neuronal groups. Imagine also that the activity of each neuronal group is subject to some source of change or variance in the absence of external inputs. This situation is not unlike the spontaneous activity that is observed in the brain during REM sleep: Groups of neurons are firing spontaneously and changing their firing patterns all the time. However, such changes are determined not by incoming stimuli, but by their mutual interactions. What information is produced within such an isolated system?

The standard approach would be to measure information by the number and probability of the states of the system that are discriminable from the point of view of an external observer. To avoid the fallacy of assuming a "homunculus" watching the brain and interpreting its activity patterns from the outside, however, we must get rid of the privileged viewpoint of an external observer. In other words, differences between activity patterns should be assessed only with reference to the system itself. It is easy to show why. A noisy TV screen, for example, goes through a large number of "activity patterns" that may look different to an external observer, but the TV, by itself, clearly cannot tell the difference among them; they make no difference to it. Since there is no homunculus watching the enchanted loom or TV screen of the brain, the only activity patterns that matter are those that make a difference to the brain itself.

How can we measure such differences that make a difference within a system like the brain? A simple approach is to consider the system as its own "observer." It is fairly straightforward to do so; all we need to do is to imagine dividing the system in two and considering how one part of the system affects the rest of the system, and vice versa. Take, for example, a bipartition between an individual element of the system and the rest of the system (its so-called complement, as indicated in figure 10.4). If the system is isolated, then from the point of view of that element, the only information available is given by the differences in the state of the rest of the system that make a difference to the state of that element. Such information can be measured by the statistical quantity we defined previously as mutual information.

Specifically, consider an isolated neural system X, a subset j of k elements (X^k_j) of that system, as well as its complement in the system, indicated as $(X - X^k_j)$. Interactions between the subset (X^k_j) and the rest of the system will be reflected in correlations of their activity (see figure 11.1). Mutual information between the subset and its complement is given by

$$MI(X^k_j ; X - X^k_j) = H(X^k_j) + H(X - X^k_j) - H(X)$$

where $H(X^k_j)$ and $H(X - X^k_j)$ are the entropies of X^k_j and $X - X^k_j$ considered independently and $H(X)$ is the entropy of the system considered as a whole. As we mentioned in chapter 10, $H(X^k_j)$, which indicates the entropy of the subset (X^k_j), is a general measure of its statistical variability, being a function of the number of possible patterns of activity that the subset of elements can take, weighted by the probability of their occurrence. Mutual information

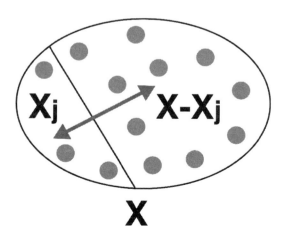

FIGURE 11.1 DIAGRAM OF MUTUAL INFORMATION. In system X, the arrow indicates how much differences in the state of subset X_j make a difference to the state of the rest of the system $X - X_j$, or vice versa. See the text.

measures to what extent the entropy of X^k_j is accounted for by the entropy of $X - X^k_j$ (and vice versa) and thereby measures the statistical dependence between any subset and the rest of the system. Thus, mutual information expresses how well the states of subset X^k_j can differentiate among the states of the rest of the system, which is to say how changes in the state of $X - X^k_j$ make a difference to the state of X^k_j.[6] Accordingly, the value of $MI(X^k_j; X - X^k_j)$

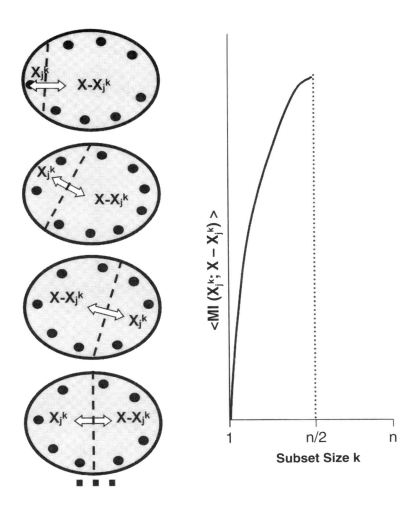

FIGURE 11.2 DIAGRAM OF COMPLEXITY. Left: the mutual information for a bipartition between a subset of elements X_j and the rest of system $X - X_j$ (double arrow) can be calculated for all bipartitions of system X. Right: the sum of mutual information values for all bipartitions of a system (averaged for subset size) corresponds to its complexity (the area under the curve).

will be high if two conditions are met. First, both X^k_j and $X - X^k_j$ must have many states, that is, their entropies must be high. Second, the states of X^k_j and of $X - X^k_j$ must be statistically dependent, that is, the entropy of X^k_j must be accounted for, in large part, by the interactions with $X - X^k_j$, and *vice versa*.[7]

NEURAL COMPLEXITY

Having determined the extent to which a given element can differentiate among the states of the rest of a neural system, it is easy to extrapolate to the entire system and define a measure of complexity. This overall measure of the degree to which the entire neural system is differentiated can be obtained by considering not just a single subset of its constitutive elements, but all its possible subsets.[8] This measure can be reached by averaging the mutual information between each subset of a neural system and the rest of the system for all possible bipartitions of the system (see figure 11.2).

The corresponding measure is called *neural complexity (C_N)*, and it is given by:

$$C_N(X) = \sum_{k=1}^{n/2} < MI(X^k_j; X - X^k_j) >$$

where we consider all subsets X^k composed of *k*-out-of-*n* elements of the system, and the *average* mutual information between subsets of size *k* and their complements is denoted as $< MI(X^k_j; X - X^k_j >$. The index *j* indicates that the average is taken over all combinations of *k* elements. According to this definition, the higher the mutual information between each subset and the rest of the system, the higher the value of complexity.

As we discussed before, the value of the average mutual information will be high if, on average, each subset can take on many different states *and* these states make a difference to the rest of the system. The fact that subsets of the system can take many different states means that individual elements are functionally segregated or specialized (if they were not specialized they would all do the same thing, which would correspond to a small number of states). On the other hand, the fact that different states of a subset of the system make a difference to the rest of the system implies that the system is integrated (if the system were not integrated, the states of different subsets of the system would be independent). Thus, we reach the important conclusion that *high values of complexity correspond to an optimal synthesis of functional specialization and functional integration within a system.* This is clearly the case for systems like the brain—different areas and groups of neurons do different things (they are differentiated) at the same time they interact to give rise to a unified conscious scene and to unified behaviors (they are integrated). By contrast, systems whose individual elements are either not integrated (such as a gas) or not specialized (like a homogeneous crystal) will have minimal complexity.[9]

An Illustration

As an illustration, it is useful to calculate complexity for three extreme examples of the organization of a cerebral cortical area corresponding to an old, diseased brain; a young, immature brain; and a normal adult brain (the simulated examples are actually based on the primary visual cortex of the cat). The simulated cortical area contained 512 neuronal groups, each of which responded preferentially to a given position in the visual field and to a given stimulus orientation.[10] The simulated cortical area was based on a detailed model that was used to investigate how the brain can give rise to the so-called Gestalt properties of visual perception—the way stimuli are grouped to form objects and are segregated from the background.[11] For the present purposes, we required that the simulated cortical area was isolated; it did not receive any visual input, and its neurons were "spontaneously" active.[12]

The first example in figure 11.3 (top row) represents a cortical area in which the density of intra-areal connections among different groups of neurons had been deliberately reduced (for example, in an old and deteriorated brain). In such a cortical area, individual groups of neurons are still active, but, because of the loss of intra-areal connections, they fire more or less independently. Such a system behaves essentially like a "neural gas" or, if examined on a computer monitor, like a TV set that is not properly tuned. The electroencephalogram of such a cortical area shows the absence of synchronization among its constituent neuronal groups.[13] The entropy of the system is high because of the large number of elements and their high individual variance: The system can take a large number of states. From the point of view of an external observer or homunculus who might assign a different meaning to each state of the system, this system would indeed appear to contain a large amount of information. But what about information from the point of view of the system itself—the number of states *that make a difference to the system itself*? Since there is little interaction between any subset of elements and the rest of the system, whatever the state of that subset might be, there is little or no effect on the rest of the system, or vice versa. The value of the mutual information is correspondingly low, and since this holds true for every possible subset, the complexity of the system is also low. In other words, although there are many differences within the system, they make no difference to it. Such a neural system is certainly noisy, but it is not differentiated.

The second example is of an immature, young cortex, in which every neuronal group is connected to all other neuronal groups in a uniform way (see figure 11.3, bottom row). In the simulations, all groups of neurons soon

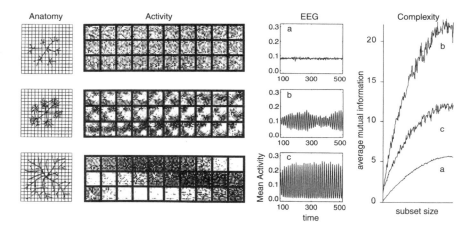

FIGURE 11.3 HOW COMPLEXITY VARIES, DEPENDING ON NEUROANATOMICAL ORGANIZATION. Complexity values were obtained from simulations of a primary visual cortical area. The figure shows three cases. In the first case (upper row), the simulated cortical area has sparse connectivity (first column: Anatomy). Neuronal groups fire almost independently (second column: Activity): the 30 small squares within the rectangle indicate the pattern of firing every 2 milliseconds (from left to right and from top to bottom) of 512 neuronal groups that are spontaneously active. The third column represents the EEG, which is essentially flat, indicating that the neuronal groups are not synchronized. Complexity (the area under the curve in the fourth column) is low. In the third case (lower row), the simulated cortical area has random connectivity. Neuronal groups are completely synchronized and oscillate together. The EEG shows hypersynchronous activity reminiscent of slow-wave sleep, epileptic seizures, or anesthesia. Complexity is low. In the second case (middle row), the simulated cortical area has a patchy connectivity that corresponds to the one found in the cortex. Neuronal groups display continually changing integrated activity patterns. The EEG shows that synchronization waxes and wanes and that different groups of neurons synchronize at different times. Complexity is high.

started oscillating together coherently almost without exception. The calculated EEG is hypersynchronous, resembling the high-voltage waves of slow-wave sleep or of generalized epilepsy. The system is highly integrated, but functional specialization is completely lost. Since the system can take up only a limited number of states, its entropy is low. The average mutual information between individual elements and the rest of the system is higher than in the previous case, since there are strong interactions. However, when larger and larger subsets are taken into consideration, the mutual information does not increase significantly because the number of different states that can be discriminated does not increase with the size of the subsets. The complexity of the system is correspondingly low. In other words, because there are few differences within the system, the difference they make to the system is small. The system is integrated but not differentiated.

In the third example, corresponding to a normal, adult cortex (see figure 11.3, middle row), groups of neurons are connected to each other according to the following rules. First, groups of neurons having similar visual orientation preferences tend to be more connected to each other. Second, they are connected so that the strength of the connections decreases with topographic distance. These rules of connectivity closely correspond to those found experimentally in the primary visual cortex.[14] In this example, the dynamic behavior of the system is far more complex than in the previous two: Groups of neurons show both an overall coherent behavior yet group and regroup themselves dynamically according to their specific functional interactions. For example, neighboring groups of similar orientation preference tend to fire synchronously more often than functionally unrelated groups, but at times, almost the entire cortical area may show short periods of coherent oscillations, as reflected by a calculated EEG that resembles that of waking or REM sleep. The entropy of the system is high, but not as high as in the first example (although the system can have a large number of states, some are more likely than others). The mutual information between individual elements and the rest of the system is, on average, high, reflecting significant interactions, just as in the second example. In contrast to the second example, however, the *average* mutual information increases considerably when we take into account subsets composed of a larger number of elements. Thus, the overall complexity is high because, in such a system, the larger the subset, the larger the number of different states that the subset can bring about in the rest of the system, and vice versa. In other words, there are many differences, and they make a lot of difference to the system. The system is both integrated and highly differentiated.

Altogether, these examples illustrate that just as the functional clustering index can be used to measure the integration of a neural process and its boundaries, complexity can be used as a statistical measure of the extent to which a neural process is differentiated: the larger the number of activity patterns that make a difference to a neural system, the higher its complexity.

Other simulations show that neuroanatomical factors can critically determine the complexity of the dynamic behavior of a neural system.[15] Neuroanatomical factors favoring complexity include dense local connections leading to the formation of neuronal groups, connections among such groups that are distributed in a patchy fashion, and an abundance of short reentrant circuits. Large-scale computer simulations of the thalamocortical system also indicate that changes in complexity can be obtained through functional modulation of neural activity without modifying the anatomical connectivity.[16] For example, during slow-wave sleep, the firing of neuromodulatory systems with diffuse projections, such as the noradrenergic and serotoninergic systems—what we have called diffusely projecting value systems in previous chapters—is dramatically reduced. As a result, individual neurons across the entire thalamocortical system fire in bursts, one to four per second, separated by pauses in which they do not fire. This pattern of burst-pause firing rapidly becomes synchronized over vast regions of the brain, leading to characteristic slow waves in the EEG. Such a hypersynchronous EEG, corresponding to the firing in unison of a large number of cortical cells, is associated with low complexity. As we noted in chapter 6, this state, lacking complexity, is not compatible with conscious awareness.

When an animal awakens, the value systems resume firing, and cells in both the thalamus and cortex undergo a transition from the burst-pause pattern of firing, typical of slow-wave sleep, to the so-called tonic pattern of firing, typical of waking. The slow waves disappear and the EEG shows much greater variability, which is associated with greater complexity. In particular, although near-coincident firings between subsets of any two neurons are only slightly more frequent than would be expected by chance, the number of near-coincidences grows proportionately larger if one considers larger subsets of neurons. This observation suggests that the system can rapidly select among a large repertoire of possible coherent states. We conclude that the complexity of neural processes in the thalamocortical system can be influenced not only by its neuroanatomy, but dynamically by its neurophysiology.[17] Because of this dynamic, the same normal brain can be more complex or less complex, depending on its level of arousal.

Why Complexity?

The analysis we have just completed represents a necessary step toward a theoretical assessment of certain fundamental properties of consciousness in terms of general principles. On the basis of the considerations and experiments discussed in chapters 3, 5, and 6, we propose that a high degree of complexity, as just defined, is a necessary requirement for any neural process that sustains conscious experience. We also argue that slow-wave sleep and epileptic seizures, two brain states characterized by highly integrated firing in most of the brain, are not associated with conscious experience because their repertoire of available neural states is diminished and their complexity is low.

Before we consider these issues further, a few questions concerning complexity need to be addressed. First, why did we call this measure of the average mutual information within a system complexity? Complexity is a widely abused term. There are complexity journals, complexity institutes, and complexity experts. But rarely is it precisely specified how one would establish whether an object of study is complex, except for the obvious fact that complex entities, such as societies, economies, biological organisms, brains, cells, and genomes, are certainly difficult to understand and even more difficult to predict.

Whatever the case, there are two aspects about which every expert on complexity agrees. First, to be complex, something must be composed of many parts that interact in heterogeneous ways. This aspect corresponds to the common use of the term. The *Oxford English Dictionary*, for example, defines *complex* as "a whole . . . comprehending various parts united or connected together." Second, it is now generally agreed that something that is completely random is not complex, nor is something that is completely regular. For example, neither an ideal gas nor a perfect crystal is considered to be complex. Only something that appears to be both orderly and disorderly, regular and irregular, variant and invariant, constant and changing, stable and unstable deserves to be called complex. Biological systems, from cells to brains to organisms to societies, are therefore paradigmatic examples of complex organizations.

The measure of complexity we have introduced satisfies both these requirements. As was shown in the previous examples, it achieves high values only for neural systems that are composed of many elements that are both functionally specialized and functionally integrated (that interact in heterogeneous ways). By contrast, complexity, as we define it, is low or zero

for systems that are composed of elements that are either completely independent (disorderly) or completely integrated (orderly and homogeneous).

The coexistence of functional specialization and integration in the behavior of the models examined earlier illustrates another important characteristic of selectional systems that are made up of diverse repertoires (see chapter
7). This characteristic distinguishes such systems from most man-made systems. It is good practice in planned engineering, for example, to develop
independent modules that each have a specific role and that interact as little
as possible. This is so because, from such a planned, computational, or
instructionist viewpoint, multiple interactions among many components are
notoriously difficult to deal with. If too many modules are allowed to interact, there are myriads of unforeseen and unforeseeable consequences, most
of them negative. From a selectionist perspective, although the consequences of diverse interactions in a population are unforeseen, they can
serve as a basis for selection. Rather than being intractable or problematic,
nonlinearities can be exploited whenever they lead to adaptive behaviors. As
a general rule, therefore, the larger the number of components and the more
extensive and nonlinear the interactions among them, the more the use of
selectional mechanisms becomes unavoidable. From this perspective, the
complexity of the anatomy and chemistry of the brain and the sheer number
of ongoing multiple interactions among specialized elements make the odds
for effective operation via nonselectional means vanishingly small.[18]

COMPLEXITY MATCHING: THE ROLE OF EXTERNAL STIMULI

Before we leave the topic of complexity, we need to confront a final question: Where does the complexity of a system, such as the brain, come from?
The previous theoretical analysis of complexity was carried out within an
isolated neural system, and it led to the conclusion that neural complexity
strikes an optimal balance between segregation and integration of function.
This conclusion is consistent with the view that a complex brain is like a collection of specialists who talk to each other a lot. Several considerations justify our initial analysis of the integration of information within an isolated
system. For instance, dreaming and imagery are striking phenomenological
demonstrations that the adult brain can spontaneously and intrinsically
produce consciousness and meaning without any direct input from the
periphery, at least for a short time. It is well known that physiologically,
the thalamocortical system—even of a fetus in utero—is spontaneously active
whether or not it receives inputs from outside. Finally, it is well established

that, anatomically, most neurons in the thalamocortical system receive signals from other neurons, rather than directly from sensory inputs.

Notwithstanding this initial emphasis on the complexity of isolated systems, it is clear that the set of dynamic relationships among functionally specialized groups of neurons that are found in a functioning adult brain must nevertheless originate somewhere. They must first be developed, selected, and refined in a long process of adaptation to the outside world. As we have argued, this process takes place during evolution, development, and experience through the mechanisms of variation, selection, and differential amplification that accompany the continuous interactions among the body, the brain, and the environment. What must be determined theoretically and measured, then, is how the intrinsic dynamic relationships among specialized neuronal groups in an adult brain become adaptively related, over time, to the statistical structure of the environment—the average, over time, of all signals characteristic of the environment received by an animal. Moreover, given that at any given time, most neuronal groups in the brain are predominantly affected by information from other parts of the brain (or intrinsic information), the moment-to-moment contribution of the information that is actually provided by the environment (extrinsic information) must also be determined.

A theoretical approach to these questions can be developed by considering in information-theoretical terms the fate of the signals transmitted from the sensory sheets during perception.[19] Although this analysis is not presented here in any detail, the main conclusions that can be drawn from it are worth mentioning. For a small value of the *extrinsic* mutual information between a stimulus and a neural system, there is generally a large change in the *intrinsic* mutual information among subsets of units within the neural system. This change can be measured by a quantity, called complexity matching, or C_M, which is the change in neural complexity that occurs as a result of the encounter with external stimuli.[20]

According to this analysis, extrinsic signals convey information not so much in themselves, but by virtue of how they modulate the intrinsic signals exchanged within a previously experienced neural system. In other words, a stimulus acts not so much by adding large amounts of extrinsic information that need to be processed as it does by amplifying the intrinsic information resulting from neural interactions selected and stabilized by memory through previous encounters with the environment. This property is entirely in line with the TNGS: The brain is a selectional system, and matching occurs within enormously varied and complex repertoires. Moreover, each selective event introduces new sources of variation within the system. At every instant, the brain goes far "beyond the information given,"[21] and in conscious animals its response to an incoming stimulus is therefore a "remembered present." According to this approach, a sharp distinction between transmission and storage of information in the brain tends to vanish. Furthermore, this conclusion corroborates the notion, described in chapter 8, that whatever memory is, it must be nonrepresentational.

The analysis also shows that the degree to which extrinsic inputs affect intrinsic signals depends on the experience that the brain has had of a set of related stimuli. In other words, high values of complexity matching indicate a high degree of "adjustment of inner to outer relations."[22] This conclusion is consistent with an everyday observation: The same stimulus, say, a Chinese character, can be meaningful to Chinese speakers and meaningless to English speakers even if the extrinsic information conveyed to the retina is the same. Attempts to explain this difference that are based solely on the processing of a previously coded message in an information channel beg the question of where this information comes from. The concept of matching in a selectional system easily resolves the issue.

Finally, this analysis shows that high complexity originates from continuing interactions between the brain and an external environment of much greater potential complexity. Simulations with simple linear systems indicate that systems with random connectivity have low complexity values.[23] However, if the connectivity of these systems is allowed to change through a selection procedure in such a way as to increase their match to the statistical regularities of an external environment, their complexity increases considerably. Moreover, everything else being equal, the more complex the environment, the larger the complexity of the systems that achieve high values of matching.[24] It is thus the adaptation of the brain's reentrant circuits to the demands posed by a rich environment, based on principles of natural, developmental, and neural selection that leads to a high complexity, as reflected by increased values of matching and degeneracy. And it is only after such a level of complexity has been achieved that an adult brain, even when relatively isolated as in dreaming, can generate integrated neural processes of sufficient complexity to sustain conscious experience. The question can now be posed: Can we use the concepts and measures developed here to specify under which conditions populations of neurons contribute to conscious experience?

CHAPTER TWELVE

Determining Where the Knot Is Tied: The Dynamic Core Hypothesis

In this chapter, we first review observations indicating that despite their wide distribution, only a subset of the neuronal groups in our brain contributes directly to conscious experience at any given time. What, then, if anything, is special about these neuronal groups, and how should they be identified both in theory and experiment? The dynamic core hypothesis is our answer to this question. This hypothesis states that the activity of a group of neurons can contribute directly to conscious experience if it is part of a functional cluster, characterized by strong mutual interactions among a set of neuronal groups over a period of hundreds of milliseconds. To sustain conscious experience, it is essential that this functional cluster be highly differentiated, as indicated by high values of complexity. Such a cluster, which we call the "dynamic core" because of its ever-changing composition yet ongoing integration, is generated largely, although not exclusively, within the thalamocortical system. The dynamic core hypothesis leads to specific predictions concerning the neural basis of conscious experience. Unlike hypotheses that merely invoke a correlation between conscious experience and this or that neural structure or group of neurons, the dynamic core hypothesis accounts instead for the general properties of conscious experience by linking these properties to the specific neural processes that can give rise to them.

The evidence examined so far suggests that to support conscious experience, the activity of distributed populations of neurons must be integrated through strong, rapid neural interactions. We have also shown that neural processes underlying conscious experience must be sufficiently differentiated, as indicated by the loss of consciousness when neural activity is globally homogenous or hypersynchronous, as is the case during slow-wave sleep and generalized epilepsy. Finally, we have noted that every conscious task seems to require the activation or deactivation of many regions of the brain. These regions typically include portions of the thalamocortical system, although they are not necessarily limited to it. The issue we consider now is whether the neural processes underlying conscious experience extend to most of the brain in some nonspecific fashion or are restricted to a particular subset of neurons therefore posing the question of what is special about this subset.

HOW MUCH OF THE BRAIN DOES A THOUGHT REQUIRE?

After reviewing the scant physiological literature of his age, William James concluded that there was as yet no evidence for restricting the neural correlates of consciousness to anything less than the entire brain.[1] Since the days of James, however, scientists have discovered that only a certain portion of the neural activity in the brain contributes to consciousness directly—as assessed by experiments with stimulation and lesions—or is directly correlated with aspects of conscious experience—as assessed by studies recording neural activity.

On the basis of studies of lesions and stimulation, we are confident that, for example, the activity of certain brain regions, such as the cerebral cortex and thalamus, is more important than the activity of other regions. Moreover, there is reason to believe that a substantial proportion of neural activity, even in the cerebral cortex, does *not* correlate with what a person is aware of. This lack of correlation is indicated by recent studies of binocular rivalry, for instance. As we discussed previously, if two incongruent images, such as a vertical and a horizontal grating, are presented simultaneously to each eye, a person perceives only one image at a time, with an alternation every few seconds in perceptual dominance—the image the person is conscious of. Studies recording neural activity in monkeys have revealed that a large proportion of neurons in the primary visual cortex and other early stages of the visual system continue to fire to their preferred stimulus even when the stimulus is not being consciously perceived. In higher visual areas, however, most of the neurons fire in response to the percept.[2] In the MEG study of rivalry in humans described in chapter 5, we found that even when the subject was not conscious of a stimulus, steady-state responses at the frequency at which a stimulus was flickered could be recorded in many regions of the brain, including the frontal cortex.[3] However, the responses of only a subset of brain regions were actually correlated with the conscious perception of a stimulus.[4]

Recording studies have also demonstrated that the activity of many neurons in sensory and motor pathways can be correlated with rapidly varying details of a sensory input or a motor output but do not seem to map to conscious experience. For example, patterns of neural activity in the retina and other early visual structures are in constant flux and correspond more or less faithfully to spatial and temporal details of the rapidly changing visual input. However, a conscious visual scene is considerably more stable, and it deals with properties of objects that are invariant under changes in position or illumination, properties that are easily recognized and manipulated. For example, when we see a hummingbird fluttering its wings, we can recognize it and grasp it, whether it is against the sunny sky or in a canopy of trees, whether it is distant or nearby, and whether it is turned toward or away from us. Moreover, much evidence indicates that during each visual fixation, we extract the meaning or gist of a scene, rather than its innumerable and rapidly varying local details.[5] We certainly could not describe the precise position of the wings during the bird's flight. In fact, we are surprisingly blind to or unconscious of considerable changes in a visual scene as long as its meaning or gist is not affected.[6] In reading a text, for instance, we usually do not take account of the typeface unless it is exotic or when we have its recognition as a specific aim. These more invariant aspects of a scene are the ones that appear to be really important and informative about it and can usefully control behavior and planning. Thus, rapidly changing patterns of activity in the retina and other early visual structures seem to contribute to conscious visual perception by affecting the responses of higher areas indirectly, rather than directly. The neurological evidence is in agreement with these observations. In adults, lesions of the retina produce blindness, but they do not eliminate the possibility of conscious visual experience, as evidenced by the persistence of visual imagery, visual memories, and visual dreams. On the other hand, lesions of certain visual cortical areas eliminate all visual aspects of perception, imagery, and dreaming.[7]

Another indication that a significant proportion of neural activity goes on without directly contributing to conscious experience comes from considering cognitive tasks that are highly practiced, as we did in chapter 5. Much of our adult cognitive life is the product of highly automated routines that make it possible to talk, listen, read, write, and so on fast and effortlessly. Neural processes devoted to carrying out such routines do not contribute directly to conscious experience, although they are essential in determining its content. For example, when we want to express a certain idea, such routines guarantee that in general the appropriate words will come to mind without any explicit conscious effort. As we mentioned, some evidence indicates that neural circuits that carry out such highly practiced neural routines may become functionally insulated. As we discuss in chapter 14, these circuits are not integrated with more distributed neural processes except at the input and output stages.

Similarly, neural events that are too fleeting or too weak to participate in *sustained*, distributed interactions are also unlikely to contribute to conscious experience. Neural activity that is sufficient for triggering a particular behavioral response but insufficient in strength or duration to affect a distributed neural process may be responsible for many examples of perception without awareness (the "DRINK COKE" example in chapter 6).[8] Experiments involving the direct or indirect stimulation of cortical areas also suggest the existence of significant limits to the spread of fast, distributed interactions in the brain. Many brain regions can be briefly stimulated or lesioned without producing direct or immediate functional effects on other regions, despite the presence of anatomical pathways linking them. Likewise, the lesioning or stimulation of these regions does not have direct consequences on conscious experience.[9] These observations suggest that transient changes in the activity of such regions are functionally insulated from those of other parts of the brain, at least for short periods.[10]

Finally, modeling studies indicate that although the sheer anatomical connectivity of the brain may hint that everything can interact with everything else, several factors ensure that the emergence of fast, effective interactions is not a global phenomenon. The organization of the anatomical connectivity of certain brain systems, such as the thalamocortical system, is much more effective in generating coherent dynamic states than that of other regions, such as the cerebellum.[11] Such studies also suggest that despite the continuity of anatomical connectivity in the cortex, nonlinear interactions among neuronal groups, that are due, for instance, to the activation of so-called voltage-dependent connections, may transiently increase the strength of the interactions among a subset of groups, leading to the formation of distinct functional boundaries.[12] Moreover, these modeling studies also suggest that although all elements of the brain are likely to be functionally interactive over a sufficiently long time scale, only certain interactions are fast enough and strong enough to lead to the formation of a functional cluster within a few hundred milliseconds (see chapter 10).

THE DYNAMIC CORE HYPOTHESIS

Taken together, these observations support the conclusion that at any given time, only a subset of the neuronal groups in the human brain—although not a small subset—contributes directly to conscious experience. This conclusion, in turn, raises a question that epitomizes the entire issue of the neural basis of consciousness—a question that is as simple to formulate as it is difficult to answer. What, if anything, is special about these neuronal groups, and how should they be identified?

Laying the ground for an adequate answer to this question has been our main goal for a good part of this book. As we have argued, assuming that certain local properties of neurons may sooner or later hold the key to the mystery of consciousness[13] is entirely unsatisfactory. How could having a specific location in the brain, firing in a particular mode or at a particular frequency, being connected to certain other neurons, or expressing a particular biochemical compound or gene endow a neuron with the remarkable property of giving rise to conscious experience? The logical and philosophical problems of hypostatization associated with such assumptions are all too obvious, as both philosophers and scientists have noted many times. Consciousness is neither a thing nor a simple property.

Instead, our approach has been to focus on the fundamental properties of conscious experience—such properties as integration and differentiation—and explain them in terms of neural processes. The previous discussions amply indicate that if integration and differentiation are indeed fundamental features of consciousness, they can be explained only by a distributed neural process, rather than by specific local properties of neurons. Can we formulate a hypothesis that explicitly states what, if anything, is special about the subsets of neuronal groups that sustain conscious experience and how they can be identified? We believe that we are now in a position to do so, and indeed to do so concisely. The hypothesis states:

1. *A group of neurons can contribute directly to conscious experience only if it is part of a distributed functional cluster that, through reentrant interactions in the thalamocortical system, achieves high integration in hundreds of milliseconds.*
2. *To sustain conscious experience, it is essential that this functional cluster be highly differentiated, as indicated by high values of complexity.*

We call such a cluster of neuronal groups that are strongly interacting among themselves and that have distinct functional borders with the rest of the brain at the time scale of fractions of a second a "dynamic core," to emphasize both its integration and its constantly changing composition. A dynamic core is therefore a process, not a thing or a place, and it is defined in terms of neural interactions, rather than in terms of specific neural location, connectivity, or activity. Although a dynamic core will have a spatial extension, it is, in general, spatially distributed, as well as changing in composition, and thus cannot be localized to a single place in the brain. Furthermore, even if a functional cluster with such properties is identified, we predict that it will be associated with conscious experience only if the reentrant interactions within it are sufficiently differentiated, as indicated by its complexity.

While we envision that a functional cluster of sufficiently high complexity can be generated through reentrant interactions among neuronal groups distributed particularly within the thalamocortical system and possibly within other brain regions, such a cluster is neither coextensive with the entire brain nor restricted to any special subset of neurons. Thus, the term *dynamic core* deliberately does not refer to a unique, invariant set of areas of the brain (whether prefrontal, extrastriate, or striate cortex), and the core may change in composition over time. Since our hypothesis highlights the role of the functional interactions among distributed groups of neurons, rather than their local properties, it considers that the same group of neurons may sometimes be part of the dynamic core and underlie conscious experience, but at other times may not be part of it and thus be involved in unconscious processes.[14] Furthermore, since participation in the dynamic core depends on the rapidly shifting functional connectivity among groups of neurons, rather than on anatomical proximity, the composition of the core can transcend traditional anatomical boundaries.[15] Finally, as suggested by imaging studies, the exact composition of the core related to particular conscious states is expected to vary significantly from person to person.

THE DYNAMIC CORE AND THE GENERAL PROPERTIES OF CONSCIOUS EXPERIENCE

The best way to flesh out the dynamic core hypothesis is to test whether it can indeed account for some of the general properties of conscious experience that we have been discussing throughout this book.

FIGURE 12.1 M83, A SPIRAL GALAXY IN HYDRA. No visual metaphor can capture the properties of the dynamic core, and a galaxy with complicated, fuzzy borders may be as good or as bad as any other. As is explained in the text, the integration of a large amount of information over fractions of a second requires a highly integrated yet differentiated organization that, as far as we know, is found only within certain brains.

Consciousness as an Integrated Process. As we discussed in chapter 2, one of William James's most valuable insights was to realize that consciousness is not a thing but a process. Although few people would disagree in principle with this conclusion, it is often ignored in practice, as indicated by the continuing attempts to identify some special intrinsic marker of those neurons that would generate conscious experience. The dynamic core hypothesis takes James's insight seriously: As a process, a dynamic core is defined in terms of neural interactions. In other words, the definition of a dynamic core is a functional one, in that it is based on the strength of an ensemble of interactions, rather than just on a structure, a property of some neurons, or their location.

Integration or Unity. As we have said, a fundamental property of conscious experience is that it is integrated—a conscious scene cannot be decomposed into independent components. Integration, as Corneille might have said of the unity of time, space, and action in classical drama, is a sine qua non of conscious experience. It is simply impossible to conceive of a conscious state that is not unified. In chapter 10, we stated that a functional cluster is a set of neural elements characterized by strong mutual interactions that cannot be subdivided into independent components. A dynamic core constitutes a functional cluster and is thus, by definition, unified and highly integrated. Another way to say it is that a dynamic core has unity because perturbing the activity of a part of the core will lead to consequences that extend to the entire core.

Privateness. Every conscious scene is not only unified, but is experienced from a single point of view. It cannot be completely shared by another person, which is to say that it is private. Both unity and inherent subjectivity, or privateness, are consistent with the definition of a functional cluster. A functional cluster is defined as a set of neural elements that interact among themselves *in a single brain* much more than they do with the surrounding neurons. Since a dynamic core constitutes a functional cluster, changes that occur inside the core affect the rest of the core strongly and rapidly, while changes that occur outside the core affect it much less strongly, much less rapidly, or not at all. Thus, there is a functional border between the environment and the informational states within a dynamic core that makes these core states effectively "private." It is also explicit in the definition of a dynamic core that, at any time, certain areas of the brain or groups of neurons are part of it while other areas or neuronal groups are not, even if they are equally active and even if they *had* been part of it at some previous instant. This is the essence of the selective nature of consciousness that James also discussed .

Coherence of Conscious States. We have shown that a person cannot be aware of two mutually incoherent scenes or objects at the same time, as demonstrated by ambiguous figures, ambiguous words, incongruous inputs to the two eyes in binocular rivalry, and so on (see figure 3.2). Coherence, meaning that the occurrence of a certain perceptual state precludes the occurrence of another one, represents another consequence of the unity of consciousness. Since a dynamic core is a unified whole, mutual interactions among its constituent neural elements will bring about certain global states of the core that automatically preclude the simultaneous occurrence of certain other global core states at a given time. What is important to note is that since the core is integrated, the competition is not between different states of a few neural elements but between integrated states of the *entire* set of elements that make up the core. We presented examples of this competition in the model of the visual system considered earlier, in which only those interactions that are mutually consistent and stable are favored by the dynamics of the system. This performance reflects the fact that the coherence characteristic of a conscious scene follows inevitably from the requirements of an integrated process.

Consciousness as a Differentiated Process. Each of us can experience an enormous number of different conscious states. These states are far from arbitrary: A person blind from birth cannot experience color, a newborn baby cannot experience the esthetic pleasures of art, and an occasional wine drinker cannot experience the discriminations available to a sommelier. By extrapolation, we must assume that confined as we are to our five senses, direct experience of countless other discriminations in countless other domains is forever precluded. Nevertheless, as we have emphasized, the number of conscious states that we can discriminate within a fraction of a second is exceedingly large, certainly much larger than anything attainable at present by a man-made artifact. It is, in fact, as large as we care to imagine. The extraordinary differentiation of conscious experience is related to some of its most important properties, such as informativeness, global access, and flexibility.

The Informativeness of Conscious Experience. As we have seen, the occurrence of a given conscious state selected among billions of others represents information, in the fundamental sense of reducing uncertainty among a large number of possible choices. How much information is at stake is what our introduction of a measure for complexity intended to address. We have focused on the relationships among the elements of an integrated process isolated from the environment—among the elements of a functional cluster—thus avoiding the ambiguities involved in introducing external observers, symbols, and codes. Within a functional cluster, the only information available is the difference that changes in the state of any subset of a system make to the rest of the system. This line of reasoning implies that every subset can act as a candidate partial "observer," and this maneuver avoids the ambiguities having to do with the idea that information must be integrated in a single place—for example, by an external observer.

The dynamic core hypothesis states that the set of interacting groups of neurons of the functional cluster supporting conscious experience must have high complexity—corresponding to high values of average mutual information between these groups. If complexity is high, changes in the state of any subset of elements of the core make a great difference to the states of the rest of the core. In other words, on average, every subset of the core has the potential to discriminate among a large number of states of the rest of the core. As we have shown, this discrimination can be achieved only if the dynamic core is simultaneously both functionally integrated and functionally specialized. The notion of neural complexity is also helpful in conceptualizing neural conditions that are characterized by hypersynchronous global activity, such as slow-wave sleep and generalized epilepsy, which are associated with the loss of consciousness. Although clearly integrated, such conditions are associated with a dramatic loss of integrated information, since functional specialization tends to vanish. In these high-integration but low-information conditions, the repertoire of neural states that can be selected is drastically reduced, and neural complexity is expected to be low.

Distribution of Information, Context-Dependency, and Global Access. When we become aware of something, whether it is an uneasiness in how we balance ourselves as we walk, a flutter in our stomach, a mistake in our reasoning, or the slow emergence of the pattern of an object out of a random dot stereogram, we can make use of that information in a large number of possible ways that can trigger all kinds of behavioral responses. It is as if, suddenly, many different parts of our brain were privy to information that was previously confined to some specialized subsystem.

These observations are fully consistent with the idea that consciousness is associated with high complexity. By definition, high complexity implies the efficient distribution of information among the elements of a neural system. A system is complex if the mutual information between any subset and the rest is high, that is, if the consequences of a change in the activity of any subset of elements are efficiently distributed to the rest of the system. The sensitivity to context is the other side of the coin. In a system in which the mutual information between any subset and the rest is high, the activity of each small subset is sensitive to whatever the different states of the rest of the system may be.[16]

The fact that consciousness can access many different behavioral outputs or, more generally, many different brain processes also fits well with the notion that cooperative interactions among a large number of brain regions, leading to the emergence of a dynamic core, can greatly increase the ability to access globally any other group of neurons in the brain, whether it is part of the dynamic core or not. For example, only if we are conscious can we access so-called episodic memory, the conscious memory of particular events in our life. This fact may indicate that the hippocampal circuits that are known to be crucial for episodic memory may be preferentially activated by the coherent firing of distributed populations of neurons in the thalamocortical system (a dynamic core). It is not surprising that biofeedback training, which shows our ability to control (often in less than one hour) the activity of any chosen neuron in our brain, actually requires consciousness.[17] Single neurons or no, the wide distribution of information is guaranteed mechanistically by thalamocortical and corticocortical reentry, which facilitates the interactions among distant regions of the brain. The distribution of information, context-dependency, and global access are all properties that contribute to the adaptive value of consciousness during evolution.

Flexibility and the Ability to Respond to and Learn Unexpected Associations. One ground for the adaptive value of consciousness may have to do with the fact that we can become aware of novel, unexpected associations to which we can then learn to respond. The example we gave before, of the animal in the jungle associating wind shifts and jungle noises as indicative of a jaguar, is a case in point. The ability to be flexible in associating signals from different modalities and submodalities or from the present and the past is an important consequence of the dynamic nature of integration, as well as of the nonlinear mechanisms that mediate it. Once the opportunity for interaction among neuronal groups is maximized through the generation of the dynamic core, any subtle change in the activity of different regions of the brain can bring about new, dynamic associations, as illustrated in the model of the visual system that we discussed in connection with the binding problem (see figure 10.2).[18] The ability to learn unexpected associations among a large variety of apparently unconnected signals has obvious adaptive significance for animals who face an open-ended world full of novelty.

The Limited Capacity of Consciousness. We saw in chapter 3 that, no matter how hard we try, we cannot keep in mind more than a few things at a time. For instance, if we are shown twelve digits arranged in four rows of three for less than 150 msec, we can consciously report only four at a time. This remarkably strict "capacity limitation" has led many to the conclusion that consciousness contains a small amount of information, just a few bits, corresponding, over time, to an information capacity of just 1 to 16 bits per sec.[19] This is an abysmal performance when judged according to engineering standards. We have argued throughout this book, however, that the informativeness of consciousness should not be based on how many more or less independent "chunks" of information a single conscious state might contain. Instead, it should be based on how many different conscious states are ruled out by the occurrence of the particular state that we are experiencing at a given moment. Since we can easily differentiate among billions of different conscious states within a fraction of a second, we have concluded that the informativeness of conscious experience must be extraordinarily high, indeed, better than any present-day engineer could dream of.[20] How should we account, then, for the so-called capacity limitation of consciousness?

As we discussed in chapter 3, it seems that the observed capacity limitation is tightly linked to the integrated nature of conscious states. In terms of the dynamic core, such a capacity limitation reflects an upper limit on *how many partially independent subprocesses can be sustained within the core without interfering with its integration and coherence.* Indeed, it is likely that the same neural mechanisms responsible for the rapid integration of the dynamic core are also responsible for this capacity limitation. We have seen in chapter 10, for example, that when our large-scale model of the visual system was presented with a visual scene containing up to three objects, functionally specialized groups of neurons distributed over many modeled areas increased their firing rate for several hundreds of milliseconds in an integrated way. However, we also observed that, at a finer time scale (tens of milliseconds), groups of neurons responding to different features of the *same* object were highly correlated among themselves and less correlated with groups of neurons responding to the features of *different* objects. Thus, the model was able to sustain both a single, integrated neural process at a time scale of hundreds of milliseconds and up to three to four partially independent subprocesses at a time scale of tens of milliseconds.

However, we also observed that when the visual scene presented to the model contained four or more different objects, units responding to two different objects were often spuriously synchronized at a finer time scale. This phenomenon is reminiscent of the so-called false conjunctions mentioned in chapter 10 that occur in human perception in similar circumstances, a clearcut manifestation of limited capacity. Thus, the need to generate a single, integrated neural process within hundreds of milliseconds requires rapid and effective interactions among distributed groups of neurons. This need puts strict limits on how many partially independent processes can be accommodated at the same time. Indeed, it would appear, based on our simulations, that the so-called capacity limitation of four to seven independent "chunks" per conscious state may be due to the specific properties of temporal summation mechanisms and to the precision and speed of synchronization needed among neurons to constitute the dynamic core.

The Serial Nature of Conscious Experience. This seemingly serial nature of conscious experience—the fact that one conscious state or thought is followed by another—can also be related to the dynamic evolution of the core. Since a dynamic core is a unified and highly integrated process, it must move from one global state to another. In other words, its temporal evolution must follow a single trajectory, and what may appear as "decisions" or "choices" can occur only one at a time. This conclusion is consistent with the well-known difficulty of dual-task paradigms involving consciousness, as well as with the phenomenon of the psychological refractory period[21] we mentioned in chapter 3, according to which conscious choices or discriminations occur one at a time. An examination of the latter phenomenon also shows that the time for such decisions is around 150 milliseconds, a figure remarkably close to the lower limit of the time typically needed for conscious integration. Although it is conceivable that, under certain conditions, it may be convenient to split one's consciousness in two or more parts and allow each part to perform separate functions—one part adding up a bill and another engaging in romantic dialogue, for example—the inevitable price to pay would be the lack of integration between parallel processes. Everything considered, this may be a less adaptive solution. Indeed, the enormous number of reciprocal pathways mediating reentry within the thalamocortical system essentially force the system to behave in an integrated way. Any major functional split within this system seems to require either a large anatomical cut (as in a split brain or various neurological disconnection syndromes) or some major psychological trauma (as in psychiatric dissociation syndromes). It is an interesting experimental question whether one may find evidence in such conditions of a corresponding split of a single, dominant dynamic core into two or more subcores.

Consciousness as a Process That Is Continuous but Continually Changing. Being a process, not a thing, consciousness is both continuous and continually changing. Conscious states typically flow seamlessly and maintain a high degree of coherence over time. Even jump cuts in a movie fail to break up the projection and flow of the story as it is consciously experienced. On the other hand, conscious experience can move at great speed; James's specious present, a rough estimate of the duration of a single conscious state, is of the order of 100 milliseconds,[22] meaning that conscious states can change very rapidly. Think of the breakneck sequences of scenes during a chase in an action movie.

It is implicit in the definition of the dynamic core that it can maintain its unity over time even if its composition may be constantly changing, which again is the signature of a process as opposed to a thing. Whether the composition of the dynamic core is changing or not, however, the process of neural integration that gives rise to the core must occur at the time scale of conscious experience—within fractions of a second. Moreover, a large repertoire of different global states must be available to the core at this rapid time scale. Thus, when a particular core state emerges, through reentrant interactions, out of this large repertoire, a large amount of information is generated over a short time. This information corresponds to the rapid reduction of uncertainty about which of many possible global states is going to occur. The various models we previously discussed indicate that ongoing, "spontaneous" reentrant interactions along corticocortical and thalamocortical connections are essential if such integration and differentiation are to occur within hundreds of milliseconds. We also noted that we are still lacking an important addition to the theoretical tools described thus far: a way of estimating integration and differentiation (complexity) over such short times, (hundreds of milliseconds). Measures of mutual information are relatively easy to obtain if a system is stationary, but other measures, most likely derivable from dynamical system theory and perturbation theory, may prove to be more appropriate over shorter periods.

SOME IMPORTANT QUESTIONS

A number of experimental questions and predictions are generated by the dynamic core hypothesis. A central prediction is that during cognitive activities involving consciousness, one should find evidence in the conscious brain for a large but distinct set of distributed neuronal groups that interact over fractions of a second much more strongly among themselves than with the rest of the brain. This prediction could, in principle, be tested by neurophysiological experiments designed to record electrical potentials from multiple neurons whose activity is correlated with conscious experience. Multielectrode recordings have already indicated that rapid changes in the functional connectivity among distributed populations of neurons can occur independently of their firing rate.[23] Recent studies of a small number of neurons in the frontal cortex of monkeys have also shown simultaneous shifts in activity states involving some but not all recorded neurons.[24]

A convincing demonstration of rapid functional clustering among distributed neuronal groups requires, however, that these studies be extended to larger populations of neurons in several areas of the brain. Another possibility would be to examine whether the effects of direct cortical microstimulation spread more widely in the brain if they are associated with conscious experience than if they are not. In humans, the extent and boundaries of neural populations exchanging coherent signals can be evaluated through methods of frequency tagging. For example, we have already stated that by exploiting frequency tagging in MEG studies of binocular rivalry, relatively direct approaches to the neural substrates of consciousness can be designed. Whether all aspects of the dynamic core hypothesis are correct or not, the criteria outlined here should facilitate the design of similar experiments using imaging methods that offer both wide spatial coverage and high temporal resolution. These methods include fMRI, topographic EEG, and MEG.

Such experiments may answer several relevant questions about the dynamics of the brain: Whenever a person is conscious, is there a set of brain regions that interact much more strongly among themselves than with the rest of the brain over fractions of a second—that is, can we directly show the existence of a dynamic core? Does the composition of the dynamic core change, depending upon the conscious activity the person is engaged in? Are certain brain regions always included or always excluded? Can this core split, or can multiple dynamic cores coexist in a normal person? Are there pathological conditions that reflect such multiple cores, or are there abnormalities of a single core? A reasonable prediction would be that certain disorders of consciousness, notably dissociative disorders and schizophrenia, should be reflected in abnormalities of the dynamic core and may result in the formation of multiple cores.

Another set of experimental questions can be posed by the prediction that the dynamic core underlying consciousness should be highly differentiated or complex over a short period. What is the complexity of the dynamic core itself, and can this complexity be correlated with the ability to differentiate, which is such a fundamental property of conscious experience? A strong prediction based on our hypothesis, is that the complexity of the dynamic core should correlate with a person's conscious state. For example, we predict that neural complexity should be much higher during waking and REM sleep, when we are conscious, than during the deep stages of slow-wave sleep, when we are not. It should be extremely low during the unconscious spells accompanying epileptic seizures, despite the overall increase in brain activity. We also predict that neural processes underlying automatic behaviors, no matter how sophisticated, should have lower complexity than neural processes underlying consciously controlled behaviors. Finally, a systematic increase in the complexity of coherent neural processes is expected to accompany cognitive development, in parallel with an extraordinary increase in discriminatory abilities.

On the basis of these considerations, we suggest that the dynamic core hypothesis, taken together with the thalamocortical mechanisms described in chapter 9, can indeed account for some of the general properties of conscious experience. The ability to define functional clustering and to estimate complexity—the repertoire of available global states—over short periods, will be particularly useful in designing experiments that can test this hypothesis directly. These questions and their associated predictions prompted by our hypothesis set an agenda that is amenable to direct experimental tests. In the meantime, there remain several important issues that can be considered, irrespective of the outcome of these investigations. These issues are the relation of subjective discriminations, or qualia, to states of the core and the relation of conscious to unconscious activity. We discuss these issues in the next part of the book in continuing our efforts to untangle the world knot.

PART FIVE

Untangling the Knot

The dynamic core hypothesis has allowed us to formulate a concise operational statement of what is special about the activity of groups of neurons underlying conscious experience. Moreover, on the basis of the dynamic core hypothesis, we were able to revisit some of the key properties of consciousness that we described before and to evaluate how they can actually be accounted for in neural terms. We have also made the case that reentry is the basic mechanism through which a unified scene, weaving perceptual categorization with value-category memory, can be rapidly generated as a result of interactions in the core.

With these hypotheses in hand, we reexamine the critical issue of qualia—the experiencing, for example, of redness, loudness, warmth, and pain—from a new standpoint. We will see that qualia are high-order discriminations among a large number of states of the dynamic core and that, as such, they are both highly integrated and extraordinarily informative. We will also make some forays into how the organization of the dynamic core can determine the phenomenological properties of different qualia. Finally, we develop a new perspective on the relationship between the conscious and the unconscious by examining the transactions between the core and the myriad functionally insulated routines related to automatic and unconscious processes. This examination clarifies the role of consciousness in learning and memory. Taken together, these efforts suggest that it may be possible, after all, to untangle the world knot.

CHAPTER THIRTEEN

Qualia and Discrimination

In this chapter we discuss what is perhaps the most daunting problem of consciousness: the problem of qualia. The specific quality, or "quale," of subjective experience—of color, warmth, pain, a loud sound—has seemed beyond scientific explanation. Our position is as follows: First, to experience qualia, one must have a body and a brain that support neural processes of the kind described in previous chapters. In no case can a theory or description substitute for an individual's experience of a quale, no matter how correct such a theory is in describing its underlying mechanisms. Second, each differentiable conscious experience represents a different quale, whether it is primarily a sensation, an image, a thought, or even a mood and whether, in retrospect, it appears simple or composite. Third, each quale corresponds to a different state of the dynamic core, which can be differentiated from billions of other states within a neural space comprising a large number of dimensions. The relevant dimensions are given by the number of neuronal groups whose activities, integrated through reentrant interactions, constitute a dynamic core of high complexity. Qualia are therefore high-dimensional discriminations. Fourth, the development of the earliest qualia occurs largely on the basis of multimodal, body-centered discriminations carried out by the proprioceptive, kinesthetic, and autonomic systems that are present in the embryo and infant's brain, particularly in the brain stem. All subsequent qualia can be referable to this initial set of discriminations, which constitute the basis of the most primitive self.

Many of the philosophical objections to a scientific explanation of consciousness have to do with qualia, and so does much of the skepticism of scientists about the whole subject. Indeed, it is often implied that the mystery of consciousness, the world knot, cannot really be unraveled unless the mystery of qualia is unraveled, too.

The prototypical qualia discussed by philosophers are simple sensations, such as the "redness" of red, the "blueness" of blue, and the "painfulness" of pain. In this view, a quale is that special subjective feeling that makes red, red and different from blue or that makes pain painful and different from both red and blue. All kinds of philosophical arguments are built on the presumed irreducibility of qualia. Why does red feel the way it does? And could it be that what both you and I call red actually looks red to me and green to you, and would this make any difference?[1] What is more, why does red feel like anything at all? Could there be a replica of you that gives exactly the same behavioral responses as you, has exactly the same neural mechanisms, and yet has no subjective experience whatsoever, no qualia associated with its experience? That is, could there be a philosophical zombie? And again, if so, how could we ever find out?

The reason qualia seem so difficult to explain in neural terms does not require such esoteric exertions. The problem of qualia can be illustrated by the simple paradox we introduced in chapter 2. A conscious human being and a photodiode can behave similarly, at least under certain circumstances: They can both differentiate between light and dark. We know how the photodiode does it. We also know reasonably well how a human being can do it, since we know that there are neurons in the retina and in the visual areas of the brain that fire differently, depending on the amount of light. But why should the human's, but not the photodiode's, ability to differentiate between light and dark be associated with a conscious experience of light or dark? Why should the firing of certain neurons in the human visual system generate a "quale" of light, a subjective feeling that there is light, while the voltage change in the photodiode does not? Or why, for that matter, should the firing of warm-sensitive neurons in the brain produce a quale of warmth, while the firing of neurons sensitive to blood pressure fails to produce any corresponding quale, or any subjective feeling of what it is like to have high blood pressure?

How qualia arise from certain kinds of neural activity is what both the neurophysiologist Charles Sherrington and the philosopher Bertrand Russell found insurmountable. They pointed out that one can give a reasonably precise neurophysiological description of the neurons that would fire when one perceives, say, a bright red object or when one perceives light or feels warmth or pain, yet, notwithstanding how precise that description is, one would still be faced with a paradox or a mystery: Why would the physical, objectively describable fact that a certain neuron is firing correspond to a conscious sensation, to a subjective feeling, to a quale? And why to that particular quale and not to another one?

Let us consider some paradigmatic qualia—the perception of red, blue, and other colors—and ask whether, on the basis of our analysis, it is possible to obtain at least an intuitive understanding of the neural bases of qualia. For the sake of argument, imagine that you are lying in a room that is quiet, comfortable, and featureless, with no other worry in the world than reporting what you are perceiving to a scientist outside, and that the only thing that happens is that every few seconds the room is aglow in a different color: pure red light, pure blue light, or pure yellow light. You have been instructed to think of nothing, just to relax and experience the pure colors. All you perceive is red, blue, or yellow, unencumbered by visual shapes or motions and undisturbed by other sensations: no sound, no deliberate tactile stimulation. Your body is as comfortable as it can be, so comfortable that you completely forget about it, or so you think. Let us say, then, that, at a certain point, you open your eyes and experience consciously a pure sensation of red or blue, as pure as possible. What neural process may account for these subjective discriminations, these qualia?

NEURAL CORRELATES OF COLOR PERCEPTION

Before we can answer this question, we must set the stage with a few words about what is known of the neural correlates of color perception. Human beings can discriminate among a vast number of colors and color gradations, up to several million.[2] Nevertheless, psychophysical investigations suggest that perceptual "color space" may actually be organized along just a few axes: Different perceived colors correspond to different points in a low-dimensional space spanned by these few axes. Much evidence exists for a set of primary axes corresponding to the opposing pairs red-green, blue-yellow, and light-dark. Studies of color naming in different cultures further indicate that colors tend to be universally categorized into certain classes. The "focal" or prototypical colors around which such categorization is organized correspond to the primary axes just mentioned (red, green, yellow, blue, black, and white) and to a few derived or composite categories (such as orange, purple, pink, brown, and gray).

Classical psychophysical experiments have demonstrated that the conscious discrimination and identification of colors are not based merely on the wavelength of the incoming light from a given object. For example, our conscious response is based on a comparison between the wavelength of the light reflected by that object and the light reflected by nearby objects. If a banana is illuminated with red light, for example, it will reflect more light in the red range than in the yellow range, but it will still reflect more yellow than a nearby avocado. This phenomenon, by which we discount the illuminant and perceive an invariant property of objects, their relative reflectance, is called color constancy. It is related to a similar phenomenon by which a piece of coal appears black under bright sunlight even if the amount of light it then reflects increases by orders of magnitude. Countless other phenomena in psychophysics indicate that perception is not merely a reflection of immediate input but involves a construction or a comparison by the brain.

Our understanding of the neurophysiological basis of color perception has progressed immensely over the past few decades. We know in great detail the properties of three classes of retinal photoreceptors, or cones, selective to long, middle, and short wavelengths, respectively, which form the basis of the ability to discriminate among colors. We also know a lot about the properties of color-selective cells in other layers of the retina, in the lateral geniculate nucleus—the thalamic relay from the retina to the visual cortex—and in the visual cortex. For example, in the lateral geniculate nucleus one finds so-called color-opponent neurons. These neurons are organized according to the three primary axes that define psychophysically opponent pairs. Some are activated by wavelengths in the red range and inhibited by those in the green range, others are activated by wavelengths in the blue range and inhibited by those in the yellow range, and others respond to the overall amount of white light and are inhibited by darkness.[3] In the visual cortex, particularly in area V4, certain neurons manifest the property of color constancy—that is, their response to the color of an object is invariant with respect to the illuminating light. Finally, in the monkey area IT (inferotemporal cortex), neurons selectively respond to a range of colors that closely correspond to perceptual color space. Their organization may even reflect the basic color categories identified in cross-cultural studies. Neuronal groups that respond to color the way a conscious human being would are clearly good candidates to be considered neural correlates of the conscious experience of color. This supposition is further strengthened by data indicating that, in humans, damage to the fusiform gyrus—the likely homologue of monkey area IT—selectively abolishes the conscious perception of color.

On the basis of these various sources of evidence, we can construct a simplified neurophysiological scenario of what goes on in the brain when we
perceive a given color. Various classes of neurons in the retina, lateral geniculate nucleus, primary visual cortex, and beyond progressively analyze the
incoming signals and contribute to the construction of new response properties in higher visual areas. Eventually, say in area IT, the firing of certain
groups of neurons begins to discriminate among different colors the same
way a conscious human being would do. For the sake of simplicity, let us
imagine that a first set of neuronal groups in IT is selectively activated when
a person reports seeing red and is inhibited when he or she reports seeing
green. A second set is activated when the person perceives blue and inhibited
when he or she perceives yellow, and a third is activated by the perception of
light and inhibited by the perception of darkness.[4]

Let us now imagine that the mean firing rate of these three sets of neuronal groups can vary from 0 (completely inhibited) to 10 Hz (spontaneous
firing range) to 100 Hz (maximum firing) and that differences in the firing
rates of as little as 5 Hz make a difference to the firing of the neurons to
which they project and connect. Clearly, the firing rates of these three sets of
neuronal groups can define a three-dimensional space within which each
color that a human being can differentiate corresponds to a distinct point
(see figure 13.1). Pure red, for example, will correspond to a point in this
space whose coordinates are 100 on the red-green axis and 10 on both the
blue-yellow and the white-black axes.

Although such a neural scenario would certainly have to be refined, it is
probably sufficient to explain many aspects of human color discrimination.[5]
For example, different combinations of the firing rates of three such sets of
neuronal groups, corresponding to different points in this three-dimensional
space, could, in principle, produce different effects on neurons elsewhere in
the brain, including neurons in the motor cortex or in executive language
areas, thus explaining our ability to discriminate among thousands of colors
behaviorally. Such discriminations would occur in accord with the principle
of color constancy.

A neurophysiologist who knew the state of these three neuronal groups
could therefore predict a subject's responses quite well. Indeed, an accurate
neural model of color vision has been constructed that essentially implements the neural scenario just described.[6] This model can account for our
ability to discriminate colors and reproduces well various phenomena in the
psychophysics of color perception, including color constancy. Thus, we may
even say that we have a reasonably good understanding of the neural mecha-

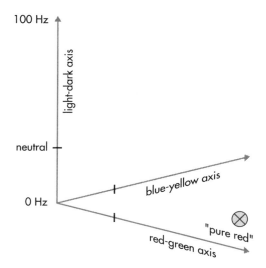

FIGURE 13.1 COLOR SPACE. The figure depicts a three-dimensional neural space that can account for many aspects of human color discrimination. Each axis corresponds to a set of neuronal groups whose firing can vary from 0 (completely inhibited) to 10 Hz (neutral or spontaneous firing range) to 100 Hz (maximum firing). The firing rates of these three sets of neuronal groups define a three-dimensional space within which each color that can be differentiated by a human being corresponds to a distinct point. Pure red, for example, would correspond to a point in this space (crossed circle) whose coordinates are 100 on the red-green axis, and 10 on both the blue-yellow and the white-black axes. Neurons with such properties are found in color areas of the cerebral cortex.

nisms of color vision, an understanding that would probably have satisfied some of the requirements of both Sherrington and Russell. One annoying problem remains, however: We have no reason to believe that the neural scenario just depicted or the model that implements it is sufficient to explain the qualia for red or blue or, for that matter, that the model can generate any qualia whatsoever. If this scenario is not enough, what else is needed?

ONE NEURONAL GROUP, ONE QUALE?

The simplest way to address the problem of qualia is to assume that for every quale, all that is needed is a group of neurons, or even a single neuron, that, when firing, explicitly represents that particular aspect of consciousness or quale.[7] With this one group of neurons, one quale, hypothesis, one may imagine, for example, that the firing of a specific group of neurons somehow explicitly represents the perception of the color red and that the firing of another neuronal group may explicitly represent the color blue, and so on. All we need to be sure of is that the neuronal group in question fires every time a person reports that she perceives red and does not fire every time that person reports that she does not.[8]

Of course, some complications arise from the simple-minded equating of the activity of specific groups of neurons with specific qualia. It is not clear, for example, how many specific neuronal groups would be required. Would there be a distinct neuronal group explicitly representing every color that a human being can discriminate, whether or not it can be adequately described in words? Furthermore, one would also have to ask how many distinct qualia there are in general, since each of them needs to be explicitly represented by a distinct neuronal group. This question has a long history. At the turn of the century, the psychologist Edward Titchener was attempting to identify the "atoms" of consciousness. Red, blue, pain, and the like were obvious candidates, but he attempted to cover the entire phenomenology of consciousness in terms of elementary sensations. His students were therefore assigned such tasks as determining the elementary atoms involved in sexual excitement, bladder distention, and other bodily functions. As may be expected, they were not successful.

A far more serious problem, however, is that beyond the dubious attempt to assign a different group of neurons to each and every quale, such an atomistic hypothesis has actually nothing to say about the very issue at stake. Why should the firing of those particular neurons in area IT generate the quale redness, with its specific subjective quality and meaning, but not, for instance, the quale greenness, or the quale pain? And why should it generate a quale at all, when the firings of neurons in the retina or in the lateral geniculate nucleus appear to generate nothing in the way of subjective feelings? How does the transformation occur that seemed so incomprehensible to both Sherrington and Russell? And what about the neural model of color vision mentioned earlier? Should we conclude that the units in the simulated area IT of that model can generate a primitive perception of color, a disembodied quale of red, blue, or yellow? And if not, what are they missing? A special biological ingredient? Or a special location in the brain? It appears that if we take the one neuronal group, one quale, approach,[9] these questions cannot be answered. Arthur Schopenhauer—pointing to the world knot—would have liked the way the situation has come full circle. The enormous *petitio principii* so unveiled, he might have said, would trigger a sudden fit of inextinguishable laughter in the Olympians.[10]

QUALIA AND THE DYNAMIC CORE

If we want to make the issue of qualia less miraculous, or at least less ridiculous, we must return to the idea of the dynamic core and explore some of its implications. Our hypothesis states that the neural processes underlying conscious experience constitute a large and changing functional cluster, the dynamic core, which includes a large number of distributed neuronal groups and has high complexity. This dynamic core emerges through rapid reentrant interactions in less than a second and includes distributed portions of the thalamocortical system, although it is not necessarily restricted to it. A key implication of our hypothesis is that the legitimate *neural reference space* for conscious experience, any conscious experience, including that of color,

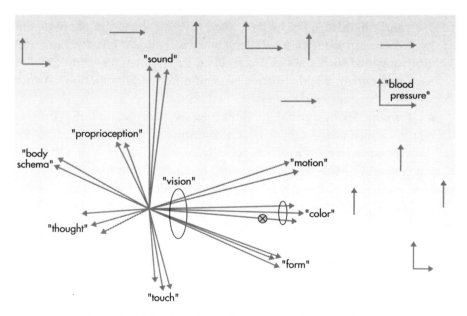

FIGURE 13.2 QUALIA SPACE. The figure depicts an *N*-dimensional neural space corresponding to the dynamic core. *N* is the number of neuronal groups that, at any given time, are part of the dynamic core, where *N* is a large number (only a minimal number of dimensions is plotted). Some of these dimensions correspond to neuronal groups that are color selective and exhibit color constancy (exactly as in figure 13.1). However, a large number of other dimensions is represented in the dynamic core, as indicated by axes corresponding to the activity of neuronal groups specialized for visual form or visual motion, for auditory or somatosensory inputs, for proprioceptive inputs, for body schemas, and so forth. The appropriate neural reference space for the conscious experience corresponding to the quale "pure red" would correspond to a discriminable point in this space (crossed circle).

is given not by the activity of any individual neuronal group (for example, a color-responsive neuronal group, as in the one group, one quale, hypothesis) or even by any small subset of neuronal groups (such as the three sets of neuronal groups that are jointly sufficient for discriminating among all colors, as in our neural model), but by the activity of *the entire dynamic core*.

To clarify this central issue, it is convenient to rephrase the dynamic-core hypothesis in terms of an N-dimensional neural space and of points within that space, as shown schematically in figure 13.2. The number of dimensions defining the neural reference space corresponding to the dynamic core is given by the number N of neuronal groups that, at any given time, are part of the dynamic core, where N is a large number, say, between 10^3 and 10^7 (only a minimal number of dimensions is plotted in the figure). Some of these dimensions correspond to neuronal groups that are color selective and exhibit color constancy (exactly as in figure 13.1). However, a large number of other dimensions are represented in the dynamic core, as indicated by axes corresponding to the activity of neuronal groups specialized for visual form or visual motion, for auditory or somatosensory inputs, for proprioceptive inputs, for body schemas, and so on. Of course, this graphic illustration should not be taken literally, since at this stage it is considerably simplified and imprecise. It may be useful, however, in obtaining an understanding of the meaning of a quale in the context of our view of consciousness as an integrated process, as well as in grasping the relevance of the various theoretical concepts that we presented earlier.

The first claim of the dynamic-core hypothesis is that these N neuronal groups constitute a functional cluster, that is, over a short period, they are highly integrated among themselves and much less so with the rest of the brain. Since a functional cluster identifies a single, unified physical process, it follows that the activity of these N neuronal groups should be considered within a single reference space. In the figure, this reference space is indicated by the common origin of all the dimensions defining the core at that moment. By the definition of a functional cluster, it follows that such a reference space cannot be decomposed into independent subspaces (corresponding to subsets of neuronal groups) without a loss of information with respect to other portions of the core.[11] By the same token, it also follows that neuronal groups that are not part of the dynamic core should be considered as constituting separate neural spaces, since within that time scale they are effectively functionally disconnected from it. Accordingly, the figure also represents several smaller neural spaces spanned by a few axes that have a separate origin. An example of such a small, functionally disconnected space may correspond to, for instance, neurons responding to the fluctuations of blood pressure. Clearly, it would be meaningless to consider neuronal groups that are not part of a single functional cluster as part of the same neural reference space because they do not correspond to an underlying unified physical process. It would be like considering the neural space spanned jointly by the neurons in the brain of a person in America and of another person in Europe and wondering what a point in that space may mean.

The second claim of the dynamic-core hypothesis is that the number of points that can be differentiated in this N-dimensional space—which make a difference to it—is vast, as indicated by high values of complexity. Clearly, the larger the number N of neuronal groups included in the dynamic core, the larger the number of points in the corresponding N-dimensional space that may be differentiated and the higher its maximum complexity. As we have shown, however, a large number of participating neuronal groups alone is not a guarantee of high complexity. If, for example, the firing of the N neuronal groups that are part of the dynamic core were synchronized to an extreme degree, as is the case during epileptic seizures, the actual repertoire of neural states available to the dynamic core would be minimal—just a few positions in the N-dimensional space. Therefore, the selection of a particular integrated state of the core over a short period would generate little information, and the complexity of the core would be correspondingly low.

We are now in a position to ask how the perception of red, blue, or any other color should be interpreted within such a framework. Given the experimental results mentioned earlier, the neural state corresponding to the sensation of red certainly involves high activity for red-sensitive neuronal groups and low activity for blue-sensitive neuronal groups and light-sensitive neuronal groups present in area IT and other cortical "color" areas. What is crucial, however, is that if we were to consider only the firing of those three sets of neuronal groups, there would not be any notion of color at all. If those three dimensions were all there was, there would be no way to discriminate between what is a color and what is not a color (everything else) within this neural space because there would be no further dimensions to make such a discrimination. For this discrimination, we need other neuronal groups responding, for example, to the shape of objects irrespective of colors, to their movement irrespective of their color and shape, and so forth. Only if the activity of these other neuronal groups is effectively part of the same neural reference space can a discrimination be made among and within different submodalities, such as color, motion, and form.

Even then, there would still be no notion that the system is dealing with visual aspects of a stimulus, rather than with aspects pertaining to some other modality. For that discrimination, the neural reference space must include other neuronal groups that are (or are not) responding to auditory, tactile, or proprioceptive inputs. We would also need neuronal groups whose firing is correlated with the particular position your body is in and its relation to the environment—the so-called body schema. In addition, we would need neuronal groups whose firing is correlated with your sense of familiarity and of congruence with the situation you are in and neuronal groups indicating whether salient events are occurring. And so on and so forth until there is a neural reference space that is sufficiently rich to allow discrimination of the conscious state corresponding to the pure perception of a given color from billions of other conscious states.

On the basis of these considerations, we can say how, in this framework, the quale corresponding to the sensation red should be conceived of: The pure sensation of red is a particular neural state identified by a point within the N-dimensional neural space defined by the integrated activity of all the groups of neurons that constitute the dynamic core. The quale of the pure sensation of red corresponds to the discrimination that has been made among billions of other states within the same neural reference space.[12] While neurons responding to the presence of red are certainly necessary for the conscious experience of red, they are clearly not sufficient. The conscious discrimination corresponding to the quale of seeing red acquires its full meaning only when considered in the appropriate, much larger, neural reference space. By this same argument, if the same neuronal groups responding to red were firing precisely in the same way but were functionally disconnected from the core, such firing would have no meaning and no associated quale.

This view differs radically from the "atomistic" or "modular" approaches we discussed earlier in this chapter. According to our hypothesis, perceiving the redness of red absolutely requires a discrimination among integrated states of the entire dynamic core, and it can never emerge magically out of the firing of a single group of neurons that are endowed with some special local or intrinsic property. By the same token, our hypothesis can account for why the firing of other neuronal groups, such as those responding to blood pressure, does not appear to "generate" any subjective experience or quale. Such neuronal groups, we propose, are not part of the dynamic core, which means that changes in their firing make a difference only locally, not in the context of a huge, N-dimensional space allowing for billions of discriminations.

A FEW COROLLARIES

It is worth examining some simple corollaries of this hypothesis. One corollary is that every discriminable point in the N-dimensional space defined by the dynamic core identifies a conscious state, while a trajectory joining points in this space would correspond to a sequence of conscious states occurring over time. Contrary to common usage by many philosophers and scientists,[13] we suggest that being uniquely specified and not reducible to independent components, *every different conscious state deserves to be called a quale*, from the state of perceiving pure red, pure darkness, or pure pain, to the state of perceiving a complicated visual scene, and to the state of "thinking of Vienna."[14] As William James correctly anticipated, there is no "pure," atomistic sensation: "No one ever had a simple sensation by itself. Consciousness, from our natal day, is of a teeming multiplicity of objects and relations, and what we call simple sensations are results of discriminative attention, pushed often to a very high degree."[15] In short, a "pure" sensation of red defines a point in this N-dimensional state space as much as the conscious perception of a busy street in New York City, full of different objects, sounds, smells, associations, and reflections, defines another point. In both cases, the meaning of the conscious perception is given by the discrimination among billions of other possible states of the core, each of which would lead to different consequences. This is exactly what we mean when we say that consciousness is informative. A pure perception of red is as informative as the perception of a busy city street because they both rule out a more or less equal number of conscious states, and this is exactly the way in which the meaning of the selected state is defined.

Another corollary is that the N-dimensional neural space that corresponds at any given time to the dynamic core is characterized by a certain metric—by precisely defined distances between points in that space. As schematically indicated in figure 13.2, the axes of this space are drawn at certain angles from each other. For example, axes corresponding to the visual submodality of color are close to each other and form a bundle, and so do axes corresponding to the visual submodality of form, but there is a much larger distance between bundles of axes corresponding to different submodalities. And the distance between more comprehensive bundles corresponding to different modalities, such as vision and touch, is even larger. This formulation corresponds to our intuitive appreciation of similarity and dissimilarity among different conscious states. It is often remarked that red is as irreducible and different from blue as it can possibly be. This irreducibility corresponds to the fact that different groups of neurons fire when we perceive red and when we perceive blue, thereby defining two irreducible dimensions of the N-dimensional space underlying conscious perception. Yet we also know that as different as red and blue may seem subjectively, they are much closer to each other than they are, say, to the blaring of a trumpet. In short, the phenomenal space obeys a certain metric within which certain conscious states are closer than others. According to our hypothesis, the topology and metric of this space should be described in terms of the appropriate neural reference—the dynamic core—and must be based on the interactions among the neuronal groups participating in it.[16]

A few other considerations about the characteristics of this N-dimensional neural space and its correspondence in terms of conscious phenomenology are worth considering. For example, for most of us, consciousness is dominated by visual experiences: We are eminently visual animals, and, indeed, a large fraction of our cortex is devoted, one way or another, to vision. It is likely that normally the number of neuronal groups that respond to visual stimuli represents a large fraction of the neuronal groups participating in the dynamic core, especially because of the prominent spatial organization of vision. This prominence implies that, everything else being equal, visual dimensions will have great weight in determining which points in neural space conscious experience will occupy. It is also generally recognized that conscious sensory experiences are especially vivid, while conscious thought is not. This contrast, too, may have a simple correspondence in neural terms: Neurons in sensory areas of the brain typically fire at high rates, while neurons in, say, the prefrontal cortex, tend to have a much more restricted dynamic range of firing. We have indicated this fact in figure 13.2 by giving a full dynamic range (from 0 to 100 Hz) to the axes corresponding to sensory neuronal groups and a more limited range (from 0 to 10 Hz) to those corresponding to neuronal groups in the prefrontal cortex that are involved with planning and thought. This difference implies that changes in neural firing along the latter dimensions would affect the position in N-dimensional neural space corresponding to the present conscious state less effectively than would changes along sensory dimensions.

QUALIA IN NEURAL TIME

Our previous discussion of qualia in terms of an N-dimensional neural reference space should help one envision that the meaning or quale of red or blue is established only within a much larger neural context than just the activity

of red or blue selective neurons. Indeed, the relevant context is the one provided by the concurrent activity of all other neuronal groups that, at a given
time, are part of the dynamic core. However, one last crucial ingredient—
time—needs to be added if we are to breathe life into this description.
Asking for a final stretch of imagination, we now try to describe how the
actual firing of neurons in real time can specify a point out of billions of
other points within an N-dimensional neural space.

Consider once more the example of lying in a room and perceiving pure
red, followed by pure blue, by pure white light, and so on. Let us try to envision what may happen, in neural terms, when the illumination switches from
red to blue. Obviously, a large number of photoreceptors in the retina will
reduce their firing almost instantaneously, while another class of photoreceptors will increase their firing. From the retina on, changes in neural
signaling will percolate upward in several early stages of the visual system,
leading, within tens of milliseconds, to the strong activation of blue-selective
neuronal groups in area IT and perhaps to the inhibition of red-selective
neuronal groups. These early neural events represent the necessary conditions for and the actual beginning of the perceptual categorization of the
color blue.

As we have argued, however, these neural events are not sufficient, by
themselves, to account for conscious experience—for the generation of
qualia corresponding to the pure perception of red or blue. Something more
is needed than just the firing of red- or blue-selective neuronal groups in
area IT. Specifically, what is needed is the causal involvement of the entire
dynamic core. We have assumed that color-selective neurons in area IT,
unlike wavelength-selective neurons in the retina, are part of a large functional cluster of high complexity, the dynamic core. This participation is
what allows us to consider their activation or inhibition as specifying different points in an N-dimensional neural reference space that corresponds to
the entire core. But what does it mean, in terms of the firing of real neurons
in real time, that a subset of neuronal groups in IT that responds to red or
blue is part of the dynamic core? And what does it mean that the activation
or inhibition of these neuronal groups can switch the state of the entire
dynamic core from one point to another in N-dimensional space?

The essential concept to grasp to obtain an intuitive picture is the following. One can tell that a neuronal group is part of a functional cluster if,
within a fraction of a second, a perturbation of its state can affect the state of
the rest of the cluster. Concretely, this means that if the firing of a group of
blue-selective neurons in IT is suddenly activated, their activation should be

able to make a difference, within a fraction of a second, not just to the firing of neurons that are directly connected to them, but to the firing of scores of other neuronal groups that participate in the dynamic core. How can this remarkable distribution of causal efficacy among distributed groups of neurons occur in such a short time? We have suggested that it occurs through the establishment of ongoing reentrant interactions among them. Only if groups of neurons are continuously exchanging signals back and forth and in parallel through reciprocal connections, thereby forming strong reentrant loops, can changes in the firing of any neuronal group be rapidly propagated to the entire extent of a functional cluster. To be sure, thanks to the specific arrangement of their connections, different groups of neurons within the functional cluster maintain their functional specificity. Through the process of reentry, however, a dynamic regime is established in which a perturbation in one group of neurons can rapidly affect the rest of the cluster.

This global spread of a perturbation within a complex system may seem difficult to visualize, and it certainly is so without the help of computer models. This is where the use of large-scale simulations, such as the model of the thalamocortical system described in chapter 10, becomes essential. That model nicely demonstrates that a small perturbation of a group of neurons can affect the entire system rapidly (within 100–200 msec) and efficaciously. However, this phenomenon occurs only if neurons are kept in a state of "readiness" by ongoing activity, that is, if the reentrant loops between thalamus and cortex or between different cortical areas are ignited and voltage-dependent connections (those that require the postsynaptic neuron to be excited in order to be activated) are actually activated.[17] By contrast, if these reentrant loops are not ignited, the effects of the same perturbation remain much more local. Thus, the thalamocortical model provides examples of the rapid propagation of a perturbation within a system that preserves its functional specificity.[18]

In addition to computer simulations, another image may help one visualize the rapid spread of a perturbation within a functionally specialized system (figure 13.3). Imagine a huge cluster of tense springs that are variously connected to each other. Surrounding this cluster are other springs loosely coupled to the cluster and arranged in separate, linearly concatenated modules. In such a system, perturbing any spring in the cluster rapidly and effectively perturbs the entire cluster, while the loosely coupled springs constitute a functional barrier beyond which the perturbations do not effectively propagate. The idea here is that if a system of coupled springs is globally connected and already under tension, even a small perturbation will

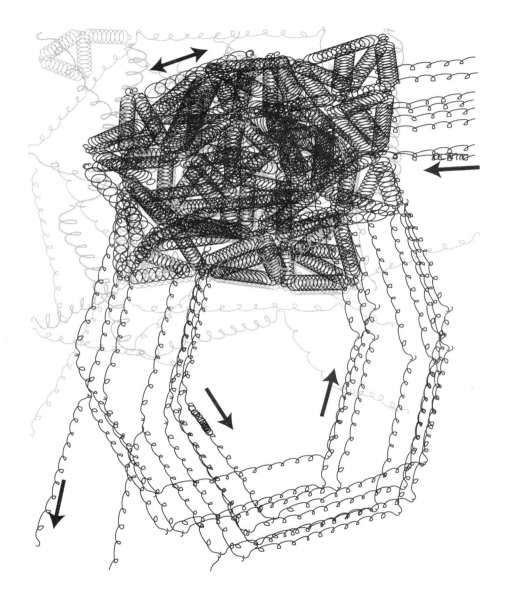

FIGURE 13.3. Coupled springs, a metaphor for the dynamics of the core and related neural systems. The tangle of connected springs under tension corresponds to the core; any perturbation rapidly spreads to the entire core (as indicated by the gray shading). By contrast, perturbations applied to parallel, functionally insulated routines remain local and propagate in one direction only (as indicated by a traveling wave).

spread rapidly and effectively, whereas if the connectivity is modular or the tension is absent, the same perturbation will be confined or dampened. In the dynamic core, the equivalent of the tension that couples the cluster of springs is provided by the ongoing reentrant interactions among its distributed populations of neurons, sustained by spontaneous activity and aided by the opening of voltage-dependent connections.

With such an image in mind, one can finally consider the functional significance of the global perturbation induced by changes in the firing of a subset of neuronal groups that are part of the dynamic core. When blue light activates a certain neuronal group in IT, its specific activation, coupled with the inhibition of other neuronal groups, leads to the perceptual categorization of incoming stimuli. If, as we have assumed, this blue-sensitive neuronal group is part of the dynamic core, a change in its firing will be capable of rapidly perturbing—thanks to ongoing reentrant interactions—the firing of many other neuronal groups throughout the core, including many neuronal groups situated in more anterior regions of the cortex. This perturbation will produce a switch from one integrated state of the entire core to the next.

If the core is complex—that is, if there is a large repertoire of different integrated states or activity patterns available for selection—the pattern of activity engendered among the neuronal groups yielding this particular quale will be highly specific. This specificity is guaranteed by the complex functional connectivity established among the distributed neuronal groups of the core in the course of evolution, development, and experience. The rapid reentrant interactions within the dynamic core thus give rise to a sort of temporally ongoing "bootstrap," according to which changes in the pattern of firing of neuronal groups involved in perceptual categorization can select one out of scores of specific activity patterns involving the entire core—an entire memory repertoire. This selection generates a large amount of information over a short time, hence creating a scene in the remembered present. The resulting integrated state of the core constitutes a memory and thereby the *meaning* of the firing of neurons involved in perceptual categorization. Therefore, in categorizing incoming stimuli, the adult brain goes well beyond the information given, and within the dynamic core, conscious perception and memory should be considered to be two aspects of one and the same process.

THE DEVELOPMENT OF QUALIA: REFERENCE TO THE SELF

One last point needs to be emphasized. As we have already mentioned, the N-dimensional neural reference space corresponding to the dynamic core is certainly not fixed; we envision it to include, from time to time, different sets of neuronal groups. But there is more. It is clear that the dynamic core must be subject to a remarkable transformation during early development and as a result of ongoing experience. It is likely that the dynamic core can evolve in terms of the number of dimensions it can include, even in the adult. For example, until we gather sufficient experience, different wines taste more or less the same. But soon, their taste will become associated with strikingly different qualia. Clearly, where there was only the ability to discriminate wine from water, there is now the ability to discriminate reds from whites and Cabernets from Pinots. This enhancement simply means that new discriminatory dimensions have been made available to the dynamic core, thereby adding a large number of subtler differentiations among conscious states.

Vastly more significant changes must be going on during development and early experience. Although at this stage many of our assertions are partially speculative, it is likely that among the earliest conscious dimensions and discriminations are those concerned with the body itself—mediated through structures in the brain stem that map the state of the body and its relation to both the inside and outside environment on the basis of multimodal signals that include proprioceptive, kinesthetic, somatosensory, and autonomic components. We may, indeed, call these components the dimensions of the protoself.[19] These components are the bodily functions of which we are usually only dimly aware, but that influence almost every aspect of our being. Equally early and central are the dimensions provided by value systems indicating salience for the entire organism. Since, memory is recategorical and there is a constant play in time between value-category systems and ongoing perceptual categorizations, this early, bodily based consciousness may provide the initial dominant axes of the N-dimensional neural reference space, out of which all subsequent memories based on signals from the world ("nonself"[20]) are elaborated. As increasing numbers of such signals are assimilated, they would be discriminated according to modality and category in reference to these initial dimensions that constitute the protoself.

Even before language and higher-order consciousness appear, a bodily based neural reference space for experienced categories and imagery in a scene will therefore be built up within primary consciousness. An animal, or even a newborn baby, with these dynamics and with primary consciousness will experience a scene but have no nameable self that is differentiable from within. With the accession of new dimensions related to language and their integration in the dynamic core, however, higher-order consciousness appears in humans. We can now imagine that while primary consciousness continues in real time, concepts of the past and future can be tied to thought and language, thus giving rise to new imagery. A discriminable and nameable self, developed through social interactions, can now be connected to the simultaneous experience of the scenes of primary consciousness and conceptually based imagery in which experiences of all kinds are linked.

Eventually, such a development permits a person to be conscious of being conscious. Qualia can actually be named and inferred through a process of higher-order categorization. But even before being named, since being precedes describing, qualia are already discriminable, and there are *hosts* of them in the complex system underlying consciousness. They *are*, in fact, all the conscious states that can be discriminated. Thus, one can see development and experience as a progressive increase in the complexity of the dynamic core, both in terms of the number of available dimensions and the number of points in the corresponding N-dimensional space that can be differentiated.

The purpose of the foregoing account was heuristic, not critical. Moreover, as we have stressed many times, such an account can lead to an understanding of how qualia should be conceived, but it cannot substitute for them. As good as that understanding may be, each of us must pass the scene by which qualia are discriminated through an experiential filter that reflects an individual history of being. The action of that filter depends as much on the behavior of the core as it does on unconscious neural processes. We therefore turn to the important issue of how conscious and unconscious processes may interact.

CHAPTER FOURTEEN

The Conscious and the Unconscious

Unconscious aspects of mental activity, such as motor and cognitive routines, and so-called unconscious memories, intentions, and expectations play a fundamental role in shaping and directing our conscious experience. In this chapter, we examine several kinds of neural processes that remain unconscious but that, by virtue of their interactions with the dynamic core, can influence conscious experience or be influenced by it. The dynamics of the core can be powerfully affected by a set of neural routines that are triggered by different core states and that, once completed, help bring about yet other core states. Such unconscious routines, which are both motor and cognitive, involve long, parallel neural loops running through cortical appendages, such as the basal ganglia and the cerebellum. As a result of conscious performance, unconscious routines can be nested or linked in sequence to give rise to sensorimotor loops that contribute to what we have called global mappings. We also discuss the possibility that islands of activity in the thalamocortical system may coexist with the core, influence its behavior, and yet not be incorporated in it. These different mechanisms provide a neurophysiological framework for understanding how unconscious processes can affect the dynamic core and thereby influence conscious experience. They also reveal how the activity of the dynamic core can affect the linkage of unconscious processes and thereby influence learned and automatic routines.

The dynamic-core hypothesis is heuristically useful not only because it specifies the kinds of neural processes that underlie conscious experience, but because it provides a rationale for distinguishing these processes from those that remain unconscious. As we have noted, the neural processes involved in the regulation of blood pressure do not and cannot contribute to conscious experience. According to our hypothesis, they cannot because the neurons dealing with the regulation of blood pressure are not part of the dynamic core—an integrated process that is generated largely in the thalamocortical system—and, in any event, they do not, by themselves, generate an integrated neural space of sufficient dimensionality and complexity. Indeed, the circuits that regulate blood pressure constitute what is, in essence, a simple reflex arc.

We have also suggested that such neural circuits are functionally insulated from the dynamic core: Perturbing the activity of a neuron in such circuits will lead to local changes, but it will not globally affect the interactions among a large number of thalamocortical regions. It is likely that, at any given time, a considerable number of such important but reflexlike functionally insulated circuits are active in the spinal cord, brainstem, and hypothalamus and that, in many cases, they never achieve functional contact with the dynamic core. Such neural activities not only remain unconscious but are completely inaccessible to the core and therefore to conscious monitoring or control. However, they can often be brought under conscious control by consciously monitoring some unconscious parameter of neural activity through the use of biofeedback.[1]

However, conscious experience does not just float freely above an ocean of functionally insulated, unconscious processes. Instead, it is constantly influencing and being influenced by many unconscious processes. Indeed, there are thousands of examples in both perception and action, thought and emotion, that demonstrate that conscious and unconscious processes are regularly in touch and that their separation is often far from clear-cut. A commonplace example is seen in a musical performance, when the player's fingers operate without conscious control until the player gives some conscious directive on noting a change in rhythm or a snag during the execution of the piece. In this chapter, we consider possible neurophysiological substrates of those scores of processes that continuously go on in our brain, which, although unconscious, can nevertheless influence or be influenced by consciousness. In doing so, we discuss not only where these processes occur in the brain, but why they remain unconscious even if they may be functionally in touch with the dynamic core. Since our understanding of many fundamental principles of brain dynamics is still primitive, this discussion is pitched in general terms. Our main goal is, on the basis of our hypotheses, to shed light on the possible modes of interaction between conscious and unconscious processes in the brain.

In order not to overindulge in speculative neurology, we resist the temptation to suggest possible neural mechanisms for aspects of unconscious cognition that, while having obvious psychological significance, are far removed from neurophysiological understanding. We refer, for instance, to the role of unconscious contexts, such as unconscious expectations and intentions, in shaping conscious experience; to the effects on consciousness of surprise or violation of expectation; to the conscious and unconscious regulation of attention; and to the substrates and mechanisms of the Freudian unconscious. The relationship of many of these unconscious mental processes to conscious experience is certainly worth considering.[2] However, at the present state of our knowledge, it seems preferable to refrain from offering specific mechanistic explanations for each, but instead to provide an overall neurophysiological framework within which such explanations may be formulated.

PORTS OUT

To consider the interactions between conscious and unconscious processes of the brain, it is useful to imagine that the core has ports, or input-output connections, at certain sites. In particular, neuronal groups that interact both with the rest of the core and with neurons that are outside the core can be considered *ports out* or *ports in*, depending on the direction of the interaction.

Let us start by considering the output side—how the core can trigger unconscious neural processes (we use the term *unconscious neural processes or circuits* as shorthand for neural circuits whose activity does not directly contribute to conscious experience). We know that when we extend our hand to grab a glass, a large number of processes go on in such structures as the basal ganglia, cerebellum, subcortical motor nuclei, and portions of the motor cortex. Such processes, which contribute to global mappings as described in chapter 8, deal with the precise timing of the contraction of muscles, the coordination of different muscles and joints, the anticipated rotation of the wrist and aperture of the finger grip on the basis of the perceived shape and size of the glass, postural adjustments for balancing weight, and many other activities that are required for the smooth performance of such acts. We are

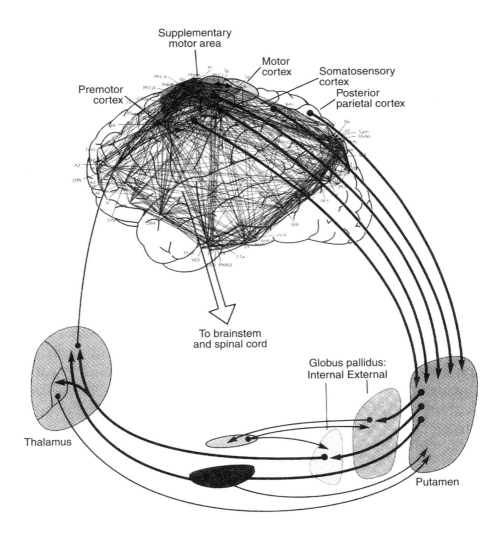

FIGURE 14.1 STRUCTURES AND CONNECTIONS MEDIATING CONSCIOUS AND UNCONSCIOUS PROCESSES. The thalamocortical system, which gives rise to the dynamic core, is represented by a fine meshwork of cortical and thalamic areas and reentrant connections. The functionally insulated routines that are triggered by the core and return to it travel along parallel, polysynaptic, one-directional pathways that leave the cortex, reach the various components of the basal ganglia and certain thalamic nuclei and finally return to the cortex. The large arrows represent connections to the brain stem and spinal cord that mediate motor outputs.

not conscious of most of these detailed processes, nor would we want to be. The situation is reminiscent of when the president and his war cabinet order a fleet to be deployed during an international crisis: They should know where, when, and why, but they should not be bothered by the details of how the fleet is put together, how the sailors are alerted, how the decks and armories are stocked, and so on.

Since we are consciously able to set these processes in motion, there must be "ports out" connecting the core with the unconscious neural circuits that bring about the motor output. These ports are likely to involve particular layers of the six-layered cortex. Neurons in layer V of the cerebral cortex (in this case, presumably those in the motor and premotor areas), for example, are in a good position to constitute ports out from the core. On the one hand, these neurons are directly connected to layer VI neurons and, through them, contribute to the reentrant circuits linking them to other cortical and thalamic regions that give rise to the core. On the other hand, the same neurons send axons that exit the thalamocortical system and, directly and indirectly, reach motor effectors—namely, the motoneurons in the spinal cord. Through such pathways, conscious decisions to act can actually produce a motor output and bring about, for example, some skilled hand movements.

This picture raises an issue that needs to be clarified. Remember that the core is defined in terms of the interactions among its participating elements. If neurons in layer V of a motor or premotor area[3] that participate in the core can function as ports out by activating motoneurons, why should the motoneurons with which they interact *not* be considered part of the core? The answer is actually simple enough. The functional interactions between neuronal groups in the dynamic core and motoneurons are exclusively one way. Changes in the firing patterns in the core typically make a difference to the firing of motoneurons, leading to a particular behavioral output. By contrast, the firing of motoneurons makes little or no difference to the core itself; stimulating a motoneuron in the spinal cord will affect muscles and behavior, but it will not be able to modify the global state of the core. (Of course, through global mappings, which sample different parts of the environment and thereby alter sensory input, the *consequences* of certain actions will be consciously appreciated, but such effects are obviously indirect).

PORTS IN

Let us now consider the input side: how certain unconscious neural processes can have an effect on the core. The obvious example is the unconscious neural activity occurring in the sensory periphery.[4] As we mentioned, when we consciously perceive a visual scene that is meaningful, coherent, and relatively stable, an enormous amount of neural activity is going on in the retina and other early visual structures of which we are not conscious. This neural activity is necessary to adapt to overall levels of light; to enhance contrast; to detect coherent motion; to identify edges; to group objects together and separate them from each other and from the background; to discover their reflectance (color) irrespective of the composition of the light that illuminates them; to identify them despite changes in position, orientation, or size; and to extract a large number of their invariant, more abstract features that are essential for recognition. In short, such neural activity is necessary for perception to reflect properties of the environment. Similar considerations apply to several other sensory processes, for example, those responsible for such extraordinary feats as the parsing of language.

Why are we ordinarily not conscious of the constantly shifting activity and of the millions of interactions that occur among neurons in the sensory periphery but are conscious of certain aspects of their outcome? For example, while we are certainly aware of the colors of objects, we are not aware of the rapidly changing activity of various kinds of cones in our retinas. Unlike the firing of motoneurons, the firing of sensory neurons is clearly able to influence the dynamic core and to determine what we ultimately perceive. But if these processes can influence the core, why do they not become part of it? The answer is, again, simple but deserves to be emphasized. As we have noted, there is reason to believe that the connectivity among neurons in the retina and in other early stages of the visual system is such that much of the activity occurring at these sites remains relatively insulated or local. In other words, these low-level interactions are like the busy activity in front of the radar screen of each ship in the aforementioned fleet that is required to reach a desired target. All this activity is necessary, just as are the communications among the various ships in the fleet the president deploys. However, none of this frenetic activity reaches the president and his cabinet at home, who remain and should remain unaware of it. Indeed, all the president and his cabinet need is an up-to-date assessment of the overall position and progress of the fleet.

Similarly, if a complicated series of local interactions eventually leads to the firing of cortical neurons that signal the presence of the color red, all that counts in the end is that those red-selective neurons did fire. Such neuronal groups can be considered ports in of the core: On the one side, their firing is affected by local processes outside the core in such a way as to respond to changing properties of the environment; on the other side, by virtue of their connectivity to the core, their firing can affect globally and effectively a much larger set of neuronal groups that are distributed over the thalamocortical system—the entire core. By contrast, stimulating neurons in the sensory periphery produces effects that are purely local except in so far as they may eventually affect groups of neurons participating in the core. According to this scheme, no information or trace of the activity occurring in the sensory periphery reaches the core above and beyond what is transmitted by the ports in of the core.

MOTOR AND COGNITIVE ROUTINES

These examples are meant to illustrate how unconscious neural processes occurring in the sensory and motor periphery can influence the core (at ports in) or be influenced by it (at ports out), yet remain informationally distinct from it. There is, however, a whole other class of unconscious neural processes that we have not yet considered: the innumerable unconscious neural processes that interface with the core *at both the output and input sides* and that may or may not be related to the sensory or motor periphery.

Consider the following example. When we speak, we know roughly what we want to say, although we typically do not know the words we are going to use. Luckily, however, words seem to pop up when we need them, in the right place at the right time, with the right sound and the right meaning. We usually do not have to search consciously for each of them or check our syntax at every step. If we had to do so, speaking would be an almost impossible task that would place an enormous burden on our conscious lives. This fact has been appreciated for a long time. In *La Parole Intérieure*,[5] M. V. Egger remarked that "before speaking, one barely knows what one intends to say, but afterwards one is filled with admiration and surprise at having said and thought it so well." The woman in E. M. Forster's novel *Howards End* said memorably: "How can I know what I think till I see what I say?" It seems that although the core moves smoothly from one conscious state to the next, particular unconscious routines and subroutines are continually triggered to find the right word, check the syntax, and deliver the results to consciousness for another iteration.

Ongoing unconscious assistance to our conscious life occurs whenever we speak aloud or only to ourselves, write or type, play a musical instrument, perform athletic routines, drive, or simply set a table. It also occurs when we perform a mental calculation or merely follow a train of thought without doing or saying anything. A suggested relationship between the core and scores of unconscious neural routines and subroutines is illustrated schematically in figure 14.1. Unconscious routines are interfaced with the core at ports out and ports in: Specific routines are triggered by specific states of the core. While they run, they may or may not bring about overt motor outputs. When they end, they again make contact with the core and help bring about specific conscious states. Like the neural processes in the motor and sensory periphery, such routines have a powerful influence on the course of conscious experience but, by themselves, are not able directly to incite conscious experience. Although they are in contact with the core at ports out and ports in, they do not participate directly in the set of global interactions that make up the core itself.

To expand on our naval crisis metaphor, think of the neural interactions within the core as being similar to the interactions taking place in a closed-door conference among top-level diplomats from different nations during an international crisis. What eventually happens at the conference clearly depends on the exchanges among the diplomats in that room. However, each diplomat is privately in touch by phone with his or her government and its various bureaucratic functionaries, who, we may consider, represent the unconscious routines. If the diplomats need to make public statements at the conference, they first ask for directions or pose technical questions to the governmental functionaries. The information exchanged between each diplomat and those functionaries is isolated: Little is communicated even among different functionaries in the same government, and there is no communication among the functionaries of different nations. However, the exchanges at the conference are clearly influenced by the ongoing exchanges between each diplomat and his or her consultants at home.

LONG LOOPS AND COGNITIVE ROUTINES

It is now worth asking what the neuroanatomical and neurophysiological bases for the automatic routines and subroutines that interface with the core may be. Many observations suggest that these routines are probably implemented by a series of polysynaptic loops that leave the thalamocortical system; run through so-called cortical appendages, such as the basal ganglia and the cerebellum; and subsequently make their way back to the thalamocortical system. Here, for the sake of simplicity, we mainly consider the possible role of the basal ganglia as an example. However, we believe that another cortical appendage, the cerebellum, may serve a similar purpose, although it differs considerably in the kinds of unconscious routines that it can implement.[6]

As we noted in chapter 4 in considering the second topological arrangement of neuroanatomy, the basal ganglia are a set of huge nuclei in the depths of the forebrain that contain a vast number of neurons and that have evolved in parallel with the thalamocortical system. Their connections are organized differently from those of the thalamocortical system. They are organized into long, parallel loops that seem to be as independent as possible from each other. As we discuss later, this organization is critical to their unconscious mode of functioning. As is shown in figure 14.1, the input portion of the basal ganglia, called the striatum, receives projections from many cortical areas through the axons of neurons in cortical layer V. However, unlike the usual modes of corticocortical and thalamocortical connectivity, there are no reciprocal projections back from the striatum to the cortex. Instead, neurons in the striatum project forward to other parts of the basal ganglia, such as the external and internal segments of a region called the pallidum. These circuits are also exclusively feedforward and are not organized reciprocally. Finally, the output portion of the basal ganglia, the internal segment of the pallidum, projects to certain thalamic nuclei, which, in turn, project back to the cortex. These projections reach the cortex in restricted and particular places (different parts of the basal ganglia connect specifically to different parts of the motor, premotor, and prefrontal cortex, as well as to some parts of the temporal lobe).[7]

The series of synaptic steps from the cortex to the basal ganglia to the thalamus and back to the cortex makes up a special kind of loop, quite unlike the reentrant loops among reciprocally connected groups of neurons that are characteristic of the thalamocortical system. First, the loops through the basal ganglia are long and include multiple synaptic steps, some of which are inhibitory. Second, these long loops are one way, rather than two way or reentrant. Third, the various long cortico-basal ganglia-cortical loops seem to be organized in parallel, having distinct areas of origin and termination in the cortex, as if they were meant to interact with each other *as little as possible*. Such a parallel organization contrasts sharply with the maze of connected reentrant circuits found in the thalamocortical system, where the architecture seems ideally suited to favor simultaneous interactions among thousands of distributed neuronal groups.

Recent recording studies have provided exceptionally clear evidence that the resulting functional connectivity within the basal ganglia is radically different from that in the thalamocortical system.[8] Whereas the activities of 20 percent to 50 percent of all pairs of neurons recorded in the cortical and thalamic areas of a monkey are broadly synchronized, the activities of neurons in the internal segment of the monkey's globus pallidus (the output station of the basal ganglia) are almost completely uncorrelated. Thus, the anatomy of the thalamocortical system favors the emergence of widespread coherence among distributed regions, which is brought about by reentrant interactions. By contrast, it appears that in the basal ganglia, different neurons are organized in parallel loops that are independent from each other and thus do not engage in the kind of cross talk one sees in the cortex.

This observation fits nicely with the hypothesis that while activity in the thalamocortical system leads to the formation of a large functional cluster of high complexity—the dynamic core—activity in the basal ganglia is organized quite differently: The parallel loops are noninteracting and therefore do not lead to the emergence of a single functional cluster. Furthermore, although the sequential activity of such parallel loops may make contact with the core at ports in or ports out, for the most part, their connections remain excluded from it. Perturbing neurons along one such long loop does not, by itself, lead to changes in the state of the core, but only to local changes within the loop. It is only when, after several synaptic steps, one or more groups of neurons constituting a port in to the core is activated that the effects of the perturbation are transmitted globally to the entire core. Thus, the long, one-way, parallel loops found in the basal ganglia seem to be just the architecture one would envision to implement a variety of *independent* unconscious neural routines and subroutines: They are triggered by the core at specific ports out; they do their job rapidly and efficiently but in a local, functionally insulated way; and at specific ports in, they provide the core with the results of their activation.[9]

The idea that parallel loops through the basal ganglia (and through the cerebellum) may be involved in setting up and executing neural routines is not novel and, as far as research on the basal ganglia goes, is reasonably well established.[10] In particular, there is considerable evidence that the basal ganglia participate in the development and expression of sequential motor acts and that neurons in a monkey's basal ganglia fire selectively in relation to specific learned motor sequences, much like the cortical regions to which these loops project.[11] What is novel is the suggestion that the type of connectivity typical of basal ganglia and similar loops—which are functionally insulated and connected to the dynamic core only at ports out and in—may be the key reason why such routines are unconscious.

If correct, this suggestion would have several important implications. For example, it is becoming increasingly clear that loops through the basal ganglia are not only involved in motor routines, but that depending on which part of the cortex they originate from, they may be involved in various kinds of cognitive activities. This conclusion prompts the generalization that in addition to automatic motor routines, there are also a large number of cognitive routines having to do with speaking, thinking, planning, and so on and that such routines may be unconscious for the same reason that automatic motor routines are unconscious. In the same way that obtains for motor routines, neuronal groups that are part of the dynamic core would be able to trigger the activity of cognitive routines (ports out), while other groups of neurons belonging to the core (corresponding to ports in) would be activated or inhibited by the results of such routines through the basal ganglia loops. Only then would the results of such routines be communicated to the entire core and be made consciously accessible.

It also seems likely that various mechanisms in the basal ganglia or at the interface between the basal ganglia and the cortex may implement a kind of winner-take-all competition between parallel routines in such a way that, at any given time, only one routine is activated sufficiently as to connect functionally back to the core. Such a mechanism would contribute to the sequential unity of behavior and thought. Thus, in general, once a person starts a movement or a thought, she must wait until it is close to completion before she starts another.

GLOBAL MAPPINGS AND LEARNING

Another important implication of the view expounded here has to do with the processes leading to the linkage and nesting of otherwise independent elementary routines within entire motor or cognitive sequences (the elements being single sweeps through a loop in the basal ganglia). Although a trip in a single loop through the basal ganglia (and possibly through the other cortical appendages) may take up to 100-150 msec., most behaviors and cognitive activities consist of sequences that are much longer and considerably more articulated. For example, in learning a musical piece consisting of a series of arpeggios, a pianist will first learn a single arpeggio, then another, and still another and finally string them together. Clearly, some mechanism is required for the linkage and nesting of such multiple elementary routines and subroutines into entire sequences that emerge during learning.

In principle, such nesting could occur by setting up links among loops at the level of the basal ganglia themselves or, more likely, at the level of the cortex. Because of its enormous associative capabilities, the dynamic core would be in an ideal position to link or hierarchically organize a series of preexisting unconscious routines into a particular sequence. This is what happens when a pianist deliberately links separate arpeggio passages. Through the vast access available to the core, the articulation of particular sequences of routines would be facilitated, thus promoting the flawless performance of integrated sensorimotor loops that may or may not involve the environment. For the musician, these loops may be activated during a performance from a musical score, from memory, or even during mental rehearsal.

In chapter 4, we pointed out that the sensorimotor loops we have been discussing are parts of global mappings. These global mappings are dynamic structures made up of multiple reentrant cortical maps and various cortical appendages that are linked to one or more of the hippocampus, basal ganglia, and cerebellum. We said that activity in a global mapping occurs in an ongoing loop that continually relates an animal's movements to the sampling of several kinds of sensory signals. This dynamic structure is maintained or altered by continual motor and sensory rehearsal in an unconscious fashion. We can now be more specific about how global mappings are related to the substrates of consciousness. Global mappings are activated when the core links, through its ports, a series of unconscious routines implemented by cortical appendages into higher-order entities that subserve an integrated sequence of sensorimotor actions. According to this view, our cognitive life is typically constituted by an ongoing sequence of core states that trigger certain unconscious routines, which, in turn, trigger certain other core states and so on in a series of cycles. At the same time, of course, as in a musician's performance, core states are also modified by sensory input (acting on other ports in), as well as partly by the intrinsic dynamics of the core itself.[12]

This view has several implications related to processes of conscious learning. As we noted, before behavior or thought become automatized and unconscious, there is a phase of conscious control in which behavioral or cognitive fragments are first painstakingly performed one by one and then linked until a single "chunk" of automated behavior can be flawlessly and effortlessly executed.

We can therefore conceive of the following scenario that is played out every time we learn a new routine (to speak, to think, to play an instrument, and so on). Initially, the dynamic core triggers elementary routines or fragments of routines, thanks to its wide access to a large number of basal ganglia circuits. Such access would most likely be arranged hierarchically (certain areas would be activated corresponding to the intention to play, the appropriate neuronal groups would then be called on to bring about the appropriate postural adjustments, the fingers would then be prepared to touch the keyboard, and finally a particular finger would be moved to hit a particular key). After several repetitions under the continuous control of the conscious core, such routines would become progressively more effective and error-free. This improvement would correspond first to the successful selection and then to the functional insulation of the appropriate polysynaptic circuit through the basal ganglia or other cortical appendages.[13] The portions of the brain responsible for the execution of each routine would soon be reduced to a specific and dedicated set of linked circuits. The resulting functional insulation would be ideal for optimizing the neural interactions within such circuits while reducing those with the rest of the brain.

In the second phase, conscious control would be necessary to link further whatever initially separate unconscious routines seem to work well together. As we noted, it would appear that the dynamic core is in an ideal position to achieve the higher-order linkage of different loops through the basal ganglia. Thanks to its wide access to diverse sources of information and its sensitivity to context, the core can mediate the transition between subsequent routines and favor the reinforcement of specific transitions.

Recent evidence indicates that the neural selection leading to the functional insulation of dedicated loops and circuits occurs through the reinforcement of basal ganglia circuits brought about by the firing of value systems, especially the so-called dopaminergic system (named after the neuromodulator dopamine that it releases). Such systems have been shown to fire when behavior is being reinforced by a reward and to stop firing once the behavior has been acquired.[14] The firing of the dopaminergic system and of other value systems that innervate both the basal ganglia and the cortical regions to which they project may also be the key mechanism for strengthening the synaptic linkages that are forged between different routines through the mediation of the core. In this way, global mappings that are related to a particular task can be constructed or linked during consciously guided learning until a smooth, apparently effortless sensorimotor loop is executed speedily, reliably, and unconsciously.

Finally, it is worth mentioning in this context that psychiatric disorders, such as obsessive compulsive disorder, may be understood, in part, as conditions in which certain motor and cognitive routines are triggered with excessive frequency. An obsessive-compulsive person experiences the repeated intrusion of certain thoughts or the urge to perform certain acts. He experiences such obsessions and complusions as ego-dystonic, that is, as unwelcome and unwilled. Obsessions and compulsions thus have the hallmarks of fixed, rigid unconscious routines that are forced upon one's consciousness as if certain ports out and ports in of the core were pathologically open. In Parkinson's disease, a reduction of the dopaminergic innervation of the basal ganglia apparently leads to the loss of independence among the normally insulated loops through the basal ganglia.[15] Just as when all muscles contract simultaneously, leading to a spastic paralysis, the simultaneous activation of multiple routines may lead, in this case, to a state of executive paralysis. It is interesting that in Parkinson's disorder, such executive paralysis does not just involve movement, but thought itself can be slowed, impeded, or even frozen.

We have deliberately limited our discussion to interactions with the basal ganglia. It is likely that similar types of relationships obtain with the cerebellum. The exercise could be carried out and suitably modified according to the particular structure and function of other cortical appendages as well. Indeed, in a full description, one must conceive of the mutual functional interactions of all these structures in the ongoing relations between conscious and unconscious activity.

THALAMOCORTICAL BREAKAWAYS: THE POSSIBILITY OF SPLINTER CORES

One last category of unconscious neural processes may occur, not in connection with cortical appendages, such as the basal ganglia, but in the thalamocortical system itself. We refer to brain areas or sets of neuronal groups in the thalamocortical system that may be active but that because of an anatomical or functional disconnection, do not become incorporated into the dominant dynamic core. We have already mentioned that part of the neural activity in primary sensory areas or in primary motor areas may be in contact with the core at ports in or ports out without contributing directly to the core. Here, however, we consider neural processes in the thalamocortical system that ordinarily participate in the core but that, under certain conditions, may remain functionally insulated from it. Is it possible that the thalamocortical system may support more than one large functional cluster at any

one time? Could some active thalamocortical islands or splinters have broken away from the mainland?

At our present state of knowledge, it is not possible to answer such questions with any certainty. It is worth mentioning, however, that such functional or anatomical disconnections may underlie several of the pathological
dissociations discussed in chapter 3. For example, a person with hysterical
blindness is capable of avoiding obstacles, yet denies seeing anything. An
interesting possibility would be that in people with hysterical blindness, a
small functional cluster that includes certain visual areas is autonomously
active, may not fuse with the dominant functional cluster, but is still capable
of accessing motor routines in the basal ganglia and elsewhere. After all,
something of the sort is clearly going on in people with split brains, in whom
at least two functional clusters appear to coexist in the same brains because
of the callosal disconnection.

The possibility that splinter cores or autonomously functioning thalamocortical breakaways may exist alongside a dominant core raises several
intriguing questions. Are certain dominant goals or intentions that we
formed consciously and intentionally at one time and then always carry with
us, say, a determination to learn a foreign language, merely an inactive set of
neural circuits that need to be activated for their influence on consciousness
to be felt? Or is it possible that they are autonomously active yet remain
unconscious until they fuse with the dominant core? Is it possible that such
active but functionally insulated thalamocortical circuits may underlie certain aspects of the psychological unconscious—aspects that, as Sigmund
Freud pointed out, share many of the hallmarks of the "mental"—except
that they do not make it into consciousness? Can such circuits be created by
mechanisms of repression? May such active thalamocortical islands be capable of triggering their own basal ganglion routines, thereby accounting for
slips of the tongue, action slips, and the like? Clearly, much work needs to be
done to clarify these issues, and means must be developed actually to assess
the activity of the core and its relationship to different cortical appendages.
In the meantime, the basic idea of a highly integrated core underlying conscious states that is linked to a series of unconscious, functionally insulated
routines sets a useful framework for such investigations.

PART SIX

Observer Time

In this section we continue our journey into the depths of the brain and the richness of conscious phenomenology to take up several related subjects at the center of human concern. We have considered the neural mechanisms that are essential to the evolutionary origin of primary consciousness. We extended this view with specific hypotheses about the neural basis of conscious experience that can account for its most general properties. But we have not yet explicitly confronted the relationship of consciousness to language, thought, and the limits of knowledge. This relationship is based on higher-order consciousness, which, as we have shown, allows for the development of concepts of the self, the past, and the future. To untie the world knot or at least to retie it in a less tangled form, we believe it fitting to end with reflections on these large issues. They relate to science, as well as to philosophy, and prompt some further insights into what we may and may not expect from a scientific view of consciousness.

Higher-order consciousness is obviously necessary for a scientific exploration of the properties of the conscious process. It is a paradox that as conscious human beings, we cannot fully rid ourselves of higher-order consciousness, leaving only the ongoing event-driven rush of primary consciousness. That may, in fact, be the state toward which mystics aim their devotions. Let us aim ours toward a brief exploration of some subjects related to higher-order consciousness: language, the self, thinking, the origins of information, and the origins and reaches of knowing. It is time to ask what we can expect of the scientific observer who seeks to understand the conscious process and report on it to himself and to others—it is observer time.

CHAPTER FIFTEEN

Language and the Self

In this chapter, we consider several issues of central human significance in a new light, relating our efforts to philosophy and to science itself, and offer insights into what we may and may not expect from a scientific view of consciousness. In particular, we argue that neural changes that lead to language are behind the emergence of higher-order consciousness, and we therefore briefly consider some aspects of the evolution of speech. Once higher-order consciousness begins to emerge, a self can be constructed from social and affective relationships. This self (entailing the development of a self-conscious agent, a subject) goes far beyond the biologically based individuality of an animal with primary consciousness. The emergence of the self leads to a refinement of phenomenological experience, tying feelings to thoughts, to culture, and to beliefs. It liberates imagination and opens thought to the vast domains of metaphor. It can even lead to a temporary escape, while still remaining conscious, from the temporal shackles of the remembered present. Three mysteries—that of ongoing awareness; that of the self; and that of the construction of stories, plans, and fictions—can be clarified if not completely dispelled by considering a combined picture of primary and higher-order consciousness.

Consider the evolution of brain structures that lead to higher-order consciousness (see figure 15.1). An animal with only primary consciousness can generate a "mental image," or a scene based on the integrated re-entrant activity in the dynamic core. This scene is determined largely by the succession of real events in the environment and, to some degree, by unconscious subcortical activity. Such an animal has biological individuality but has no true self, a self aware of itself. Although it has a "remembered present," maintained by the activity in real time of the dynamic core, it has no concept of the past or future. These concepts emerged only when semantic capabilities—the ability to express feelings and refer to objects and events by symbolic means—appeared in the course of evolution. Necessarily, higher-order consciousness involves social interactions. When full linguistic capability based on syntax appeared in precursors of Homo sapiens, higher-order consciousness flowered, partly as a result of exchanges in a community of speakers. Syntactical and semantic systems provided a new means for symbolic construction and a new type of memory mediating higher-order consciousness. Consciousness of consciousness became possible.

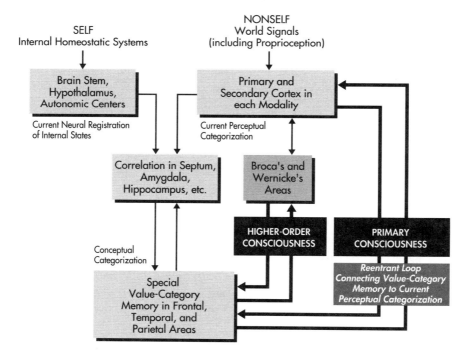

FIGURE 15.1 A SCHEME FOR HIGHER-ORDER CONSCIOUSNESS. (The reader may relate this scheme to the scheme for primary consciousness shown in figure 9.1). A new reentrant loop appears during the evolution of hominids and the emergence of language. The acquisition of a new kind of memory via semantic capabilities and ultimately language leads to a conceptual explosion. As a result, concepts of the self, the past, and the future can be connected to primary consciousness. Consciousness of consciousness becomes possible.

As in the case of primary consciousness, a key step in the evolution of higher-order consciousness was the development of a specific kind of reentrant connectivity, this time between the brain systems for language (see figure 15.1) and the existing conceptual regions of the brain. The emergence of these neural connections and the appearance of speech allowed reference to inner states and objects or events by means of symbols. The acquisition of a growing lexicon of such symbols through social interactions, probably initially based on the nurturing and emotive relationships between mother and child, allowed for the discrimination of a self within each individual consciousness. When narrative capabilities emerged and affected linguistic and conceptual memory, higher-order consciousness could foster the development of concepts of the past and future related to that self and to others.

At such a point, an individual is freed, to some extent, from bondage to the remembered present. If primary consciousness marries the individual to real time, higher-order consciousness allows for at least a temporary divorce, which is made possible by the creation of concepts of time past and time future. A whole new world of intentionality, categorization, and discrimination can be experienced and remembered. As a result, concepts and thinking flourish. Relationships that promise positive rewards can be fostered, resentments can be nourished, and plots can be laid. Scenes are enriched by symbols. Value connects to meaning and intentionality and can itself be modified in more richly adaptive ways by evolving neural systems that link individual learning back to the alteration of the value systems themselves.

When one contemplates the phenotypic changes that had to be put in place before true language appeared or was invented, the difficulty in reconstructing the evolutionary origins of language becomes painfully obvious. First, the precursor of hominids had to possess primary consciousness—the ability in the remembered present to construct a scene in which both causally related and unrelated objects or events, taken *together*, have significance with respect to the values and historically influenced memories of the individual animal. A series of morphological changes occurred that led to bipedalism, a prehensile grasp with a heightened tactile sense, and a reshaped basicranium. At some time, the changes in the skull permitted the developmental descent of the larynx, with the appearance of a supralaryngeal space and the ability to produce coarticulated speech sounds. Communicating hominids must have used gestures and sounds to develop social interactions that had some selective advantage in hunting and breeding.

What about the brain? At the least, by this time, cortical and subcortical structures for the rich phonological categorization and memory of speech sounds must have evolved. The critical step to higher-order consciousness depended on the evolutionary emergence of reentrant connectivity between these structures and those areas of the brain that are responsible for concept formation. According to the TNGS, the repertoires of different brain areas, operating according to selection, are sufficiently plastic to adapt somatically to a wide range of bodily phenotypic changes, such as the emergence of a supralaryngeal space. This plasticity relieves us of the genetic and evolutionary dilemma of requiring simultaneous correlated mutations that are reflected both in altered body parts *and* in correspondingly altered neuronal mappings. (Of course, subsequent to the *somatic* adjustment of the brain to a mutation affecting the body, later mutations in neurally significant genes *could* then accumulate *evolutionarily* to the advantage of the organism.)[1]

What is required for meaning and semantics to emerge from the exchanges within a developing hominid speech community? First, those exchanges must have affective or emotional components related to reward or punishment. The emotional early mother-child relationship and grooming are likely prototypes but not the only ones. Second, primary consciousness and enhanced conceptual abilities must already have been in place. (Before language is present, concepts depend on the brain's ability to construct "universals" through higher-order mapping of the activity of the brain's own perceptual and motor maps.) Third, sounds must become words—in the species, historically developed vocalizations within the otherwise arbitrary history of a speech community must be exchanged and remembered in connection with referents. Finally, certain areas of the brain must respond to these vocalizations, categorize them, and connect the memory of their symbolic significance to concepts, values, and motor responses. The evolutionary value of these developments derives from an enhanced memory of events that would arise as a result of reentrant connections between areas that mediate memory for speech symbols and the conceptual areas of the brain.

The fundamental relationship in linguistic exchange is a tetradic one between at least two participants, a symbol, and an object. It is the stability of this object (which can be an event) and the degeneracy of the selectional networks in each brain that together permit the building of a stable lexicon with meaning. It does not matter that the symbols used are more or less arbitrary and that because of degeneracy, different neurons are engaged in the two exchanging participants' brains. The constancy of reference to an object and the fixation of the object's connection to the conventionalized symbol in each brain are sufficient to ensure transactions with meaning.

In these transactions, it is likely that the unit of exchange was not an atomic word but the equivalent of a primitive sentence. Such a sentence, like a gesture, can convey action or immanence and can refer to events or things. The emergence of syntax from a gesturally related "protosyntax"[2] connecting pointing actions and objects in sequences of motor acts resulted in the ability to categorize word order. This ability probably required selection for enlarged repertoires in parts of the cortex, such as Wernicke's area and Broca's area and their associated subcortical loops. The sequence during development goes from phonology to semantics and then, in an overlapping fashion, from protosyntax to syntax. These transactions are all affective and are strongly linked to value systems. Besides permitting the designation of objects and events, language has expressive functions that allow for exchanges of feelings and judgments.[3]

In chapter 14, we mentioned that many aspects of speech are carried out via unconscious routines. These routines and the consciousness of word meaning lead to an enormously rich new memory system that is mediated, in part, by these language areas. Although the language areas are not themselves responsible for thinking, their reentrant interactions with conceptual areas allow the creation of a vast number of symbolic constructions, or sentences. An enhanced symbolic memory allows for an increasing number of verbal tokens. At a certain lexicon size, a person's conceptual range becomes enormously enlarged, promoting the use of metaphor.

Once higher-order consciousness begins to emerge along with language, a self can be constructed from social and affective relationships. Here we must consider two related issues that are fundamental to the understanding of higher-order consciousness. The first has to do with how critically the subjective world depends on language. The second is related to how qualia are affected by higher-order consciousness.

Views differ strongly about the relation of subjectivity to the development of the self. The two extremes may be called the internalist and externalist positions on the subjective.[4] According to the internalist view, there is first a subjective experience (say, that of a young baby) and then increasing differentiation of the self with self-consciousness occurring as a result of both social *and* linguistic interactions. Although there is no direct way to know the nature of the early subjective state, it is considered to be the necessary basis for the subsequent emergence of the true self. In this internalist view, some thinking is ontogenetically possible even before language is acquired. Thus, young children can know and figure out the intentions of their parents even before they have language.

According to the alternative, externalist view, it is meaningless to talk about subjective responses or inner states *until* language is acquired. Language is acquired through interpersonal interactions that are social. When enough language is in place, the conceptual bases of the self emerge. Only when that emergence occurs can one consider that a conscious and, above all, a self-conscious, individual is present. In this view, prior subjectivity is indeterminate, and it is meaningless to ask what it is like to be X, whether X is a prelinguistic baby or a bat.[5]

Like all extremes, these two views are useful but are not likely to be correct in their pure form. The notions of primary consciousness and higher-order consciousness allow us to consider a mix. An animal with just primary consciousness that lacks symbolic capabilities has no possibility of developing a notion of a self, of time past, or of time future. But from early times in a baby with linguistic capabilities, cues from the outside are transformed by emotional exchanges with the mother that begin to have motor and, therefore, conceptual significance. The grounds for phonological and semantic development are in place at an early stage, and so are the rewards for exchanges with the mother. There is a continuous drive toward language from the earliest times. This does not appear to be the case for higher apes, such as chimpanzees, even though they appear to have semantic capabilities with some degree of self-differentiation. But unlike humans, such apes do not appear to be compelled toward language in their native environment and do not seem to be able to master syntax. In the case of a baby, higher-order consciousness, a self-concept, and a notion of past and future emerge rapidly with language and socialization. While we cannot say when the "true subject" starts, we can be sure that, from birth, the baby is constructing his or her own "scenes" via primary consciousness and that these scenes rapidly begin to be accompanied by the refurbishment of concepts through gesture, speech, and language. From the earliest times, the thought that accompanies language and that flowers with its development is likely to be metaphorical and narrative. A child can play house with an imaginary companion and make up entire scenarios in which roles and properties are attributed to all kinds of objects. According to this picture, internalism and externalism are too extreme—components of both play major roles in subjective development.

Resolution of the internalist-externalist argument has an important bearing on the question of how qualia are affected by the emergence of the self.

We have already pointed out that a primarily conscious animal has the necessary neural structures to discriminate among billions of different scenes and qualia through the operation of the dynamic core. Moreover, that animal responds in ways that appear to be consonant with these experiences. With the possible exception of mystics, however, as humans we cannot directly experience primary consciousness in the absence of higher-order consciousness. Therefore, we cannot say whether an animal's experience of vision, noise, or pain is quite like ours.

What we can say, however, is that an animal without semantic or linguistic capabilities lacks the symbolic memory that would allow it explicitly to relate its various qualitative experiences to a self. It also lacks the set of neural events that mediate that relationship by consciously linking past, present, and future. As humans, we can not only remember the history of our sensations and categorize them, but, unlike the chimpanzee, we can reflect on our own sensations and talk about them to others. Through such exchanges, we can even refine our discriminatory capacities for certain qualia (consider wine connoisseurs again). It is not amiss to reserve the term *describable qualia* to refer to human conscious experience.

As linguistically communicating persons, we know what it is like to be human. We can also communicate what it is like with less danger of false projection than when we attempt to map our experience onto other animals in nonlinguistic species. From the standpoint of a person, qualia are higher-order categorizations by the self of the conscious experiences of that self that are mediated by the interaction between value-category memory and perception. The ability to describe and further elaborate various qualia requires the simultaneous presence of both higher-order and primary consciousness. Such an elaboration, which is denied to cats or bats, by no means implies that these animals do not experience pain, for example. It is unlikely, however, that they can actually refine qualia as humans can but simply lack the means to report. Although they have rich means for qualitative phenomenal experience, they have no self-conscious self explicitly to memorialize and refine that experience. In their case, long-term memory (which is unconscious) has to carry the main burden in any future enactment based on previous phenomenal experience. For human beings, long-term memory *and* the explicit memory of pain or pleasure phenomenally experienced by a linguistically grounded self share that burden together. The unfolding of thought, of inner narrative, and of a rich emotional life are consequences that provide some recompense for the occasional onerousness of that burden.

CHAPTER   SIXTEEN

Thinking

In this chapter, we ask the question: What goes on in your head when you have a thought? Despite the advances in neuroscience, there is no hiding the fact that we still do not know the answer in sufficient detail. Some would even say the answer is: "We don't have the faintest idea." William James was perhaps the first to attempt this exercise seriously. Repeating the exercise in the light of our present understanding of the neural basis of consciousness supports the conclusion that an awful lot goes on in the brain every time we have a thought, most of it in parallel and of an awe-inspiring complexity and richness of association. A good deal of it is information having a complexity that is far beyond the capabilities of present-day computers.

What Goes On In Your Head When You Have A Thought? This question is posed here as if context, environment, and circumstance did not matter but, of course, they do. But even if these factors were all tightly specified, the answer must still be: We do not really know. Suppose we said: WGOIYH-WYHAT? and you connected this cryptic sequence with the first letters of the words in the original question. How do your mental contents alter when you make such a connection after you have thought about the meaning of the question? To attempt to answer this question, we construct a hypothetical scenario around the human head within which we have no doubt that thoughts occur. We know the anatomy of human brains, we have pathology and neurosurgery to give us clues, and we undoubtedly will be able to devise new imaging techniques to correlate the activity of the brain with verbal instructions and reports. As long as we are aware of the pitfalls that they entail, we can also make use of first-person reports, introspection, and the consciousness of consciousness.

Before we embark on an exercise in speculative neurology, trying to imagine what goes on in the brain during a thought, we must clear up a few important issues. First, we have to take into account that a subjective domain is embodied in each person: Whatever thought I entertain, fragments reflecting my past history are likely to be at the fringe of my consciousness. Given the number and kinds of processes that are going on in parallel in any individual at a particular moment—perceptions, images, feelings, beliefs, desires, moods, emotions, plans, recollections—it is easy to become confused. If we do not discriminate those processes that are aided by language or for which language may be essential from those that do not require language, we may not be able to learn what a thought entails.

To make this discrimination, we must review the relationship between internalist and externalist views of the mental. The internalist view (a first-person view) is that as we interact with the world to establish our beliefs, their content is determined by particular kinds of brain activity that are reachable by introspection. The externalist view (a third-person view) is that mental life is a construct that is mainly dependent on the interpersonal or social exchanges that are based on language. According to this view, the whole system of language is essential to thought; it is the public aspect of language that gives thought its meaning and that is the basis of mental content. This does not mean that we cannot have "thoughts" without putting them into words. For example, Albert Einstein claimed that his most creative thoughts about physics did not explicitly involve words. Nevertheless, the externalist view claims that to the extent we think about something, our sustained thought is based on the emergence of a mental life through language. As before, we have to sort out which parts of these two extreme positions are necessary and which are sufficient before we go ahead. It should then be possible to discriminate at least some of the brain processes that we choose to call mental.

As far as perceptions, images, and feelings are concerned, the internalist view needs no defense. The subjective life of an organism with primary consciousness only (such as a young chimp or a baby before he or she acquires language) *is* supportable as a process that is uniquely embodied in each individual. And with experience leading to the development of concepts in the nonsentential sense, such an individual can almost certainly connect perceptions and images with feelings in a more or less autonomous manner. But extended narrative, logic, or highly abstract thought are out of the question. And beliefs and desires *in the rich sense* of the demands of a true self seeking satisfactions in a social setting based on linguistic exchange remain more or less inaccessible. We would nevertheless hesitate to declare that such an animal has no mental life. What must be conceded is that an individual can have a mental life in the absence of linguistically based beliefs and desires. Only if we restrict the mental to a linguistically based self—the externalist view—do we exclude this possibility. According to the externalist view, a mature chimpanzee with semantic capability but no true language still cannot think. We doubt this conclusion.

Roughly speaking, the internalist view describes primary consciousness while the externalist position describes higher-order consciousness seen in humans. In humans, both kinds of consciousness operate concurrently, and with the exception of mystical, drugged, or confused states, this simultaneous operation is unavoidable. In contrast, while a nonlinguistic animal can have a mental life, that life is necessarily a restricted one because the animal lacks a self-concept. Although such an animal has a unique mental history, it is not a subject—a self who is able to be conscious of being conscious.

Another disputed issue—concerning imagery and imagination—must be cleared up before we ask, WGOIYHWYHAT? The dispute over the existence of mental images began with the Greeks and continues unabated to this day. Pictorialists insist that there are mental images, pictures in the head. Propositionalists insist that we may *think* there are mental images, but the real processes underlying these vague accompaniments are actually propositional and syntactical structures. The pictorialists rely on a strong body of evidence showing that the times required, for example, to carry out the mental rotation of geometric figures or to move mentally from one point on a map to another are linearly related to the actual degrees or distance originally traveled when such acts are carried out "in the real world."

The body of evidence indicating that a "language of thought" does not exist would seem to undercut the claims of the propositionalists. A propositionalist would have to show, for example, how an animal like a dog or a chimpanzee could actually have a language of thought. But even if the inability to make this demonstration favors the pictorialists, are we forced to support the idea of an explicit picture in the head? We all know that when we consciously experience an image, it is usually vague, partial, and "not real." It is entirely possible to account for the pictorialists' experimental results by considering that the brain generates concepts that are based on a nonrepresentational memory. To establish a mental relationship, such a memory, which must operate in terms of global mappings based on prior real-world movements, may well be constrained neurally to relate the time taken to carry out its reconstructions to the original times or distances actually traveled. Such a correlation, therefore, does not, in itself, prove the pictorialists' claim. This is not to deny that we *consciously* experience images, just that the images exist as "representations." We are truly imagining, and short of schizophrenic hallucinations and dreams, we know it. Given the close relationship between perception and memory in a complex brain whose functional connectivity matches the statistics of the environment, it is perhaps no surprise that what we perceive or image in the waking state and what we imagine in dreams is remarkably similar. There is certainly no need to posit that there are actual images in the brain simply because we experience them in conscious states.

Now we come to an important question: Is the expression of a thought ever isolated, or is it always accompanied by images, perceptions, sensations, and feelings? To answer this question, let us designate the products of primary consciousness as mental life I and those of higher-order consciousness as mental life II. There is no harm in this distinction as long as it is understood that these forms of consciousness coexist, overlap, and feed each other. We suspect that no event in mental life II is ever completely divorced from the happenings in mental life I. Consider images: We can have images without words or images with words (or even images stimulated by words). We can have imageless thoughts with or without words. But always in the background, there is the parallel buzz of perception, feeling, mood, and fleeting memories. Of course, mechanisms of attention can come into play, reducing this buzz to near-silence in extreme states of concentration. But most thoughts come into being in the presence of a clamor, however muted, from mental life I.

What keeps a thought going? The answer is likely an intricate combination of ongoing perception, attention, memory, habit, and reward, including aspects of previous learning. Again the drive comes from a mixture of mental life I and mental life II. If someone's thought concerns a recollection, it may be rich in associated imagery. If it concerns willed action, it may or may not be accompanied by any imagery, and if it concerns mathematical objects, it may have associated imagery or just a sequence of habitual symbolic operations without pictures.

If I have the thought "I must go to the store before it is too late," I am deep into mental life II and implicitly assume social interactions, highly developed language, richly connected memories, and relations to others. The thought may have arisen when I entered the kitchen for a drink of water and remembered belatedly that I promised that I would do the shopping on this day. Entering the kitchen, I see the clock: near closing time, a strong prompting for the thought that drives me.

Now consider what is going on in my head. First, my basal ganglia, cerebellum, and motor cortex are involved in my walking and in unconscious habitual procedures, such as turning on the water tap. As I move, global mappings are sending signals to my body, arms, and legs, of which I am also mostly unconscious. A series of reentrant interactions among my visual maps, parietal cortex, and forebrain areas are involved in immediately translating the signals from the clock face into the time. The activity of the dynamic core plays out a complex contextual scene, along with images from my body. At that moment, a strong surge from mental life I—a feeling of slight fear converted through mental life II into an emotion with necessary cognitive components: anxiety. "The store may be closed." Ascending value systems—the locus coeruleus, basal forebrain nuclei, raphé nucleus, and hypothalamus—send out a particular combination of neurotransmitters that reflect the salience of these various signals. The core must register the neural consequences of this activity—feelings as well as perceptions and recollections.

At this point, a clear elicitation of language and of the true subjective (and emotional) life may emerge: an inner paraphrase (possibly vocalized) "Damn! I *must* go to the store." And with this paraphrase, the entire memory system of language is engaged, coupled in the core specifically to the temporal cortex; to the frontal cortex for concepts; and, through ports out, to the basal ganglia again for plans to go down to the garage, followed finally by motor cortical signals.

All this still accompanied by little wisps of discomfort from my meal and possibly fleeting memories of opportunities missed. To add a Freudian touch to this little play, we might say that the "reason" I was late to realize my promise concerned a repressed episode related to early punishments by my mother over failed errands, connected to failed performances in later life.

In this account, we are richly into emotions, beliefs, and desires. But notice that whatever the combination, an extraordinary number of brain events are going on simultaneously. Some are directly related to my anxiety, some are subsequently related to my plans to reduce it, and some are simply contemporaneous. In other words, some brain events may be considered causally connected, while others are coincidental, occurring in parallel.

Nevertheless, depending on external events or memories or my reactions to anxiety, what was coincidental and not causally significant may unexpectedly become strongly causal, change my conscious attention, and alter my feelings and actions in an unpredicted fashion.

This near-simultaneous evocation of complexity in the dynamic core and its connection to unconscious routines may be called the Jamesian scenario. The first thing we can say about it is that even in an animal without language, once its nervous system can carry out perceptual categorization and develop conceptual memory, a huge set of possible actions opens up. In an animal with primary consciousness, the activities of the nervous system are driven by value systems, perception, movement, memory, and habit. The reward or threat of a scene consisting of both causally connected and causally unrelated events is assessed in terms of the past experience of that individual animal, and that scene drives behavior. The dynamic, temporally ongoing, bootstrap between a value-category memory and perceptual categorization reflects an individual history, one illuminated at each moment by a remembered present—primary consciousness, mental life I.

With the emergence of a higher-order consciousness through language, there is a consciously explicit coupling of feelings and values, yielding emotions with cognitive components that are experienced by a person—a self. When this coupling occurs, the already complex events of mental life I become intercalated with those of mental life II, which is even more complex. A true subjectivity emerges with narrative and metaphorical powers and concepts of self and of past and future, with an interlacing fabric of beliefs and desires that can be voiced or expressed. Fiction becomes possible.

The driving force for weaving this remarkable fabric is still provided by the componentry of primary consciousness and memory itself, not to speak of animal appetites. The number of brain areas contributing to the dynamic core and the global mappings that are simultaneously engaged is large, fluctuating, and subject to various linkages. Still, what appears to be a large number of circuits and cells that are actually engaged at any one time is only a small fraction of the number of combinations that are possible in the repertoires of a selectional brain. It is the possibility of enlisting new combinations that gives flexibility to what would otherwise appear to be routine behavior. Like evolution itself, the workings of the brain are a play between constancy and variation, selection and diversity. Given the additional power that language exerts in such a selectional system, meaning can emerge from value through the development of a conscious self.

Is thought necessarily always conscious? Whatever the play between the conscious and the unconscious and however strongly unconscious routines may, at times, overwhelm conscious decisions, thought itself, in our view, requires consciousness. To declare that what is mental is conscious and that thinking is conscious does not, however, exclude the enormous impact of unconscious learned routines or emotions on thought. Nor does it exclude the possibility that what is threatening to the self can be repressed. The reflections described in chapter 14 make it possible to take this position without claiming constant or exclusive control of our behavior by either conscious processes or unconscious routines.

It will be some time before we can visualize and track in detail the actual brain processes that accompany a thought in all their glory and remarkable complexity. For now, we may conclude that what goes on in the head when each self has a thought is an awful lot. A good part of it for humans is conscious information. We may usefully ask some interesting questions: Where and when in nature did information and then conscious information arise? And how free are humans in their thoughts and knowledge when the informativenesss of higher-order consciousness comes into play? We take up these and other questions in the final chapter.

CHAPTER SEVENTEEN

Prisoners of Description

This final chapter reconsiders the conclusions reached in the rest of the book from a philosophical point of view, one that we call qualified realism. They include the conclusions that there is no judge in nature deciding categories except for natural selection, that consciousness is a physical process embodied in each unique individual, and that this embodiment can never be substituted for by a mere description. Our embodiment is the ultimate source of our descriptions and provides the bases of how we know—the proper concern of the branch of philosophy known as epistemology. The insistence on embodiment as a critical factor carries with it the need to pay heed to how our brains actually develop. Detached philosophical thinking is not sufficient; it must be complemented by an analysis of brain mechanisms. Although it has been proposed that epistemology should be "naturalized" and take its grounds from psychology, we suggest here that this is not nearly enough: Given how information and consciousness have arisen in nature, one should go one step further and say that epistemology should be grounded in biology, specifically in neuroscience. We suggest that three important philosophical consequences can be drawn from this view: that being is prior to describing; that selection is prior to logic; and that, in the development of thought, doing is prior to understanding.

Our scientific analysis of consciousness as a process and our emphasis on the fundamental properties of primary consciousness may appear paradoxical inasmuch as we ourselves—human beings endowed with higher-order consciousness—provide the only direct referent for asking and answering questions about consciousness. Of course, humans have primary consciousness, and it is primary in the sense that it is essential for the development of higher-order consciousness. This is why we have paid so much attention to it. But given our concerns in this final chapter, it is higher-order consciousness that is at center stage. Our position has been that higher-order consciousness, which includes the ability to be conscious of being conscious, is dependent on the emergence of semantic capabilities and, ultimately, of language. Concomitant with these traits is the emergence of a true self, born of social interactions, along with concepts of the past and future. Driven by primary consciousness and the remembered present, we can, through symbolic exchange and higher-order consciousness, create narratives, fictions, and histories. We can ask questions about how we can know and thereby deliver our selves to the doorstep of philosophy.

Let us consider further the implications of our view of consciousness, particularly for what we have called biologically based epistemology.[1] As we discussed in the first chapters of this book, the study of consciousness as a scientific subject casts a sharp light on a special problem faced by the scientific observer. As long as his description leaves out his phenomenal experience and he can assume that such experience is present in another observer, they both can give a description of the physical world from a "God's-eye" view. When the observer turns his attention to the description of consciousness, however, he must face some challenging issues. These issues include the fact that consciousness is embodied uniquely and privately in each individual; that no description, scientific or otherwise, is equivalent to the experience of individual embodiment; that there is no judge deciding categories in nature except for natural selection; and that the external description of information by the observers as a code in the brain leads to paradox. These issues pose a challenging set of problems: how to provide an adequate description of higher brain functions; how information arises in nature; and, finally, how we know—the central concern of epistemology.

THE ORIGIN OF INFORMATION IN NATURE

We have made the case that a most remarkable property of conscious states is their informativeness: The occurrence of a particular conscious state rules out, in a fraction of a second, an enormous number of possibilities. This ruling-out process represents the integration of an extraordinary amount of information in a short time. This capability has not been matched by any of our inventions, including the computer. It certainly did not spring forth without evolutionary precedent. Rather, it arose from structures and systems that were reconfigured over millions of years as a result of natural selection. Indeed, a defensible case can be made that conscious brains are the most creative sources of information in all of nature. But just as there are different phenotypes, there are different sources and types of information.

When can we say that information first appeared in nature? To answer this question, we must confront a set of subsidiary questions. Can information exist without a conscious interpreter? Should we consider a potentially observable order in nature in the absence of humans as information? Is the genetic code the true origin of information? Does the "existence" of natural laws imply that nature is like a computer?

As these questions suggest, inquiry about the origin of information in nature faces several definitional problems, many of which are concerned with the distinction between the describer and the thing described. First, we must ask whether the term *information* can be used to describe a state of nature in the total absence of a human observer. Can *information* be solely an objective term? If it is defined by a physicist as a measure of order in a far-from-equilibrium state, then by the terms of that definition, in a "God's-eye view," it is objective. If, however, information is defined in a way that requires a historical process involving either memory or a heritable state, then information can have arisen only with the origin of life.

It seems clear that systems that are capable of actually *processing* information appeared for the first time as a result of evolution by natural selection. This statement implies that the origin of information not only requires prior variation and selection, but that such selection must lead to some degree of heritable change. In this view, the presence of heritability, variation, and selection are critical factors in the emergence of information. This emergence involves a kind of matching and stabilization of responses to environmental states. But although such heritable processes are concerned with the transition to the living from the nonliving, they still do not involve a sentient observer.

It is noteworthy that the selective events that led to the genetic code followed a different set of rules than the laws of chemistry and physics that govern the covalent bonding of nucleic acids. For a set of Darwinian rules to apply certainly required the existence of stable covalent chemical bonds to ensure the growth of nucleic acid polymers, that such polymers could be replicated, and that mutations could occur. But the ingredient that supervened over the laws of chemistry and physics was that selection for fitness in the phenotype could stabilize some DNA or RNA sequences over others. Such code sequences represent the historical residues of generally irreversible selection events that acted on whole organisms at a much higher level of organization than DNA itself. So the actual nucleotide sequences of genes reflect historical events, as well as chemical laws, and both together ultimately constrained how processing of information eventually arose in nature.

Elsewhere,[2] we have suggested that the ability to repeat a performance with variation under changing contexts actually first appeared with the emergence of life, that is, of self-replicating systems under natural selection. The continued action of natural selection during evolution then gave rise to a variety of systems for which memory was critical, each having different structures within a given animal species. Examples of such structures range from the immune system to reflexes and, finally, to consciousness. In this view, there are as many memory systems as there are systems capable of autocorrelation with their previous states over time, whether such systems are constituted by DNA itself or by the phenotype it constrains. It is morphology that underlies the particular properties of any memory system. Memory itself is a system property that allows the binding in time of selected characteristics having adaptive value. If symmetry is a great binding principle of the physical universe that guarantees conservation laws in physics, memory in selectional systems, from the genetic code to consciousness, may be seen as a great binding principle in the biological domain.

Why not, then, consider that information actually arose with the genetic code itself? The fact that the code, acting through complex protein-nucleic acid interactions, results in the formation of proteins with defined structures and functions makes it tempting to consider that the so-called open-reading frame of sequential triplet bases is information. Indeed, when as scientists we "read" the code, that is exactly what it is. Likewise when, at different stages of an organism's development, different regions of the genetic code are transcribed and translated into different proteins, we may say that what is being "read out" is information.

Nevertheless, calling any manifestation of biological order or memory "information" may not be as useful as requiring that some symbolic exchange or, at least, signification must be involved in actual informational transactions. According to this view, information did not appear until the evolutionary emergence of animals that were capable of mutual symbolic exchange. In this case, honeybees would have to be considered as trafficking in information. We can then say that for signals or physical states to constitute information, several conditions should be met: (1) pattern recognition must be involved that includes but goes beyond the scientific laws of physics or chemistry: A bee dance involves information, but formation of a crystal does not. The reason is that some prototypical value, based on historical and evolutionary constraints, is involved in the first case but not in the second. (2) Living organisms with brains and physiology permitting choice and communication must be at the origin or the terminus (or both) of a stimulus or signal for it to constitute information. This requirement rules out molecular interactions, however sophisticated, events at submicroscopic or cosmic scales, and organisms (for example, amoebas) that are incapable of rich memories. We can ask, for example, whether bacterial tropisms or protozoan feeding events involve the exchange of information. Given our agreed-upon terms, such behaviors should not be conflated with those of animals that have rich nervous systems that allow them to communicate, remember, and learn.

In any case, information is a biological concept. In humans, capable of speech, it can show exquisite refinements—artificial codes, scientific analyses, logical proofs, mathematical creations, or bizarre manifestations like stock market frenzies or the madness of crowds. These achievements based on higher-order consciousness should not tempt us to assume, however, that there is a unique pattern of syntax existing in nature (like the syntax we insert into a computer tape) or even that there is a special code in the workings of neurons. Such assumptions are badly framed; although it takes a transaction with an evolved structure to construct information, that process is not driven by syntax. Nature is not a computer, and syntax did not emerge in nature until hominids capable of language arrived on the scene.

Whatever evolutionary event we wish to consider as representing the beginning of true information—for example, the exchange of signals among individuals driven by adaptive needs—our conclusions in this book suggest that perhaps the most momentous achievement of evolution happened later. It is the transcendent leap from simple nervous systems, in which signals are exchanged in a relatively insulated manner within separate neural subsystems, to complex nervous systems based on reentrant dynamics, in which an enormous number of signals are rapidly integrated within a single neural process constituting the dynamic core. Such integration leads to the construction of a scene relating signals from many different modalities with memory based on an entire evolutionary history and an individual's experience—it is a remembered present. This scene integrates and generates an extraordinary amount of information within less than a second. For the first time in evolution, information acquires a new potential—the possibility of subjectivity. It is information "for somebody"; in short, it becomes consciousness itself.

We have claimed that the sophisticated forms of information exchange developed by humans would not be conceivable in the absence of consciousness. After Homo sapiens and higher-order consciousness appeared, it became possible to create syntactically rich symbol systems, to create codes, and even to create logic. Eventually, methods of scientific analysis were invented, resulting in the formulation of natural laws. To us, those laws are information. To nature, outside of us, is it energy or coded information that is being exchanged? Does it come from bit or bit from it?[3] What came first: biology or logic?

SELECTIONISM AND LOGIC

We live in a world dominated by computers and computing. It has become commonplace these days to think about the brain as a computer, a device based on logic. Although we do not believe that this is a tenable point of view, it does pose an interesting epistemological question: At the most fundamental level, how many modes of thought are there: Is logic the only one?

In a purely formal sense, some philosophers have defined logic as the study of all sentential relations invariant with respect to lexical substitution. "All A are B. X is an A; therefore, X is a B," no matter what A, B, or X refer to. In a broader, more psychological framework, logic may be considered the study of the relationships between such formal issues and intuition (or pattern recognition). This latter framework is much less tidy, but it does prompt one to ask: What is the connection between the ability to recognize and match patterns, the ability to think, and the ability to carry out logical operations? This last ability can be mechanized, but as Gödel's theorem implies, there are certain patterned mathematical relationships whose truth cannot be proved or disproved within a consistent axiom system. Nevertheless, the argument has often been made that the brain is some kind of computer and therefore is describable as a Turing machine.

A universal Turing machine can carry out any sequence of logical operations and, according to the Church-Post thesis, can carry out any sequence of effective procedures or precisely specified algorithms (see figure 17.1). This is a powerful capability, and we suppose that it is this capability that has prompted the suggestion that the brain is a Turing machine. We have considered elsewhere why this cannot be the case. Briefly, the argument goes as follows: Each brain is formed in such a way that its wiring and dynamics are enormously variable at the level of its synapses. It is a selectional system, and each brain is therefore unique. That uniqueness and unpredictability can be significant in carrying out certain brain operations and must be taken into account in considering any particular brain operation. Moreover, brain function is degenerate: When presented with an unpredictable context, non-isomorphic brain structures at more than one level of construction and operation can lead to the same output or function. Furthermore, many brain operations in perception and memory are nonrepresentational, constructive, and context dependent and are not necessarily guided by an effective proce-

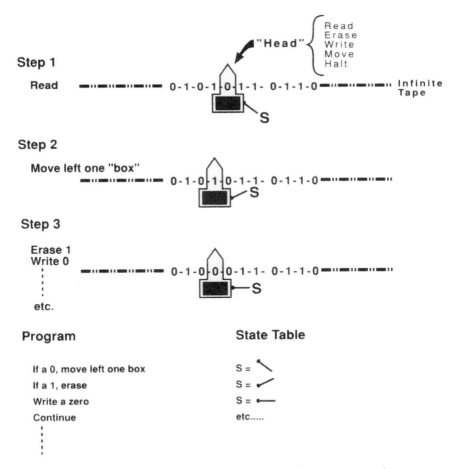

FIGURE 17.1 DIAGRAM OF A TURING MACHINE. When a program designates an action, as shown in the figure, the machine state *S* changes, and this change alters the next step prescribed by the set of precise instructions. Brains do not work this way.

dure. This is so because their key operations involve selection, not instruction, and there is no evidence for rigorous or preestablished neural codes resembling those of computers. Finally, the environmental input and the context of signals to the brain are not uniquely specified or single valued; that is, the world, although it obeys physical laws, does not behave like a computer tape.

If the brain is not a Turing machine, we need another explanation for its workings. That explanation is provided by the theory of neuronal group selection (TNGS). As we have seen, a series of simulations based on the TNGS can actually carry out pattern recognition and perceptual categorization. Moreover, a large body of disparate experimental evidence not only indicates that selectional events occur in the brain, but suggests that much of that apparently disparate evidence can actually be reconciled by an analysis of such events. We have taken it as established that after the brain arose in evolution by natural selection, which set up value constraints and major structures, each individual brain operates by a process of somatic selection. Instead of being guided mainly by a set of *effective procedures*, it is governed by a degenerate set of *effective structures*, the dynamics of which allow its correlated activities to arise by selection, rather than by the rules of logic.

Clearly, if the brain evolved in such a fashion, and this evolution provided the biological basis for the eventual discovery and refinement of logical systems in human culture, then we may conclude that, in the generative sense, selection is more powerful than logic. It is selection—natural and somatic— that gave rise to language and to metaphor, and it is selection, not logic, that underlies pattern recognition and thinking in metaphorical terms. Thought is thus ultimately based on our bodily interactions and structure, and its powers are therefore limited to some degree. Our capacity for pattern recognition may nevertheless exceed the power to prove propositions by logical means. Indeed, conscious human thought can create new axioms, which a computer cannot do. This realization does not, of course, imply that selection can take the place of logic, nor does it deny the enormous power of logical operations.

In the realm of either organisms or of the synthetic artifacts that we may someday build, we conjecture that there are only two fundamental kinds— Turing machines and selectional systems. Inasmuch as the latter preceded the emergence of the former in evolution, we conclude that selection is biologically the more fundamental process. In any case, the interesting conjecture is that there appear to be only two deeply fundamental ways of patterning thought: selectionism and logic. It would be a momentous occasion in the history of philosophy if a third way were found or demonstrated.

PHILOSOPHICAL CLAIMS

Whatever the powers and limits of a thought process that is embodied and is the result of natural and neuronal group selection, that thought process has given rise to a remarkable propensity for asking questions about the ultimate significance of things—questions of philosophy. Two grand areas of philosophy are metaphysics, which is concerned with the ultimate nature of reality, and epistemology, which is concerned with the basis and justification of knowledge and belief. These two areas are linked to some extent, and they touch on others of human concern that are connected to values, for example, ethics and esthetics. Does a theory of consciousness have implications for our approach to such questions? We believe it does.

Perhaps the best way to support our belief is to consider certain matters of epistemology and metaphysics and their connection to scientific matters. We believe that there is a real world, the one described by the laws of physics, which so far appear to apply everywhere. As humans, we must follow such laws without exception because we have evolved in that world from ancient animal origins. As living systems, we are also subject to evolutionary constraints not considered by the laws of physics. Consciousness, while special, arose as a result of evolutionary innovations in the morphology of the brain and body. The mind arises from the body and its development; it is embodied and therefore part of nature. All these statements follow from what we called, in chapter 2, the physics assumption and the evolutionary assumption, both of which underlie our theory.

Once we agree that these assumptions are justified by a large body of evidence, a number of consequences can be identified. First, we must reject the Cartesian assumption of dualism and any form of idealism. Thus, we cannot accept the position taken by those who embrace a materialist metaphysics combined with a dualist, rationalist or idealist, epistemology. On the other hand, we must be skeptical about extreme reductionist accounts that attempt to explain consciousness on the basis of quantum mechanics but ignore the facts of evolution and neurology. The same skepticism holds for attempts to imbue the world at large with conscious properties—the view of panpsychism.

The metaphysical and epistemological positions that we do espouse we have called, respectively, qualified realism and biologically based epistemology.[4] A key idea on which qualified realism and biologically based epistemology both depend is the notion that concepts are not, in the first instance, sentential. That is, concepts are not propositions in a language (the common usage of this term); rather, they are constructs the brain develops by mapping its own responses prior to language. Just as signals from the world are not organized as information before interaction with the brain, neither is language specified in terms of a genetically inherited universal grammar. Concepts, in our view, precede language, which develops by epigenetic means to further enhance our conceptual and emotional exchanges.

Consciousness is a dynamic property of a special kind of morphology—the reentrant meshwork of the thalamocortical system—as it interacts with the environment. Our knowledge of the real world comes as a result of the physical, psychological, and social interactions of our minds and bodies with that world. Those interactions do not involve a direct transfer of information, however, and we must therefore reject naive realism, the position that the perception of objects is direct and that the qualities we perceive are, in fact, those of the objects that are perceived. Realism based on perception must be qualified by the bodily means we have available for perception. Most of these means, while enormously powerful, are nevertheless indirect and of limited range. They constrain how our brains develop their conceptual systems, and we therefore conclude that our realism must be qualified, at least to some extent.

Of course, as conscious persons capable of language develop and communicate in a culture, their conceptual abilities become enormously enriched. The products of that enrichment, for example, logic and mathematics, can transcend some of the phenotypic constraints on the embodied mind and remove some of the qualifications imposed on us by the limitations of our phenotype. Indeed, perceptual categories based on neural structures, buttressed by conceptual categorization and aided by conscious planning and choice in a linguistic milieu, have led to the extraordinary systems of thought that underlie the scientific investigation of the world. The important point that emerges from the work reviewed in this book is that a scientific investigation of consciousness is also consistent with the facts of human individuality and subjectivity.

Before the advent of modern experimental psychology and neuroscience, epistemology was based solely on normative issues and thinking about thinking. But from the time of Charles Darwin on, and in light of recent scientific advances, it has been proposed that epistemology should be "naturalized" and take its grounds from a behavioristic psychology.[5] Naturalized epistemology necessarily stops, however, at the stimulation of receptor sheets—the retina, the skin, the taste buds—and while it includes the analysis of language, it leaves the inner workings of the body and brain untouched. We claim that this position is insufficient: Epistemology should be grounded in biology, notably neuroscience and a theory of consciousness, which, of course, includes psychology. We therefore reject the effort by philosophical behaviorists to naturalize epistemology via behavioral psychology alone.[6] A move to a biologically based epistemology would not only recast certain arguments about, for example, the possibility of a "synthetic a priori," but would create a much broader base for thinking about thinking and feeling. Moreover, it would not limit our descriptions to the boundary between our skin and the rest of our world. Most important, it would open our inquiry to include feelings and emotions in terms of bodily mechanisms that go far beyond computation.

While these attempts give due scientific recognition to the subjective domain, subjectivism itself is no basis for a sound scientific understanding of the mind. Consequently, we reject phenomenology and introspectionism, along with philosophical behaviorism. We believe that the inner mechanisms of consciousness can be explored scientifically without exclusive resort to either simple behaviorism or introspection. The first puts the observer outside the key phenomena, while the second assumes falsely that by taking thought alone, one can analyze the underlying bases of conscious experience.

Taking the position of biologically based epistemology changes how we look upon that fictive but useful agent, the scientific observer. As Erwin Schrödinger once noted, a physical scientist does not introduce sensation or perception into his theories. Having removed the mind from nature, he cannot therefore expect to find it there. Taking a God's-eye view to observe an individual person from the outside leaves the scientific observer with an impoverished picture of mind. It can lead to the paradoxical conclusion that consciousness is merely a bottleneck in an information-processing cascade, a bottleneck that at any given time can contain "just a few chunks" of information. We have insisted, instead, that the observer must consider consciousness by viewing the brain from within, in terms of what makes a difference to its underlying neural processes. From that vantage point, the observer will discover a unified physical process of the utmost complexity—a process that, unlike anything we have built so far, can rapidly integrate immense amounts of information.

Taking the position of a biologically based epistemology offers a major opportunity to extend our scientific view of animal behavior and human nature. This position accepts physics and evolution as two main pillars for philosophical reflection. It then proposes that the efficacious role of consciousness is to construct an informative scene ("the remembered present") that connects present reality to the past value-ridden history of each individual, conscious animal. The efficacy of consciousness for the rapid integration of information and planning yields significant evolutionary advantages. The translation of such planning into unconscious learned routines is also essential for survival, and such routines constitute a vast proportion of the basic mechanisms of behavior. Indeed, consciousness plays upon such routines to give the possibility of enhanced planning and of ever more complex learned acts.

While the efficacy of nonconscious mechanisms cannot be denied, biologically based epistemology considers consciousness to be a sine qua non of mental acts. Without entering into definitional controversies, we take the position that thought is a conscious process underlaid by a deep structure of necessary nonconscious mechanisms, including nonrepresentational memory, value constraints, and the action of cortical appendages like the basal ganglia, hippocampus, and cerebellum.

The incorporation of value systems as necessary constraints on the workings of the brain as a selectional system ties the view of biologically based epistemology to the view that emotions are fundamental both to the origins of and the appetite for conscious thought. As described by Spinoza, emotions may represent human bondage, but despite the apparent paradox, we think it likely that it was mainly emotions that impelled him to create his magnificent edifice of thought. Value systems and emotions are essential to the selectional workings of the brain that underlie consciousness. Further neuroscientific research on these systems and their modification by learning should shed light on an important issue: the place of value in a world of facts.[7]

A final word on the causal efficacy of consciousness: If anyone doubts the efficacy of consciousness, let him compare the workings of eusocial insects to the abstract constructions of poets, composers, mathematicians, and scientists. Without life, the intricate behavioral webs of wasps and the structures of termite colonies certainly are not likely to arise spontaneously. But as impressive as these colonies are, they cannot be compared to the grand view of the universe that has emerged from the workings of higher-order consciousness in human beings. We continue to describe our place in the universe by scientific means and, at the same time, give ourselves comfort and significance in that place by artistic means. In the realization of both ends, it is consciousness that provides the freedom and the warrant.

CONSCIOUSNESS AS A PHYSICAL PROCESS

We have argued throughout this book that consciousness arises from certain arrangements in the material order of the brain. There is a common prejudice that to call something material is somehow to refuse its entry into the realm of exalted things—mind, spirit, pure thought. The word *material* can be used to refer to many things or states. As it is used in these pages, it applies to what we commonly call the real world of sensible or measurable things, the world that scientists study. That world is considerably more subtle than it first appears. A chair is material (shaped by us, of course), a star is material, atoms and fundamental particles are material—they are made of matter-energy. The thought, "thinking about Vienna," however, while couched in material terms, is, as Willard Van Orman Quine pointed out, a materially based process but is, itself, not material.

What is the difference? It is that conscious thought is a set of relations with a meaning that goes beyond just energy or matter (although it involves both). And what of the mind that gave rise to that thought? The answer is, it is both material and meaningful. There is a material basis for the mind as a set of relations: The action of your brain and all its mechanisms, bottom to top, atoms to behavior, results in a mind that can be concerned with processes of meaning. While generating such immaterial relationships that are recognized by it and other minds, this mind is completely based in and dependent on the physical processes that occur in its own workings, in those of other minds, and in the events involved in communication. There are no completely separate domains of matter and mind and no grounds for dualism. But obviously, there is a realm created by the physical order of the brain, the body, and the social world in which meaning is consciously made. That meaning is essential both to our description of the world and to our scientific understanding of it. It is the amazingly complex material structures of the nervous system and body that give rise to dynamic mental processes and to meaning. Nothing else need be assumed—neither other worlds, or spirits, or remarkable forces as yet unplumbed, such as quantum gravity.[8]

There is a web to untangle here: Humans were capable of meaning and of thought before they had a scientific description of the world. Any such scientific description, even when clarified, cannot be fully tested or sustained by just one person for an indefinite period of time. It needs social interactions or, at least, two persons to make an ongoing experimental science. Yet a single person can have both private thoughts, not fully capturable by a scientific description, at the same time that he or she has a quite correct scientific understanding. So, what happens when we turn scientific inquiry in the direction of the individual human brain and mind? What are the limits? What can we expect to capture and understand by such a scientific adventure?

Our claim is that we may capture the material bases of mind even to the extent of having a satisfactory understanding of the origins of exalted things, such as the mental. To do so, we may have to invent further ways of looking at brains and their activities. We may even have to synthesize artifacts resembling brains connected to bodily functions in order fully to understand those processes. Although the day when we shall be able to create such conscious artifacts is far off, we may have to make them—that is, use synthetic means—before we deeply understand the processes of thought itself. However far off the date of their construction, such artifacts shall be made. After all, it has been done at least once by evolution. The history of science, particularly of biological science, has shown repeatedly that apparently mysterious or impassable barriers to our understanding were based on false views or technical limitations. The material bases of mind are no exception.

This position does not contradict the conclusion that each mind is unique, not fully exhaustible by scientific means, and not a machine. Do not search for the mystical here. Our statements about the material order and immaterial meaning are not only mutually consistent within a scientific framework, but live in a useful symbiosis.

PRISONERS OF DESCRIPTION OR MASTERS OF MEANING?

Our analysis has been predicated on the notion that while we can construct a sensible scientific theory of consciousness that explains how matter becomes imagination, that theory cannot replace experience: Being is not describing. A scientific description can have predictive and explanatory power, but it cannot directly convey the phenomenal experience that depends on having an individual brain and body. In our theory of brain complexity, we have removed the paradoxes that arise by assuming only the God's-eye view of the external observer and, by adhering to selectionism, we have removed the homunculus. Nevertheless, because of the nature of embodiment, we still remain, to some extent, prisoners of description, only somewhat better off than the occupants of Plato's cave. Can we get around this limitation—this qualification of our realism? Not completely, but we return to the extravagant thought that we may transcend our analytic limits by synthetic means. Even if, some long time into the future, we can eventually construct a con-

FIGURE 17.2 The world knot can be expressed in many ways, as, for example, in this figure *Counterpart* by Giuseppe Arcimboldo (1527–93) and in this fragment of a poem by Emily Dickinson (1830–86):

> The Brain—is wider than the Sky—
> For—put them side by side—
> The one the other will contain
> With ease—and You—beside.

scious artifact that, *mirabile dictu*, has linguistic capability, we will, even then, not directly know the actual phenomenal experience of that artifactual individual; the qualia we experience, each of us, artifact or person, rests in our own embodiment, our own phenotype.

There is no real mystery here; embodiment in the individual corpus is the price of admission for any such qualitative experience. There is, however, one new expanse of knowledge that would open up at that remarkable moment in our intellectual journey. It is the opportunity to see how a radically different phenotype capable of higher-order consciousness actually categorized the same world, the world we would share with it. The likelihood that this phenotype will be like ours or even like that of a complex animal appears diminishingly small. But could such an artifact, in its descriptions, reach a lawful generality identical to ours, even if its body and mind carved up the signals of this world in a radically different fashion than we do? If it did, some of the qualifications constraining our position of realism might be removed.

The limits and ranges of exploration of the material order as it gives rise to mind may or may not fall out according to our speculations here. But there is one fascinating point that, here and now, bears on the exhaustiveness of the scientific pursuit. It concerns whether *all* meaningful relations at the level of consciousness constitute objects for scientific study. Think, for example, of meaningful sentences in ordinary language or, even better, of poetic exchanges as they are enacted by sentient humans. Our conjecture is that they are, here and now, not fit objects for scientific study except in some trivial sense. Their meaning and description rest on too many unique historical patterns; on multiple ambiguous references; and, in the case of a unique poetic utterance (see figure 17.2), on an incomparable sample. To grasp their meaning requires both the unique phenomenal experience and the historically based culture of each participating individual.

We do not wish to be misunderstood: Just as consciousness itself may be explained, the *bases* of such objects and utterances can be fully explained by scientific inquiry as arising in the material order. But even though they may be more directly accessible as objects for study than the origin of the cosmos, they are unfit (except in the most trivial sense) to be scientific subjects, and they will not yield up their significance through scientific inquiry alone. They do yield significance, however, as a result of our individual embodiment and the mutual grammatical exchanges that allow us to experience higher-order consciousness.

If we consider that most of our lives take on meaning in the rich soup of such exchanges, we need not fear exhaustion by scientific reduction. But neither need we call upon mystical explanations to account for such richness. It is enough to recognize that some scientifically founded objects are not appropriate scientific subjects. Rejoice in it. While we remain prisoners of description, our freedom is in the grammar.

Notes

PART ONE

1. C. Sherrington, *Man on His Nature*, 2nd ed. (Cambridge, England: Cambridge University Press, 1951).
2. B. Russell, quoted in Sir J. Jeans, *Physics and Philosophy* (Cambridge, England: Cambridge University Press, 1943).
3. A. Schopenhauer, *On the Fourfold Root of the Principle of Sufficient Reason*, trans. E. F. J. Payne (La Salle, Ill.: Open Court, 1974), Chapter 7, §42.

CHAPTER ONE

1. W. James, *The Principles of Psychology* (New York: Henry Holt, 1890).
2. R. Descartes, *Meditationes de prima philosophia, in quibus Dei existentia, & animae humanae à corpore distinctio, demonstrantur* (Amstelodami: Apud Danielem Elsevirium, 1642).
3. T. H. Huxley, *Methods and Results: Essays* (New York: D. Appleton, 1901), 241.
4. See, for example, N. J. Block, O. J. Flanagan, and G. Güzeldere, *The Nature of Consciousness: Philosophical Debates* (Cambridge, Mass: MIT Press, 1997); J. Shear, *Explaining Consciousness: The "Hard Problem"* (Cambridge, Mass.: MIT Press, 1997); R. Warner and T. Szubka, *The Mind-Body Problem: A Guide to the Current Debate* (Cambridge, Mass.: Blackwell, 1994); N. Humphrey, *A History of the Mind* (New York: HarperPerennial, 1993); O. Flanagan, *Consciousness Reconsidered* (Cambridge, Mass.: MIT Press, 1992); D. J. Chalmers, "The Puzzle of Conscious Experience," *Scientific American* 273 (1995), 80–86; D. C. Dennett, *Consciousness Explained* (Boston: Little, Brown, 1991); and J. R. Searle, *The Rediscovery of the Mind* (Cambridge, Mass.: MIT Press, 1992).
5. C. McGinn, "Can We Solve the Mind-Body Problem?" *Mind*, 98 (1989), 349.
6. See, for example, D. J. Chalmers, "The Puzzle of Conscious Experience," *Scientific American* 273 (1995), 80–86.
7. See, for example, E. B. Titchener, *An Outline of Psychology* (New York: Macmillan, 1901); and O. Külpe and E. B. Titchener, *Outlines of Psychology, Based upon the Results of Experimental Investigation* (New York: Macmillan, 1909).
8. B. J. Baars, *A Cognitive Theory of Consciousness* (New York: Cambridge University Press, 1988); and B. J. Baars, *Inside the Theater of Consciousness: The Workspace of the Mind* (New York: Oxford University Press, 1997).

9. Ibid.

10. J. Eccles, "A Unitary Hypothesis of Mind-Brain Interaction in the Cerebral Cortex," *Proceedings of the Royal Society of London, Series B—Biological Sciences,* 240 (1990), 433–51.

11. R. Penrose, *The Emperor's New Mind: Concerning Computers, Minds, and the Laws of Physics* (New York: Oxford University Press, 1989) .

12. W. James, *The Principles of Psychology* (New York: Henry Holt, 1890).

13. S. Zeki and A. Bartels, "The Asynchrony of Consciousness," *Proceedings of the Royal Society of London Series B—Biological Sciences,* 265 (1998), 1583–85.

14. G. Ryle, *The Concept of Mind* (New York: Hutchinson, 1949).

CHAPTER TWO

1. T. Nagel, "What Is It Like to Be a Bat?" reprinted in T. Nagel, *Mortal Questions* (New York: Cambridge University Press, 1979).

2. See also a letter to John Locke by the philosopher William Molyneux in 1690 (J. Locke, W. Molyneux, T. Molyneux, and P. V. Limborch, *Familiar Letters Between Mr. John Locke, and Several of His Friends: In Which Are Explained His Notions in His Essay Concerning Human Understanding, and in Some of His Other Works* (London: Printed for F. Noble, 1742). Molyneux's suggestion was not taken seriously until the twentieth century, after surgical methods had been found to restore the sight of people born blind because of cataract (clouded lens within the eye). See also M. J. Morgan, *Molyneux's Question: Vision, Touch, and the Philosophy of Perception* (Cambridge, England: Cambridge University Press, 1977).

3. J. Locke, and P. H. Nidditch, *An Essay Concerning Human Understanding* (Oxford, England: Clarendon Press, 1975), 389.

4. J. Dewey, *Experience and Education* (New York: Simon & Schuster, 1997).

5. This is described very well in A. R. Damasio, *Descartes' Error: Emotion, Reason, and the Human Brain* (New York: Putnam, 1994).

6. G. M. Edelman, *Neural Darwinism: The Theory of Neuronal Group Selection* (New York: Basic Books, 1987); and O. Sporns and G. Tononi, eds., *Selectionism and the Brain* (San Diego, Calif.: Academic Press, 1994).

7. G. Tononi and G. M. Edelman, "Consciousness and Complexity," *Science,* 282 (1998), 1846–51.

8. G. Ryle, *The Concept of Mind* (New York: Hutchinson, 1949).

CHAPTER THREE

1. D. Foulkes, *Dreaming: A Cognitive-Psychological Analysis* (Hillsdale, N.J.: Lawrence Erlbaum Associates, 1985); and A. Rechtschaffen, "The Singlemindedness and Isolation of Dreams," *Sleep,* 1 (1978), 97-109.

2. W. James, *The Principles of Psychology* (New York: Henry Holt, 1890), 225-26. Note that by thought, James meant consciousness, having decided to use the word *thought* for every form or state of consciousness indiscriminately (see pp. 186, 224).

3. J. D. Holtzman and M. S. Gazzaniga, "Enhanced Dual Task Performance Following Callosal Commissurotomy," *Neuropsychologia,* 23 (1985), 315-21.

4. For references and a discussion, see T. Nørretranders, *The User Illusion: Cutting Consciousness Down to Size* (New York: Viking, 1998). In chapter 10, we present a neural model that perceptually and behaviorally integrates several attributes of a visual scene

and manifests a surprisingly similar capacity limitation, suggesting a possible neural substrate for this aspect of consciousness.

5. H. Pashler, "Dual Task Interference in Simple Tasks: Data and Theory," *Psychological Bulletin*, 116 (1994), 220-44.

6. C. Trevarthen and R. W. Sperry, "Perceptual Unity of the Ambient Visual Field in Human Commissurotomy Patients," *Brain*, 96 (1973), 547-70.

7. J. McFie and O. L. Zangwill, "Visual-Constructive Disabilities Associated with Lesions of the Left Cerebral Hemisphere," *Brain*, 83 (1960), 243-60. A painter with hemineglect painted a self-portrait of just half his face and did not find anything wrong with it. Unawareness of a hole or break in consciousness can extend even to memory. A famous case described by E. Bisiach and C. Luzzatti, in "Unilateral Neglect of Representational Space," *Cortex*, 14 (1978), 129-33, showed that neglect can extend to material in memory and imagination. Two Milanese patients were asked to imagine standing on one end of the Piazza del Duomo in Milan and to describe what they would see. The patients described only the buildings and landmarks on the right-hand side. Later, they were asked to imagine standing on the opposite side of the piazza. This time, they described only the buildings on the other side. In both cases, the patients thought they were giving a reasonably complete reconstruction.

8. In some cases, it appears that such gaps and holes are obliterated by a shrinking and warping of consciousness, but they may actually be partially mended by confabulation (extrapolation) or filling in (interpolation). Confabulation occurs often at the cognitive level and represents an attempt to make sense of what would otherwise be perceived as an unaccountable emptiness or absence in one's existence. For example, a patient with Anton's syndrome may deny his total blindness but, at the same time, confabulate that the room is too dark, that his vision has grown weak, that he is tired, or that his goggles are missing. Filling in is an attempt to preserve the order and coherence of consciousness and obliterate any hole or discontinuity by stretching the fabric around it. It happens even in normal people. Everyone has a blind spot in the visual field of each eye. The blind spot is due to a hole in the retina, a small area called the optic disk where photoreceptors are absent because of the passage of the optic nerve when it emerges from the retina. The blind spot can be demonstrated by placing a small object in that portion of the visual field and closing the other eye; the object will disappear as soon as it enters the blind spot. Despite this unavoidable blindness, we are not aware of any gaping hole in our visual field; visual perception seems remarkably seamless and coherent. In people with neurological conditions, localized lesions of the retina or of the primary visual pathway lead to localized blindness or scotomas that are not different in principle from the physiological blind spot. In most of these cases, the people are unaware of a hole in their vision (they may be aware that their vision is blurred), and in all these cases, filling in phenomena have been demonstrated. Recently, a new technique for inducing transient scotomas has been developed. If a random texture containing a small blank patch is flickered, within a few seconds the patch becomes invisible and is filled in by the random texture; see V. S. Ramachandran, and R. L. Gregory, "Perceptual Filling in of Artificially Induced Scotomas in Human Vision," *Nature*, 350 (1991), 699-702. Using such stimuli, it has been shown that perceptual filling in corresponds to the increasing activity of neurons in the corresponding part of the visual field of the extrastriate area V3 of the monkey (to a lesser extent of neurons in V2 and V1; see P. De Weerd, R. Gattass, R. Desimone, and L. G. Ungerleider, "Responses of Cells in Monkey Visual Cortex During Perceptual Filling-in of an Artificial Scotoma," *Nature*, (1995), 731-34.

9. Whether a conscious state is an intricate visual scene or, as happens in some rare instances, just one simple sensation, such as an all-encompassing sensation of darkness

and silence, the richness of information is not in how many chunks the psychologist (or the person) can use to categorize the situation or in how many chunks the person can remember. It is in how many different internal states can be effectively discriminated. This is the reason why constructing an artifact capable of emulating the discriminatory capacity of a conscious human being is so difficult, while constructing artifacts capable of dealing with more than just four chunks of information is so easy. We discuss this topic in further detail in chapter 13.

10. C. E. Shannon and W. Weaver, *The Mathematical Theory of Communication* (Urbana: University of Illinois Press, 1963); D. S. Jones, *Elementary Information Theory* (Oxford, England: Clarendon Press, 1979).

11. The idea that information is "a difference that makes a difference" can be found in G. Bateson, *Steps to an Ecology of Mind* (New York: Ballantine Books, 1972).

12. G. Sperling, "The Information Available in Brief Visual Presentations" (doctoral diss.), (Washington, D.C.: American Psychological Association, 1960).

13. To simplify matters, let us also consider a discrete conscious state, recognizing that it is just an abstraction, since consciousness is continuous and continually changing. We can, however, approximate a discrete and discriminable conscious state by rapidly closing and reopening our eyes or by the rapid flashing of different stimuli with a tachistoscope.

14. H. Intraub, "Rapid Conceptual Identification of Sequentially Presented Pictures," *Journal of Experimental Psychology: Human Perception & Performance*, 7 (1981), 604-10; cf. I. Biederman, "Perceiving Real-World Scenes," *Science*, 177 (1972), 77-80; I. Biederman, J. C., Rabinowitz, A. L. Glass, and E. W. Stacy, "On the Information Extracted from a Glance at a Scene," *Journal of Experimental Psychology*, 103 (1974), 597-600; I. Biederman, R. J. Mezzanotte, and J. C. Rabinowitz, "Scene Perception: Detecting and Judging Objects Undergoing Relational Violations," *Cognitive Psychology*, 14 (1982), 143-77. Monkeys are also good at such tasks; see, for example, M. Fabre-Thorpe, G. Richard, and S. J. Thorpe, "Rapid Categorization of Natural Images by Rhesus Monkeys," *Neuroreport*, 9 (1998), 303-08.

15. Of course, a 16-bit camera would be able to discriminate among 2^{16} light levels, but in this example, this is beside the point.

16. If there is nobody "reading" the camera display, the camera has no way of "seeing" that there is a vertical column of black pixels or any other configuration of pixels. In other words, configurations are such only insofar as they are integrated as such.

17. C. H. Schenck, S. R. Bundlie, M. G. Ettinger, and M. W. Mahowald, "Chronic Behavioral Disorders of Human REM Sleep: A New Category of Parasomnia," *Sleep*, 9 (1986), 293-308.

18. The first demonstration of such dissociative behavior was given by J. P. Sastre and M. Jouvet, "Oneiric Behavior in Cats," *Physiology and Behavior*, 22 (1979) , 979-89. They found that lesions in a limited region of the pontine tegmentum of cats eliminates the muscle atonia that is characteristic of REM sleep, the stage of sleep in which dreams are most frequent and vivid. When cats with these lesions enter REM sleep, they engage in various instinctive behaviors; they may attack an imaginary prey, freeze in front of imaginary enemies, or approach a nonexistent source of food and start licking it, all while not responding to environmental stimuli— in short, they act out their dreams.

PART TWO

1. A. Schopenhauer, *On the Fourfold Root of the Principle of Sufficient Reason*, trans. E. F. J. Payne (La Salle, Ill.: Open Court, 1974), chap. 4, §21.

CHAPTER FOUR

1. One should keep in mind that in graph-theoretical terms, neuronal groups may be thought as including both cortical and thalamic neurons, since columns of functionally specialized cortical neurons are tightly and reciprocally connected to a dedicated set of neurons in the thalamus.

2. G. M. Edelman and V. B. Mountcastle, *The Mindful Brain: Cortical Organization and the Group-Selective Theory of Higher Brain Function* (Cambridge, Mass.: MIT Press, 1978); G. M. Edelman, *Neural Darwinism: The Theory of Neuronal Group Selection* (New York: Basic Books, 1987).

3. G. Tononi, C. Cirelli, and M. Pompeiano,"Changes in Gene Expression During the Sleep-Waking Cycle: A New View of Activating Systems," *Archives Italiennes de Biologie*, 134 (1995), 21–37.; G. M. Edelman, G. N. J. Reeke, W. E. Gall, G. Tononi, D. Williams, and O. Sporns, "Synthetic Neural Modeling Applied to a Real-World Artifact," *Proceedings of the National Academy of Sciences of the United States of America*, 89 (1992), 7267–71.

4. Edelman, *Neural Darwinism*.

CHAPTER FIVE

1. See, for example, F. H. C. Crick, *The Astonishing Hypothesis: The Scientific Search For the Soul* (New York: Charles Scribner's Sons, 1994); *Experimental and Theoretical Studies of Consciousness, Ciba Foundation Symposium*, 174 (Chichester, England: John Wiley & Sons, 1993); A. J. Marcel and E. Bisiach, eds., *Consciousness in Contemporary Science* (Oxford, England: Clarendon Press, 1988); H. C. Kinney and M. A. Samuels, "Neuropathology of the Persistent Vegetative State: A Review," *Journal of Neuropathology & Experimental Neurology*, 53 (1994), 548–58; M. Kinsbourne, "Integrated Cortical Field Model of Consciousness," *Ciba Foundation Symposium*, 174 (1993), 43–50; C. Koch and J. Braun, "Towards the Neuronal Correlate of Visual Awareness," *Current Opinion in Neurobiology*, 6 (1996), 158–64; M. Velmans, ed., *The Science of Consciousness: Psychological, Neuropsychological and Clinical Reviews* (London, England: Routledge, 1996); W. Penfield, *The Mystery of the Mind: A Critical Study of Consciousness and the Human Brain* (Princeton, N.J.: Princeton University Press, 1975); T. W. Picton and D. T. Stuss, "Neurobiology of Conscious Experience," *Current Opinion in Neurobiology*, 4 (1994), 256–65; M. I. Posner, "Attention: The Mechanisms of Consciousness," *Proceedings of the National Academy of Sciences of the United States of America*, 91 (1994), 7398–403; and L. Weiskrantz, *Consciousness Lost and Found: A Neuropsychological Exploration* (New York: Oxford University Press, 1997).

2. E. P. Vining, J. M. Freeman, D. J. Pillas, S. Uematsu, B. S. Carson, J. Brandt, D. Boatman, M. B. Pulsifer, and A. Zuckerberg, "Why Would You Remove Half a Brain? The Outcome of 58 Children after Hemispherectomy—The Johns Hopkins Experience: 1968 to 1996," *Pediatrics*, 100 (1997), 163–71; and F. Müller, E. Kunesch, F. Binkofski, and H. J. Freund, "Residual Sensorimotor Functions in a Patient after Right-Sided Hemispherectomy," *Neuropsychologia*, 29 (1991), 125–45.

3. A. P. Lonton, *Zeitschrift für Kinderchirurgie*, 45 (1990) Suppl. 1, 18–19.

4. V. B. Mountcastle, "An Organizing Principle for Cerebral Function: The Unit Module and the Distributed System," in *The Mindful Brain: Cortical Organization and the Group-Selective Theory of Higher Brain Function*, eds., G. M. Edelman and V. B. Mountcastle (Cambridge, Mass.: MIT Press, 1978), 7–50; A. R. Damasio, "Time-Locked

Multiregional Retroactivation," *Cognition*, 33 (1989), 25–62; and Picton and Stuss, "Neurobiology of Conscious Experience."

5. R. S. J. Frackowiak, K. J. Friston, C. D. Frith, R. J. Dolan, and J. C. Mazziotta, *Human Brain Function* (San Diego, Calif.: Academic Press, 1997); P. E. Roland, *Brain Activation* (New York: Wiley-Liss, 1993); and M. I. Posner and M. E. Raichle, *Images of Mind* (New York: Scientific American Library, 1994).

6. O. D. Creutzfeldt, "Neurophysiological Mechanisms and Consciousness," *Ciba Foundation Symposium*, 69 (1979), 217–33.

7. G. Moruzzi and H. W. Magoun, "Brain Stem Reticular Formation and Activation of the EEG," *Electroencephalography and Clinical Neurophysiology*, 1 (1949), 455–73.

8. F. Plum,"Coma and Related Global Disturbances of the Human Conscious State," in *Normal and Altered States of Function* (vol. 9), eds. A. Peters and E. G. Jones (New York: Plenum Press, 1991), 359–425.

9. M. Steriade and R. W. McCarley, *Brainstem Control of Wakefulness and Sleep* (New York: Plenum Press, 1990).

10. Plum, "Coma and Related Global Disturbances of the Human Conscious State"; and Kinney and Samuels, "Neuropathology of the Persistent Vegetative State: A Review."

11. See, for example, J. E. Bogen, "On the Neurophysiology of Consciousness: I. An Overview," *Consciousness and Cognition*, 4 (1995), 52–62.

12. It should be pointed out, however, that the reticular system may offer a more specific contribution to conscious experience than merely sustaining the activation of the thalamocortical system. Some evidence (see A. B. Scheibel, "Anatomical and Physiological Substrates of Arousal: A View from the Bridge," in *The Reticular Formation Revisited*, eds. J. A. Hobson and M. A. B. Brazier [New York: Raven Press, 1980], 55–66) indicates that neurons in the upper brainstem (such as those in the cuneiform nucleus of the mesencephalon) are multimodal, responding, in particular, to visual, somatic, and auditory stimuli. Neural maps in the cuneiform nucleus and in the neighboring tectum seem to map the three-dimensional spatial envelope surrounding an organism. The axons from these maps sweep forward on a broad front, investing the reticular thalamic nucleus and other thalamic nuclei in a topographically organized way. Axons from the frontal cortex also reach the same areas of the thalamus. It appears that the interactions between the ascending reticular activating system and the thalamocortical system implement a gate that facilitates thalamocortical interactions related to a particular portion of the organism's spatial envelope and selectively block other portions. It is possible that the activity of reticular structures that map the body and the surrounding space based on multiple sensory and motor modalities, and in conjunction with analogous maps in the thalamus, the parietal cortex, and possibly other brain areas may provide fundamental dimensions to the multimodal scene that constitutes conscious experience.

13. Both increases or decreases in regional brain activity are important. An example is selective attention. In PET studies of visual selective attention, the blood flow (reflecting synaptic activity) in auditory and somatosensory regions decreases while visual regions are activated; see J. V. Haxby, B. Horwitz, L. G. Ungerleider, J. M. Maisog, P. Pietrini, and C. L. Grady, "The Functional Organization of Human Extrastriate Cortex: A PET-rCBF Study of Selective Attention to Faces and Locations," *Journal of Neuroscience*, 14 (1994), 6336–53. In other studies, the same visual activation can occur without the concomitant deactivation of the auditory cortex. This pattern may signal a different cognitive process, perhaps that both visual and auditory domains are being attended; see A. R. McIntosh, "Understanding Neural Interactions in Learning and Memory Using

Functional Neuroimaging," *Annals of the New York Academy of Sciences*, 855 (1998), 556–71; and L. Nyberg, A. R. McIntosh, R. Cabeza, L. G. Nilsson, S. Houle, R. Habib, and E. Tulving, "Network Analysis of Positron Emission Tomography Regional Cerebral Blood Flow Data: Ensemble Inhibition During Episodic Memory Retrieval," *Journal of Neuroscience*, 16 (1996), 3753–59.

14. D. Kahn, E. F. Pace-Schott, and J. A. Hobson, "Consciousness in Waking and Dreaming: The Roles of Neuronal Oscillation and Neuromodulation in Determining Similarities and Differences," *Neuroscience*, 78 (1997), 13–38; and J. A. Hobson, R. Stickgold, and E. F. Pace-Schott, "The Neuropsychology of REM Sleep Dreaming," *Neuroreport*, 9 (1998), R1-R14; but see D. Foulkes, *Dreaming: A Cognitive-Psychological Analysis* (Hillsdale, N.J.: Lawrence Erlbaum Associates, 1985).

15. A. R. Braun, T. J. Balkin, N. J. Wesenten, R. E. Carson, M. Varga, P. Baldwin, S. Selbie, G. Belenky, and P. Herscovitch, "Regional Cerebral Blood Flow Throughout the Sleep-Wake Cycle," *Brain*, 120 (1997), 1173–97; and P. Maquet, C. Degueldre, G. Delfiore, J. Aerts, J. M. Péters, A. Luxen, and G. Franck, "Functional Neuroanatomy of Human Slow Wave Sleep," *Journal of Neuroscience*, 17 (1997), 2807–12. A regional analysis indicated that the brain regions in which neural activity is deeply reduced during slow-wave sleep include paralimbic structures, such as the anterior insula, anterior cingulate cortex, and polar temporal cortex; neocortical regions, such as frontoparietal association areas and centrencephalic structures, such as the reticular activating system, the thalamus, and the basal ganglia. On the other hand, unimodal sensory areas were comparatively not depressed.

16. F. Plum, "Coma and Related Global Disturbances of the Human Conscious State"; and G. B. Young, A. H. Ropper, and C. F. Bolton, *Coma and Impaired Consciousness: A Clinical Perspective* (New York: McGraw-Hill, 1998).

17. W. James, *The Principles of Psychology* (New York: Henry Holt, 1890).

18. H. Maudsley, *The Physiology of Mind: Being the First Part of a 3d Ed., Rev., Enl., and in Great Part Rewritten*, of "The Physiology and Pathology of Mind" (London: Macmillan, 1876). In psychology, the distinction between conscious control of action and its automatic performance has been conceptualized in several different ways. M. I. Posner and C. R. R. Snyder ("Attention and Cognitive Control," in *Information Processing and Cognition, the Loyola Symposium*, ed. R. L. Solso [Hillsdale, N.J.: Lawrence Erlbaum Associates, 1975], 55–85) proposed three criteria for a process to be purely automatic: if it occurs without giving rise to conscious awareness, without intention, and without interfering with other ongoing mental activity. Schneider and Shiffrin (W. Schneider and R. M. Shiffrin, "Controlled and Automatic Human Information Processing: I. Detection, Search, and Attention," *Psychological Review*, 84 [1977], 1–66; and R. M. Shiffrin and W. Schneider, "Controlled and Automatic Human Information Processing: II. Perceptual Learning, Automatic Attending, and a General Theory," *Psychological Review*, 84 [1977], 127–90) argued for a theoretical distinction between automatic and controlled processing, where the first is of limited capacity, requires attention, and can be used flexibly in changing circumstances, while the latter has no capacity limitations, does not require attention, and is difficult to modify after it has been learned. D. A. Norman and T. Shallice, "Attention to Action: Willed and Automatic Control of Behavior," in *Consciousness and Self-Regulation*, (vol. 4), eds. R. J. Davidson, G. E. Schwartz, and D. Shapiro, (New York: Plenum, 1986), 1–18, distinguished between fully automatic processing controlled by action schemas (organized plans); partially automatic processing involving contention scheduling among conflicting schemas; and deliberate control by a supervisory attentional system, involved in decision making, troubleshooting, and flexible

responding in novel situations. G. D. Logan ("Toward an Instance Theory of Automatization," *Psychological Review*, 95 [1988], 492–527) argued that automatic performance should be differentiated not on the basis of the absence of attentional involvement or of resource limitations, but of access to memory. In his view, performance is automatic when it is based on the "single-step direct-access retrieval of past solutions from memory." This feature is well illustrated by children learning simple arithmetic: Initially children add single-digit numbers by counting, a slow and laborious process. With practice, they learn by rote the sums of all pairs of single digits and rely on memory retrieval, rather than counting.

19. The presumed limited capacity of consciousness is discussed in chapters 10 and 12.

20. The impressive capabilities of automatic, unconscious processes in terms of speed and accuracy should not obscure some features that make conscious control of vital importance. Whereas conscious control is flexible, receptive to novelty, and context-sensitive, automatic performance is rigid, impervious to novelty, and context-insensitive. Most important, conscious control is necessary to learn new tasks whenever a large amount of information needs to be integrated to select what the appropriate inputs and outputs should be. Only when an economical mapping from inputs to outputs can be discovered, that is, when the information required is much more restricted, does automatic performance set in. In fact, it has been shown that automaticity is acquired only in consistent task environments, as when the same stimuli are mapped consistently onto the same responses throughout practice; conscious control remains necessary when such mapping varies from task to task; see Schneider and Shiffrin, "Controlled and Automatic Human Information Processing: I."; and Shiffrin and Schneider, "Controlled and Automatic Human Information Processing: II." At times, automatisms can even become counterproductive. A well-studied example in the laboratory is the Stroop effect: Naming the color of the ink that a disparate color word is printed in produces a hesitation and slows reaction times considerably (see J. R. Stroop, "Studies of Interference in Serial Verbal Reactions," *Journal of Experimental Psychology*, 18 [1935], 643–62). Another example may be semantic blindness (D. G. MacKay and M. D. Miller, "Semantic Blindness: Repeated Concepts Are Difficult to Encode and Recall Under Time Pressure," *Psychological Science*, 5 [1994], 52–55). A more familiar example is an action slip, the performance of an action that was not intended or inappropriate, such as using one's key instead of ringing the doorbell when visiting, jingling coins in one's pocket; kneading breadcrumbs; fiddling with one's clothes, adjusting one's hair, and fingering one's chin. Sigmund Freud listed many such action slips, or parapraxias, and attempted to analyze their unconscious motives. More recently, action slips have been investigated by means of diary studies that have distinguished among many different categories. For example, J. T. Reason and K. Mycielska (*Absent-minded? The Psychology of Mental Lapses and Everyday Errors* [Englewood Cliffs, N.J.: Prentice-Hall, 1982], 73) gave the following typical one: "I sat down to do some work and before starting to write I put my hand up to my face to take my glasses off, but my fingers snapped together rather abruptly because I hadn't being wearing them in the first place." Whatever their categories, motives, or degree of unconsciousness, all action slips involve highly practiced activities.

21. James, *The Principles of Psychology*, 114.

22. Ibid., 112–13.

23. Durup and Fessard (1935), cited in E. R. John, *Mechanisms of Memory* (New York: Academic Press, 1967). The electrocorticogram is the electrical activity recorded at the surface of the brain. It is similar to but more accurate than the EEG, which is recorded at the scalp.

24. E. R. John and K. F. Killam, "Electrophysiological Correlates of Avoidance Conditioning in the Cat," *Journal of Pharmacological and Experimental Therapeutics*, 125 (1959), 252. A more recent article (I. N. Pigarev, H. C. Nothdurft, and S. Kastner, *Neuroreport*, 8 [1997], 2557–60) provided a surprising indication that behavior may continue in an automatic way in the (presumed) absence of conscious experience. Young monkeys were trained to signal, by pressing one of two pedals, whether a simple stimulus, such as a single vertical line, was present in a display containing many oriented lines that was shown 0.5–1.5 seconds afterward. It was noticed that the monkeys often continued to respond appropriately even if they showed clear signs of drowsiness and of falling asleep. What was most interesting was that neurons in the visual area V4 stopped responding to their preferred stimuli during the periods of sleep. Thus, a portion of the cerebral cortex may "fall asleep" while another, presumably V1, is performing behavioral discriminations that have become automatic. Neural activity in both areas may still be going on yet not contribute to conscious experience.

25. R. J. Haier, B. V. Siegel, Jr., A. MacLachlan, E. Soderling, S. Lottenberg, and M. S. Buchsbaum, "Regional Glucose Metabolic Changes after Learning a Complex Visuospatial/Motor Task: A Positron Emission Tomographic Study," *Brain Research*, 570 (1992), 134–43. Unfortunately, the amount of hand movement was not controlled in this study.

26. S. E. Petersen, H. vanMier, J. A. Fiez, and M. E. Raichle, "The Effects of Practice on the Functional Anatomy of Task Performance," *Proceedings of the National Academy of Sciences of the United States of America*, 95 (1998), 853–60.

27. Changes in the opposite direction were seen in a few cortical areas.

28. With continuing practice, however, the extent of motor cortex activated by the practiced sequence enlarged compared with the unpracticed sequence; see A. Karni, G. Meyer, P. Jezzard, M. M. Adams, R. Turner, and L. G. Ungerleider, "Functional MRI Evidence for Adult Motor Cortex Plasticity During Motor Skill Learning," *Nature*, 377 (1995), 155–58, possibly because of the local recruitment of additional cells. Whether the initial decrease reflects a localized "habituation" or priming effect (cf. R. L. Buckner, S. E. Petersen, J. G. Ojemann, F. M. Miezin, L. R. Squire, and M. E. Raichle, "Functional Anatomical Studies of Explicit and Implicit Memory Retrieval Tasks," *Journal of Neuroscience*, 15 (1995), 12–29; and repetition suppression, described by R. Desimone, "Neural Mechanisms for Visual Memory and Their Role in Attention," *Proceedings of the National Academy of Sciences of the United States of America*, 93 [1996], 13494–99), or a decreased input from the rest of the brain, was not determined because of the limited sampling.

CHAPTER SIX

1. The subject of disconnection syndromes goes back to the nineteenth century. The first to consider seriously the clinical effects of disconnection was Karl Wernicke, who predicted conduction aphasia, a syndrome that would result from the disconnection of the anterior and posterior areas of speech. Joseph Dejerine was the first to show actual behavioral abnormalities following a lesion of the corpus callosum. Around 1900, Hugo Liepmann published a series of papers in which he demonstrated the clinical impact of damage to connections among brain areas. On the basis of the careful study of a single subject, he predicted several disconnections in his patient's cortex. He then published the postmortem neuropathological findings in that case and argued that his hypotheses were confirmed. In recent times, disconnection syndromes have been carefully analyzed and tested experimentally by R. W. Sperry ("Lateral Specialization in the Surgically

Separated Hemispheres," in *Neurosciences: Third Study Program*, eds. F. O. Schmitt and F. G. Worden, [Cambridge, Mass.: MIT Press, 1974]); N. Geschwind ("Disconnexion Syndromes in Animals and Man," *Brain*, 88 [1965], 237–84,585–644); and M. Mishkin ("Analogous Neural Models for Tactual and Visual Learning," *Neuropsychologia*, 17 [1979], 139–51). In a striking demonstration, R. K. Nakamura and M. Mishkin ("Chronic 'Blindness' Following Lesions of Nonvisual Cortex in the Monkey," *Experimental Brain Research*, 63 [1986], 173–84) showed that chronic "blindness" can be produced in monkeys by a large cortical disconnection that spares the visual cortices. After complete disconnection of the two hemispheres, a large ablation of the left hemisphere that spared the visual striate, prestriate, and inferior temporal cortex eliminated visual behavior. However, single-unit activity recorded from the striate cortex of these blind monkeys was similar to that of the normal monkeys; see R. K. Nakamura, S. J. Schein, and R. Desimone, "Visual Responses from Cells in Striate Cortex of Monkeys Rendered Chronically 'Blind' by Lesions of Nonvisual Cortex," *Experimental Brain Research*, 63 (1986), 185–90. The chronic blindness is therefore probably due not to dysfunction within the striate cortex but to a disconnection from critical processing stages within the ablated territory; see below.

2. Under strict laboratory conditions, however, it was soon confirmed that the two hemispheres, if tested separately, show different specializations. For instance, the left brain is dominant for language, speech, and major problem solving and has an uncanny tendency to interpret behavior and make up stories; see M. S. Gazzaniga, "Principles of Human Brain Organization Derived from Split-Brain Studies," *Neuron*, 14 (1995), 217–28. The right hemisphere usually has some advantage in visuospatial tasks, such as drawing, the recognition of upright faces, and attentional monitoring.

3. R. W. Sperry, "Brain Bisection and Consciousness," in *Brain and Conscious Experience*, ed. J. C. Eccles (New York: Springer Verlag, 1966), 299.

4. P. G. Gasquoine, "Alien Hand Sign," *Journal of Clinical and Experimental Neuropsychology*, 15 (1993), 653–67; D. H. Geschwind, M. Iacoboni, M. S. Mega, D. W. Zaidel, T. Cloughesy, and E. Zaidel, "Alien Hand Syndrome: Interhemispheric Motor Disconnection Due to a Lesion in the Midbody of the Corpus Callosum," *Neurology*, 45 (1995), 802–08. In reviewing the split-brain literature, some investigators, notably M. S. Gazzaniga (*The Social Brain: Discovering the Networks of the Mind* [New York: Basic Books, 1985]) concluded that only the left hemisphere is conscious, containing an "interpreter" that constantly tries to make sense of the outputs of various nonconscious modules and weaves them together into a coherent, rationalized narrative. However, regardless of what one makes of the interpreter construct, this criterion for consciousness seems to be too strictly biased toward verbal report and may exclude, for instance, animals from consciousness. The distinction between primary and higher-order consciousness seems to be particularly appropriate here. Some implicit-explicit dissociations, such as amnesia, may also be due to a partial disconnection of a lesioned area from the more global pattern of neural activity that is associated with consciousness; see D. L. Schacter, "Implicit Knowledge: New Perspectives on Unconscious Processes," *Proceedings of the National Academy of Sciences of the United States of America*, 89 (1992), 11113–17.

5. W. D. TenHouten, D. O. Walter, K. D. Hoppe, and J. E. Bogen, "Alexithymia and the Split Brain: V. EEG Alpha-Band Interhemispheric Coherence Analysis," *Psychotherapy and Psychosomatics*, 47 (1987), 1–10; T. Nielsen, J. Montplaisir, and M. Lassonde, "Decreased Interhemispheric EEG Coherence During Sleep in Agenesis of the Corpus Callosum," *European Neurology*, 33 (1993), 173–76; J. Montplaisir, T. Nielsen, J. Côté, D. Boivin, Rouleau, and G. Lapierre, "Interhemispheric EEG

Coherence Before and After Partial Callosotomy," *Clinical Electroencephalography*, 21 (1990), 42–47; and M. Knyazeva, T. Koeda, C. Njiokiktjien, E. J. Jonkman, M. Kurganskaya, L. de Sonneville, and V. Vildavsky, "EEG Coherence Changes During Finger Tapping in Acallosal and Normal Children: A Study of Inter- and Intrahemispheric Connectivity," *Behavioural Brain Research*, 89 (1997), 243–58.

6. W. Singer, "Bilateral EEG Synchronization and Interhemispheric Transfer of Somato-Sensory and Visual Evoked Potentials in Chronic and Acute Split-Brain Preparations of Cat," *Electroencephalography and Clinical Neurophysiology*, 26 (1969), 434; and A. K. Engel, P. Konig, A. K. Kreiter, and W. Singer, "Interhemispheric Synchronization of Oscillatory Neuronal Responses in Cat Visual Cortex," *Science*, 252 (1991), 1177–79.

7. P. Janet, *L'automatisme psychologique; essai de psychologie expérimentale sur les formes inférieures de l'activité humaine* (Paris: F. Alcan, 1930).

8. S. Freud, J. Strachey, and A. Freud, *The Psychopathology of Everyday Life* (London: Benn, 1966).

9. E. R. Hilgard, *Divided Consciousness: Multiple Controls in Human Thought and Action* (New York: John Wiley & Sons, 1986).

10. *Diagnostic and Statistical Manual of Mental Disorders: Fourth Edition* (Washington, D.C.: American Psychiatric Association, 1994), 477.

11. A confusion about pathogenetic mechanisms is probably responsible for the separate listing of hysterical paralysis and anesthesia as conversion disorders under the heading of somatoform disorders; see J. Nehmiah, "Dissociation, Conversion, and Somatization," in *American Psychiatric Press Review of Psychiatry*, Vol. 10, eds. A. Tasman and S. M. Goldfinger (Washington, D.C.: American Psychiatric Press, 1991), 248–260.; and J. F. Kihlstrom, "The Rediscovery of the Unconscious," in *The Mind, the Brain, and Complex Adaptive Systems: Santa Fe Institute Studies in the Sciences of Complexity*, Vol. 22, ed. J. L. S. Harold Morowitz, (Reading, MA: Addison-Wesley, 1994), 123–43. These mechanisms are rightly classified as dissociative sensory and motor disorders according to the international classification of diseases (ICD10). In fact, differences between dissociative motor and sensory symptoms and dissociative splitting of the self and autobiographical memory are likely to be differences in level, the former reflecting disorders of primary consciousness and the latter of higher-order consciousness, rather than differences in pathogenetic mechanisms.

12. G. Tononi and G. M. Edelman, "Schizophrenia and the Mechanisms of Conscious Integration," *Brain Research Reviews*, in press.

13. A. J. Marcel, "Conscious and Unconscious Perception: An Approach to the Relations Between Phenomenal Experience and Perceptual Processes," *Cognitive Psychology*, 15 (1983), 238–300; A. J. Marcel, "Conscious and Unconscious Perception: Experiments on Visual Masking and Word Recognition," *Cognitive Psychology*, 15 (1983), 197–237; and P. M. Merikle, "Perception Without Awareness: Critical Issues," *American Psychologist*, 47 (1992), 792–95.

14. V. O. Packard, *The Hidden Persuaders* (New York: D. McKay, 1957).

15. N. F. Dixon, *Subliminal Perception: The Nature of a Controversy* (New York: McGraw-Hill, 1971); N. F. Dixon, *Preconscious Processing* (New York: John Wiley & Sons, 1981); Marcel, "Conscious and Unconscious Perception: An Approach to the Relations Between Phenomenal Experience and Perceptual Processes"; Marcel, "Conscious and Unconscious Perception: Experiments on Visual Masking and Word Recognition"; J. M. Cheesman and P. M. Merikle, "Priming with and without Awareness," *Perception & Psychophysics*, 36 (1984), 387–95; and J. M. Cheesman,

"Distinguishing Conscious from Unconscious Perceptual Processes," *Canadian Journal of Psychology*, 40 (1986), 343–67.

16. The distinction between an objective and a subjective threshold was first made in this context; see Cheesman and Merikle, "Priming with and without Awareness"; and Cheesman, "Distinguishing Conscious from Unconscious Perceptual Processes." As we mentioned earlier, the objective threshold is a level of stimulus presentation above which forced-choice testing produces responses above chance that indicate detection, while the subjective threshold is a level of stimulus presentation above which the subject reports conscious perception.

17. In some cases, perception without awareness has been shown to occur with stimuli that are neither short lasting nor weak. For instance, a form of "functional blindsight" in normal subjects was reported by F. C. Kolb and J. Braun, "Blindsight in Normal Observers," *Nature*, 377 (1995), 336–38. A textural contrast, such as a patch of vertical bars in a field of horizontal bars, is presented for a fraction of a second to one eye, while the complementary picture is presented to the other eye. Observers report that they do not consciously experience the textural contrast, as judged by either subjective or objective measures, but if they are forced to guess, they can reliably detect and locate the contrasting patch. In another experiment, high-contrast gratings that were so finely spaced that they were perceived not as gratings but as uniformly gray could nevertheless change the viewer's ability to detect less finely spaced, readily visible gratings; see S. He, H. S. Smallman, and D. I. A. MacLeod, "Neural and Cortical Limits on Visual Resolution," *Investigative Ophthalmology & Visual Science*, 36 (1995), S438. An observer can also habituate to the orientation of a patch of bars without perceiving them if they are surrounded by adjacent patches of bars (an effect called perceptual "crowding"); see S. He, P. Cavanagh, and J. Intriligator, "Attentional resolution and the Locus of Visual Awareness," *Nature*, 383 (1996), 334–37. Since it is likely that the primary visual cortex is involved in these effects, some have suggested that neural activity in the primary visual cortex may not contribute to consciousness; see, for example, F. Crick and C. Koch, "Are We Aware of Neural Activity in Primary Visual Cortex?" *Nature*, 375 (1995), 121–23. It should be said that at present, we have no idea about the pattern of firing and the intracortical connections of the neurons responsible for any of these effects.

18. B. Libet, D. K. Pearl, D. E. Morledge, C. A. Gleason, Y. Hosobuchi, and N. M. Barbaro, "Control of the Transition from Sensory Detection to Sensory Awareness in Man by the Duration of a Thalamic Stimulus: The Cerebral 'Time-On' Factor," *Brain*, 114 (1991), 1731–57.

19. L. Cauller, "Layer I of Primary Sensory Neocortex: Where Top-down Converges upon Bottom-up," *Behavioural Brain Research*, 71 (1995), 163–70.

20. B. Libet, C. A. Gleason, E. W. Wright, and D. K. Pearl, "Time of Conscious Intention to Act in Relation to Onset of Cerebral Activity (Readiness-Potential: The Unconscious Initiation of a Freely Voluntary Act," *Brain*, 106 (1983), 623–42.

21. A. Baddeley, "The Fractionation of Working Memory," *Proceedings of the National Academy of Sciences of the United States of America*, 93 (1996), 13468–72.

22. J. M. Fuster, R. H. Bauer, and J. P. Jervey, "Functional Interactions Between Inferotemporal and Prefrontal Cortex in a Cognitive Task," *Brain Research*, 330 (1985), 299–307; and P. S. Goldman-Rakic, and M. Chafee, "Feedback Processing in Prefronto-Parietal Circuits During Memory-Guided Saccades," *Society for Neuroscience Abstracts*, 20 (1994), 808.

23. The idea that neural activity must persist for a minimum period to contribute to conscious experience is also suggested by the phenomenon of masking. See V. Menon, W. J. Freeman, B. A. Cutillo, J. E. Desmond, M. F. Ward, S. L. Bressler, K. D. Laxer, N. Barbaro, and A. S. Gevins, "Spatio-Temporal Correlations in Human Gamma Band Electrocorticograms," *Electroencephalography & Clinical Neurophysiology*, 98 (1996), 89–102; and K. J. Meador, P. G. Ray, L. Day, H. Ghelani, and D. W. Loring, "Physiology of Somatosensory Perception: Cerebral Lateralization and Extinction," *Neurology*, 51 (1998), 721–27.

24. S. L. Bressler, "Interareal Synchronization in the Visual Cortex," *Brain Research—Brain Research Reviews*, 20 (1995), 288–304; W. Singer and C. M. Gray, "Visual Feature Integration and the Temporal Correlation Hypothesis," *Annual Review of Neuroscience*, 18 (1995), 555–86.; M. Joliot, U. Ribary, and R. Llinas, "Human Oscillatory Brain Activity Near 40 Hz Coexists with Cognitive Temporal Binding," *Proceedings of the National Academy of Sciences of the United States of America*, 91 (1994), 11748–51; and A. Gevins, M. E. Smith, J. Le, H. Leong, J. Bennett, N. Martin, L. McEvoy, R. Du, and S. Whitfield, "High Resolution Evoked Potential Imaging of the Cortical Dynamics of Human Working Memory," *Electroencephalography & Clinical Neurophysiology*, 98 (1996), 327–48.

25. R. Srinivasan, D. P. Russell, G. M. Edelman, and G. J. Tononi, "Increased Synchronization of Magnetic Responses During Conscious Perception," *Neuroscience*, 19 (1999), 5435–4.

26. In a recent study, electrical brain activity was recorded from human subjects who were viewing ambiguous visual stimuli that were perceived either as faces or as meaningless shapes. Only when the subjects perceived a face, was there a long-distance pattern of synchronization, corresponding to the moment of perception itself and to the ensuing motor response. A period of desynchronization marked the transition between the moment of perception and the motor response. Just as the long-range synchronization may reflect the integration of distributed populations of neurons that underlie a unified conscious state, the brief desynchronization may reflect their uncoupling, which is necessary to select another unified state. See E. Rodriguez, N. George, J. P. Lachaux, J. Martinerie, B. Renault, and F. J. Varela, "Perception's Shadow: Long-Distance Synchronization of Human Brain Activity," *Nature*, 397 (1999), 430–33. In another recent imaging study , human subjects could be divided on the basis of whether they were aware that one tone predicted a visual event and another did not. Only aware subjects acquired a differential behavioral response to the tones. The results of PET scans indicated that the correlations among the activities of several brain regions functionally connected to the left prefrontal cortex (for example, the occipital and temporal regions) showed a strong increase at the time when awareness likely emerged. The authors concluded that awareness occurs through the integration of distributed regions. See A. R. McIntosh, M. N. Rajah, and N. J. Lobaugh, "Interactions of Prefrontal Cortex in Relation to Awareness in Sensory Learning," *Science*, 284 (1999), 1531–33.

27. It should be noted that verbal reports can also be elicited at awakenings from slow-wave sleep, although with less frequency and different characteristics than after REM sleep. Dream fragments are typically much shorter and much less vivid. It appears, however, that awakening from the deepest phases of slow-wave sleep rarely leads to any report. See D. Kahn, E. F. Pace-Schott, and J. A. Hobson, "Consciousness in Waking and Dreaming: The Roles of Neuronal Oscillation and Neuromodulation in Determining Similarities and Differences," *Neuroscience*, 78 (1997), 13–38; and J. A. Hobson, R. Stickgold, and E. F. Pace-Schott, "The Neuropsychology of REM Sleep Dreaming,"

Neuroreport, 9 (1998), R1-R14; but cf. D. Foulkes, "Dream Research," *Sleep*, 19 (1996), 609–24.

28. cf. M. S. Livingstone and D. H. Hubel, "Effects of Sleep and Arousal on the Processing of Visual Information in the Cat," *Nature*, 291 (1981), 554–61.

29. A familiar example of dissociation midway between the physiological and the pathological is sleepwalking. Sleepwalkers are clearly able to engage in various motor routines, but they are deeply asleep. If they are awakened, which typically is not easy, they act confused and do not report dreams. Sleepwalking occurs in the deep phases of slow-wave sleep, not in the dream-rich REM sleep.

30. M. Steriade, D. A. McCormick, and T. J. Sejnowski, "Thalamocortical Oscillations in the Sleeping and Aroused Brain," *Science*, 262 (1993), 679–85; and M. Steriade and J. Hobson, "Neuronal Activity During the Sleep-Waking Cycle," *Progress in Neurobiology*, 6 (1976), 155–376.

31. Another example is general anesthesia. Unconsciousness that is produced by many volatile anesthetics is associated with slow-waves in the EEG that are similar to those seen during NREM sleep and that indicate the hypersynchronous activity of distributed populations of neurons.

32. Short-lasting visual stimuli become invisible if the transient neuronal responses associated with their onset and offset are suppressed by masking stimuli; see S. L. Macknik and M. S. Livingstone, "Neuronal Correlates of Visibility and Invisibility in the Primate Visual System," *Nature Neuroscience*, 1 (1998), 144–9. Attentional modulation also works by increasing the contrast between certain foci of increased neural activity and others of decreased neural activity; see J. H. Maunsell, "The Brain's Visual World: Representation of Visual Targets in Cerebral Cortex," *Science*, 270 (1995), 764–69; and K. J. Friston, "Imaging Neuroscience: Principles or Maps?" *Proceedings of the National Academy of Sciences of the United States of America*, 95 (1998), 796–802. These considerations also suggest that, everything else being equal, neuronal groups that are more capable of differentiating among a large number of possibilities are more likely to contribute to conscious experience. On a neuron-by-neuron basis, the firing of neurons at later stages in the visual system, such as those in area IT, is more informative than that of neurons at earlier stages, such as the retina, lateral geniculate nucleus, or V1, in the sense that the firing of an IT neuron is highly unlikely a priori, while the firing of a retinal neuron is highly likely. Specifically, the firing of a face-sensitive neuron in IT considerably reduces uncertainty about the nature of a visual scene (a face is seen, rather than countless other visual scenes), while the firing of a retinal neuron reduces uncertainty to a lesser degree (any of countless visual scenes could be seen that contain a bright spot in a certain position of the visual field). The results of studies of binocular rivalry in monkeys are consistent with this view; see D. A. Leopold and N. K. Logothetis, "Activity Changes in Early Visual Cortex Reflect Monkeys' Percepts During Binocular Rivalry," *Nature*, 379 (1996), 549–53; and D. L. Shenberg and N. K. Logothetis, "The Role of Temporal Cortical Areas in Perceptual Organization," *Proceedings of the National Academy of Sciences of the United States of America*, 94 (1997), 3408–13. In visual areas, such as V1, V4, and MT, only some 18 percent to 25 percent of the recorded neurons increased their firing rate when their preferred stimulus was perceived. By contrast, almost all recorded neurons in IT responded when their preferred stimulus was perceptually dominant. Also consistent with this view is the fact that attentional effects are stronger and easier to demonstrate in higher areas. Correspondingly, it has often been remarked that a conscious scene, whether a visual scene or a sentence, captures the gist of a situation with a broad brush in the service of action and planning and is typically unencumbered by local

details; see, for example, R. Jackendoff, *Consciousness and the Computational Mind* (Cambridge, Mass.: MIT Press, 1987). Does this mean that neurons whose firing corresponds to more invariant aspects of the world are more likely to contribute to conscious perception?

CHAPTER SEVEN

1. Quoted in M. J. Kottler, "Charles Darwin and Alfred Russel Wallace: Two Decades of Debate over Natural Selection," in *The Darwinian Heritage*, ed. D. Kohn (Princeton, N.J.: Princeton University Press, 1985), 420.

2. F. M. Burnet, *The Clonal Selection Theory of Acquired Immunity* (Nashville, Tenn.: Vanderbilt University Press, 1959); G. M. Edelman, "Origins and Mechanisms of Specificity in Clonal Selection," in *Cellular Selection and Regulation in the Immune Response*, ed. G. M. Edelman (New York: Raven Press, 1974), 1–37.

3. G. M. Edelman and V. B. Mountcastle, *The Mindful Brain: Cortical Organization and the Group-Selective Theory of Higher Brain Function* (Cambridge, Mass.: MIT Press, 1978); G. M. Edelman, *Neural Darwinism: The Theory of Neuronal Group Selection* (New York: Basic Books, 1987); O. Sporns and G. Tononi, eds., *Selectionism and the Brain* (San Diego, Calif.: Academic Press, 1994).

4. G. Tononi, "Reentry and the Problem of Cortical Integration," *International Review of Neurobiology*, 37 (1994), 127–52.

5. See, for example, G. Tononi, O. Sporns, and G. M. Edelman, "Reentry and the Problem of Integrating Multiple Cortical Areas: Simulation of Dynamic Integration in the Visual System," *Cerebral Cortex*, 2 (1992), 310–35; and S. Zeki, *A Vision of the Brain* (Boston: Blackwell Scientific Publications, 1993).

6. L. H. Finkel and G. M. Edelman, "Integration of Distributed Cortical Systems by Reentry: A Computer Simulation of Interactive Functionally Segregated Visual Areas," *Journal of Neuroscience*, 9 (1989), 3188–208.

7. Edelman and Mountcastle, *The Mindful Brain*; Edelman, *Neural Darwinism*; G. Tononi, O. Sporns, and G. M. Edelman, "Measures of Degeneracy and Redundancy in Biological Networks," *Proceedings of the National Academy of Sciences of the United States of America*, 96 (1999), 3257–62.

8. G. Tononi, C. Cirelli, and M. Pompeiano, "Changes in Gene Expression During the Sleep-Waking Cycle: A New View of Activating Systems," *Archives Italiennes de Biologie*, 134 (1995), 21–37.

9. C. Cirelli, M. Pompeiano, and G. Tononi, "Neuronal Gene Expression in the Waking State: A Role for the Locus Coeruleus," *Science*, 274 (1996), 1211–15.

10. G. M. Edelman, G. N. J. Reeke, W. E. Gall, G. Tononi, D. Williams, and O. Sporns, "Synthetic Neural Modeling Applied to a Real-World Artifact," *Proceedings of the National Academy of Sciences of the United States of America*, 89 (1992), 7267–71; and N. Almássy, G. M. Edelman, and O. Sporns, "Behavioral Constraints in the Development of Neuronal Properties: A Cortical Model Embedded in a Real-World Device," *Cerebral Cortex*, 8 (1998), 346–61.

11. K. J. Friston, G. Tononi, G. N. J. Reeke, O. Sporns, and G. M. Edelman, "Value-Dependent Selection in the Brain: Simulation in a Synthetic Neural Model," *Neuroscience*, 59 (1994), 229–43.

12. M. Rucci, G. Tononi, and G. M. Edelman, "Registration of Neural Maps Through Value-Dependent Learning: Modeling the Alignment of Auditory and Visual Maps in the Barn Owl's Optic Tectum," *Journal of Neuroscience*, 17 (1997), 334–52.

13. A. R. Damasio, *Descartes' Error: Emotion, Reason, and the Human Brain* (New York: G. P. Putnam's Sons, 1994).

CHAPTER EIGHT

1. G. M. Edelman, *Neural Darwinism: The Theory of Neuronal Group Selection* (New York: Basic Books, 1987).

2. It may be argued that even in a selectional system, the entire set of all the responses that give a repeated performance can be considered to be a representation. To accept this possibility, however, would tend to weaken the notion of selection, which is a dynamic one. Selection is ex post facto; no code or symbol stands for a given memory, and different structures and dynamics can give rise to the same memory. Above all, the set of responses and the structures underlying memory change continually over time. It seems senseless to conflate such dynamic properties of the brain with those that we know are characteristic of symbolic representational systems—whether language or a computer code—systems that we have consciously constructed for human communication and for cultural purposes.

CHAPTER NINE

1. G. M. Edelman, *Neural Darwinism: The Theory of Neuronal Group Selection* (New York: Basic Books, 1987); and G. M. Edelman, *The Remembered Present: A Biological Theory of Consciousness* (New York: Basic Books, 1989).

CHAPTER TEN

1. O. Sporns, G. Tononi, and G. M. Edelman, "Modeling Perceptual Grouping and Figure-Ground Segregation by Means of Active Reentrant Connections," *Proceedings of the National Academy of Sciences of the United States of America*, 88 (1991), 129–33; G. Tononi, O. Sporns, and G. M. Edelman, "Reentry and the Program of Integrating Multiple Cortical Areas: Simulation of Dynamic Integration in the Visual System," *Cerebral Cortex*, 2 (1992), 310–35; E. D. Lumer, G. M. Edelman, and G. Tononi, "Neural Dynamics in a Model of the Thalamacortical System, 1: Layers, Loops, and the Emergence of Fast Synchronous Rhythms," *Cerebral Cortex*, 7 (1997), 207–27; and E. D. Lumer, G. M. Edelman, and G. Tononi, "Neural Dynamics in a Model of the Thalamo-cortical System, 2: The Role of Neural Synchrony Tested Through Perturbations of Spike Timing," *Cerebral Cortex*, 7 (1997), 228–36.

2. Tononi, Sporns, and Edelman, "Reentry and the Program of Integrating Multiple Cortical Areas."

3. Given the complexity of the model, the reader is referred to the original publication for a detailed description of how anatomical and physiological properties of the visual system were simulated; see ibid.

4. For example, they were observed between the primary visual area, V1, which was topographically organized and responded to detailed features of the objects, and less topographically organized regions, such as area IT, which responded to invariant properties of the objects.

5. A. Treisman and H. Schmidt, "Illusory Conjunctions in the Perception of Objects," *Cognitive Psychology*, 14 (1982), 107–41.

6. Other simulations with this model provided evidence that the process of reentry is able rapidly to distribute signals from different neuronal groups to the rest of the system in a global way, to make the responses of any neuronal group in the model highly context-dependent, and to provide global access to many different outputs. This model system

could also flexibly accommodate new combinations of features it never encountered before without requiring the deployment of new committed neural units. These aspects of the model's performance are of particular importance in the present context because they are directly relevant to the explanation of properties of conscious experience, such as context-sensitivity, access, and flexibility of association; see G. Tononi and G. M. Edelman, "Consciousness and the Integration of Information in the Brain," in *Consciousness*, eds. H. H. Jasper, L. Descarries, V. F. Castellucci, and S. Rossignol (New York: Plenum Press, 1998).

7. In view of the extreme complexity of the brain, it is almost impossible, without the aid of detailed simulations, to envision how the interplay between corticocortical loops and thalamocortical loops may take place and to imagine the dynamic consequences of the peculiar structural organization of the thalamocortical system in terms of realistic cellular and synaptic properties. To overcome this barrier, we have recently constructed a large-scale model that embodies the minimum features necessary for operation of the basic thalamocortical circuitry; see Lumer, Edelman, and Tononi, "Neural Dynamics in a Model of the Thalamacortical System, 1"; and Lumer, Edelman, and Tononi, "Neural Dynamics in a Model of the Thalamacortical System, 2, *Cerebral Cortex*, 7 (1997), 207–36." The model includes more than 65,000 spiking neurons with over five million connections. A full description of the model and of the results obtained cannot be presented here, and interested readers are referred to the original publications; we provide here only a short summary for experts. The brain regions modeled consisted of in-register sectors in a primary and a secondary area of the visual cortex (Vp and Vs), two corresponding regions of the dorsal thalamus (Tp and Ts), and two regions of the reticular thalamic nucleus (Rp and Rs). Individual neurons, both excitatory and inhibitory, were modeled as single-compartment integrate-and-fire units using cellular constants from regular-spiking and fast-spiking neurons, respectively. Synaptic interactions occurred through simulated channels that provided voltage-dependent (NMDA-like) and voltage-independent (AMPA-like) excitation, as well as fast (GABA$_A$-like) and slow (GABA$_B$-like) inhibition. All connections were endowed with conduction delays. In addition, units were endowed with a background level of irregular, spontaneous activity through balanced Poissonian excitation and inhibition.

8. In a standard experiment, the model was presented for 250 milliseconds with a simulated stimulus consisting of two superimposed gratings, one vertical and one horizontal, moving in perpendicular directions. Records of the membrane potential for all units in the model showed a clear-cut, spatiotemporal pattern of both subthreshold and action potentials that was shared by a large number of units. This quasi-stable activity pattern revealed a considerable degree of synchronous firing as well as oscillatory behavior. High-frequency synchronous oscillations occurred at every level of the model, as indicated by a measure of global synchrony. However, there were also many units in the model that, though active, did not participate in such globally synchronous firing. The ensemble of synchronously firing units has the characteristics of a rapidly established "functional cluster," with strong interactions among the synchronously firing units and much weaker interactions with other active units. Simulations based on this model have been used to investigate in detail the influences on the emergence of synchronous rhythms of physiological parameters, such as synaptic strength, time constant of inhibition, transmission delays, and structural parameters affecting horizontal or intralaminar circuits, vertical or interlaminar circuits, thalamocortical circuits, and thalamoreticular macrocircuits. Experiments in which one- or two-way lesions of the polysynaptic loops were introduced revealed that the emergence of high-frequency synchronous firing in

population-averaged activities depends critically on the dynamics of corticothalamic and corticocortical reentrant circuits. Voltage-dependent channels with kinetic characteristics typical of NMDA receptors in the horizontal corticocortical connections of the model proved essential for the development of the widespread coherence within and among cortical regions. A simulated blockade of these receptors resulted not only in the reduction of the efficacy of individual synapses, but in the abolition of the global coherence that occurred in the intact model. Furthermore, it was observed that synchrony within the thalamocortical system showed a nonlinear dependence on activity levels, and activity showed a nonlinear dependence on synchrony. The sudden increase in the degree of synchrony and of the effectiveness of synchrony when the stimulus intensity reached a certain level was associated with a sudden increase in the mean level and variance of neural activity. This abrupt, nonlinear effect is characteristic of a nonequilibrium phase transition; see H. G. Schuster, *Deterministic Chaos: An Introduction* (New York: VCH Distribution, 1988). These simulations suggest that the "ignition" of corticothalamic and thalamocortical reentrant loops, in conjunction with the opening of voltage-dependent channels, represents a necessary condition for the emergence of an integrated, coherent thalamocortical process.

9. G. Tononi, A. R. McIntosh, D. P. Russell, and G. M. Edelman, "Functional Clustering: Identifying Strongly Interactive Brain Regions in Neuroimaging Data," *Neuroimage*, 7 (1998), 133–49.

10. B. Everitt, *Cluster Analysis* (London: E. Arnold, 1993).

11. Tononi, McIntosh, Russell, and Edelman, "Functional Clustering."

12. If the patterns of activity of the system are expressed by a discrete variable X, $H(X) = K\sum p_j \log_2 p_j$, where κ is an arbitrary constant, p_j is the probability of the jth system state, and the sum goes from $j = 1$ to N, the number of possible system states (if the N states are equally likely, $p_j = 1/N$, and this expression reduces to $H(X) = \log_2 N$ bits). If the states of the system have a continuous range of values: $H(X) = -\kappa \int dX\, P(X) \log_2 P(X)$, where $P(X)$ is the probability distribution function of the system. Note that although the entropy for continuous variables is not well defined because of the infinite number of possible states, it is well defined once one assumes a finite precision of measurements. Furthermore, entropy *differences*, such as those indicated by integration and mutual information, are always well defined; cf. F. Rieke, D. Warland, B. de Ruyter van Steveninck, and W. Bialek, *Spikes: Exploring the Neural Code* (Cambridge, Mass.: MIT Press, 1997).

13. G. Tononi, O. Sporns, and G. M. Edelman, "A Measure for Brain Complexity: Relating Functional Segregation and Integration in the Nervous System," *Proceedings of the National Academy of Sciences of the United Sates of America*, 91 (1994), 5033–37.

14. As measures of statistical dependence, respectively, inside and outside a subset of elements, integration and mutual information have the virtue of being highly general, since they are multivariate and sensitive to high-order moments of statistical dependence; see A. Papoulis, *Probability, Random Variables, and Stochastic Processes* (New York: McGraw-Hill, 1991). They can easily be calculated provided that certain conditions, such as stationarity, are satisfied. Under conditions of nonstationarity, or for short periods, their calculation is more difficult.

15. Tononi, McIntosh, Russell, and Edelman, "Functional Clustering."

16. To be precise, we consider that the corresponding subset represents a functional cluster only if such values are statistically higher than those expected for a homogeneous system and if it does not contain smaller subsets with higher CI values; see ibid.

17. Ibid.

18. S. L. Bressler,"Interareal Synchronization in the Visual Cortex," *Behavioural Brain Research*, 76 (1996), 37–49; M. Joliot, U. Ribary, and R. Llinas, "Human Oscillatory Brain

Activity Near 40 HZ Coexists with Cognitive Temporal Binding," *Proceedings of the National Academy of Sciences of the United States of America*, 91 (1994), 11748–51; A. Gevins, "High-Resolution Electroencephalographic Studies of Cognition," *Advances in Neurology*, 66 (1995), 181–95; R. Srinivasan, D. P. Russell, G. M. Edelman, and G. Tononi, "Frequency Tagging Competing Stimuli in Binocular Rivalry Reveals Increased Synchronization of Magnetic Responses During Conscious Perception," *Journal of Neuroscience*, 19 (1999), 5435–48; E. Rodriguez, N. George, J. P. Lachaux, J. Martinerie, B. Renault, and F. J. Varela, "Perception's Shadow: Long-Distance Synchronization of Human Brain Activity," *Nature*, 397 (1999), 430–33.

19. W. Singer and C. M. Gray, "Visual Feature Integration and the Temporal Correlation Hypothesis," *Annual Review of Neuroscience*, 18 (1995), 555–86.

20. A. K. Engel, P. Konig, A. K. Kreiter, and W. Singer, "Interhemispheric Synchronization of Oscillatory Neuronal Responses in Cat Visual Cortex," *Science*, 252 (1991), 1177–79.

CHAPTER ELEVEN

1. C. E. Shannon and W. Weaver, *The Mathematical Theory of Communication* (Urbana: University of Illinois Press, 1963).

2. The present discussion is framed, for simplicity, in terms of discrete variables and therefore discrete states, but continuous variables can also be considered once one assumes a finite precision of measurement, see note 12, chapter 10.

3. Shannon and Weaver, *The Mathematical Theory of Communication*; and A. Papoulis, *Probability, Random Variables, and Stochastic Processes* (New York: McGraw-Hill, 1991).

4. It is acceptable to do so as long as the currencies used are multidimensional variance (measured by entropy) and statistical dependence (measured by mutual information) within the system. We introduced these terms in chapter 10 and describe them further later in this chapter. Such a purely statistical approach has been used successfully to address, for example, a growing number of fundamental issues in physics; cf. W. H. Zurek, *Complexity, Entropy, and the Physics of Information: The Proceedings of the 1988 Workshop on Complexity, Entropy, and the Physics of Information Held May-June, 1989, in Santa Fe, New Mexico* (Redwood City, Calif.: Addison-Wesley, 1990).

5. G. Tononi, O. Sporns, and G. M. Edelman, "A Measure for Brain Complexity: Relating Functional Segregation and Integration in the Nervous System," *Proceedings of the National Academy of Sciences of the United States of America*, 91 (1994), 5033-37.

6. In other words, while entropy measures the variability of a system as assessed by an external observer, mutual information measures the variability of the system as can be assessed by the system itself (by its various subsets).

7. If, for example, X^k_j had only two available states, even if these states were statistically dependent on the states of $X - X^k_j$, X^k_j could differentiate between at most two sets of states of $X - X^k_j$, and $MI(X^k_j; X - X^k_j)$ would be correspondingly low. Conversely, if X^k_j and $X - X^k_j$ were statistically independent, X^k_j could not differentiate among the states of $X - X^k_j$ irrespective of the number of states, and $MI(X^k_j; X - X^k_j)$ would be zero. On the other hand, if X^k_j had many states *and* these states were statistically dependent on the states of $X - X^k_j$, $MI(X^k_j; X - X^k_j)$ would be high.

8. cf. Tononi, Sporns, and Edelman, "A Measure for Brain Complexity." In many of their writings, both William James and Rudolf Lotze continued to struggle with the notion of integration. Their problem arose mainly because they were trying to understand integration from the outside of the system, rather than from the inside; cf. W. James, *The Principles of Psychology* (New York: Henry Holt, 1890), 159.

9. This conclusion is consistent with intuitive notions and current attempts in physics and biology to conceptualize complex systems; see Zurek, *Complexity, Entropy, and the Physics of Information*. A measure of complexity that does not involve the calculation of average values of integration and mutual information can also be defined as the amount of the entropy of a system that is accounted for by the interactions among its elements and is given by $\Sigma MI(X_j^1; X - X_j^1) - I(X)$; see G. Tononi, G. M. Edelman, and O. Sporns, "Complexity and the Integration of Information in the Brain," *Trends in Cognitive Science*, 2 (1998), 44-52. One can also consider the direction of the actual causal interactions among the elements of a system by injecting variance (stimulating a subset of them) and observing the change in mutual information between them and the rest of the system; see G. Tononi, O. Sporns, and G. M. Edelman, "Measures of Degeneracy and Redundancy in Biological Networks," *Proceedings of the National Academy of Sciences of the United States of America*, 96 (1999), 3257-62. Note that measures of complexity should be applied to a single system (a functional cluster), not to a collection of independent or nearly independent subsystems.

10. cf. Tononi, Sporns, and Edelman, "A Measure for Brain Complexity."

11. O. Sporns, G. Tononi, and G. M. Edelman, "Modeling Perceptual Grouping and Figure-Ground Segregation by Means of Active Reentrant Connections," *Proceedings of the National Academy of Sciences of the United States of America*, 88 (1991), 129-33.

12. That is to say, neuronal activity was triggered by random noise provided independently to each neuron.

13. In this case, of course, the EEG was not recorded; it was calculated on the basis of the activity of thousands of simulated neurons.

14. Note that as long as the system is isolated, it is the intrinsic connectivity among its elements that defines their functional specificity (reflected here in topography and orientation specificity), rather than vice versa.

15. Tononi, Sporns, and Edelman, "A Measure for Brain Complexity"; O. Sporns, G. Tononi, and G. M. Edelman, "Theoretical Neuroanatomy: Relating Anatomical and Functional Connectivity in Graphs and Cortical Connection Matrices," *Cerebral Cortex*, 10 (2000), 127–41.

16. C. G. Habeck, G. M. Edelman, and G. Tononi, "Dynamics of Sleep and Waking in a Large-Scale Model of the Cat Thalamocortical System," *Society Neuroscience Abstracts*, 25 (1999), 361.

17. The measure of complexity described here was validated on the basis of neurophysiological data; see K. J. Friston, G. Tononi, O. Sporns, and G. M. Edelman, "Characterising the Complexity of Neuronal Interactions," *Human Brain Mapping*, 3 (1995), 302-14.

18. A number of other biological systems exhibit complexity and appear to be susceptible to the kind of analysis described here. The circuits of gene regulation in prokaryotes and eukaryotes, various endocrine loops, and the coordinative events observed during embryological development are significant examples. It remains to be seen whether our approach will prove useful in more widespread applications, such as the analysis of parallel computation and communication networks. It is also an open question whether our measure of complexity may be extended to a consideration of temporal patterns, particularly since complex dynamical systems have temporal evolutions that, especially near phase transitions at the so-called edge of chaos, are in between the two extremes of complete randomness (like the flip of a coin) and complete regularity (such as a clock); see Zurek, *Complexity, Entropy, and the Physics of Information*.

19. G. Tononi, O. Sporns, and G. M. Edelman, "A Complexity Measure for Selective Matching of Signals by the Brain," *Proceedings of the National Academy of Sciences of the United States of America*, 93 (1996), 3422-27.

20. Tononi, Edelman, and Sporns, "Complexity and the Integration of Information in the Brain"; G. Tononi and G. M. Edelman, "Information: In the Stimulus or in the Context?" *Behavioral and Brain Sciences*, 20 (1997), 698-99.

21. cf. J. S. Bruner, *Beyond the Information Given: Studies in the Psychology of Knowing* (New York: W. W. Norton, 1973).

22. This expression is borrowed from Herbert Spencer; see H. Spencer, *First Principles* (New York: Appleton, 1920).

23. Tononi, Sporns, and Edelman, "A Complexity Measure for Selective Matching of Signals by the Brain."

24. Complexity increases also when the connectivity of a system is allowed to change to increase degeneracy—the number of possible ways of achieving certain desirable outputs. This, too, represents an adaptation to an environment. See Tononi, Sporns, and Edelman, "Measures of Degeneracy and Redundancy in Biological Networks"; see also chapter 7.

CHAPTER TWELVE

1. W. James, *The Principles of Psychology* (New York: Henry Holt, 1890), 78.

2. See D. A. Leopold and N. K. Logothetis, "Activity Changes in Early Visual Cortex Reflect Monkeys' Percepts During Binocular Rivalry," *Nature*, 379 (1996), 549-53; and D. L. Shenberg and N. K. Logothetis, "The Role of Temporal Cortical Areas in Perceptual Organization," *Proceedings of the National Academy of Sciences of the United States of America*, 94 (1997), 3408-13.

3. G. Tononi, R. Srinivasan, D. P. Russell, and G. M. Edelman, "Investigating Neural Correlates of Conscious Perception by Frequency-Tagged Neuromagnetic Responses," *Proceedings of the National Academy of Sciences of the United States of America*, 95 (1998), 3198-203; and R. Srinivasan, D. P. Russell, G. M. Edelman, and G. Tononi, "Increased Synchronization of Magnetic Responses During Conscious Perception," *Journal of Neuroscience*, 19 (1999), 5435-48.

4. The apparent discrepancy between the limited number of single units in early visual areas whose firing levels were correlated with the percept and the finding of a significant modulation of MEG signals over the occipital cortex is partly explained by the fact that MEG signals are sensitive to the correlated firing of large populations of neurons. Consistent with this fact, a recent study of strabismic cats showed that perceptual dominance under conditions of binocular rivalry is associated with increased synchronization in early visual areas, while perceptual suppression is associated with reduced synchronization; see G. Rager and W. Singer, "The Response of Cat Visual Cortex to Flicker Stimuli of Variable Frequency," *European Journal of Neuroscience*, 10 (1998), 1856-77. Thus the changes in the firing levels of individual units may represent only the tip of the iceberg.

5. Just as the spatial "grain" of conscious experience appears to be coarser than that of individual neurons, the temporal "grain" appears to be coarser that that of individual spikes: While neurons signal in milliseconds, our conscious life unfolds in fractions of seconds; see A. L. Blumenthal, *The Process of Cognition*, (Englewood Cliffs, N.J.: Prentice-Hall, 1977). This observation suggests that the search for neural correlates of conscious experience should focus on those aspects of neural dynamics that unfold on a similar time scale.

6. D. J. Simons, and D. T. Levin, "Change Blindness," *Trends in Cognitive Sciences*, 1 (1997), 261-67.

7. M. Solms, *The Neuropsychology of Dreams: A Clinico-Anatomical Study* (Mahwah, N.J.: Lawrence Erlbaum Associates, 1997).

8. As we mentioned before, in some cases, perception without awareness has been shown to occur with stimuli that are not short lasting or weak. See F. C. Kolb and J. Braun, "Blindsight in Normal Observers," *Nature*, 377 (1995), 336-38; S. He, H. S. Smallman, and D. I. A. MacLeod, "Neural and Cortical Limits on Visual Resolution," *Investigative Ophthalmology & Visual Science*, 36 (1995), S438; and S. He, P. Cavanagh, and J. Intriligator, "Attentional Resolution and the Locus of Visual Awareness," *Nature*, 383 (1996), 334-37.

9. W. Penfield, *The Excitable Cortex in Conscious Man*, Springfield, Ill.: Charles C. Thomas, 1958); W. Penfield, *The Mystery of the Mind: A Critical Study of Consciousness and the Human Brain* (Princeton, N.J.: Princeton University Press, 1975); and E. Halgren and P. Chauvel, "Experimental Phenomena Evoked by Human Brain Electrical Stimulation," *Advances in Neurology*, 63 (1993), 123-40; cf. W. T. D. Newsome, and C. D. Salzman, "The Neuronal Basis of Motion Perception," *Ciba Foundation Symposium*, 174 (1993), 217-30.

10. Similar results are being obtained with the new technique of transcranial magnetic stimulation. See V. E. Amassian, R. Q. Cracco, P. J. Maccabee, J. B. Cracco, A. P. Rudell, and L. Eberle, "Transcranial Magnetic Stimulation in Study of the Visual Pathway," *Journal Of Clinical Neurophysiology*, 15 (1998), 288-304; U. Ziemann, B. J. Steinhoff, F. Tergau, and W. Paulus, "Transcranial Magnetic Stimulation: Its Current Role in Epilepsy Research," *Epilepsy Research*, 30 (1998), 11-30; and R. Q. Cracco, J. B. Cracco, P. J. Maccabee, and V. E. Amassian, *Journal Of Neuroscience Methods*, 86 (1999), 209-19).

11. G. Tononi, unpublished observations.

12. E. D. Lumer, G. M. Edelman, and G. Tononi, "Neural Dynamics in a Model of the Thalamorcortical system. 1: Layers, Loops, and the Emergence of Fast Synchronous Rhythms," *Cerebral Cortex*, 7 (1997), 207-27.; E. D. Lumer, G. M. Edelman, and G. Tononi, "Neural Dynamics in a Model of the Thalamocortical System. 2: The Role of Neural Synchrony Tested Through Perturbations of Spike Timing," *Cerebral Cortex*, 7 (1997), 228-36; and G. Tononi, O. Sporns, and G. M. Edelman, "Reentry and the Problem of Integrating Multiple Cortical Areas: Simulation of Dynamic Integration in the Visual System," *Cerebral Cortex*, 2 (1992), 310-35.

13. See, for example, F. Crick and C. Koch, "Some Reflections on Visual Awareness," *Cold Spring Harbor Symposia on Quantitative Biology*, 55 (1990), 953-62; F. Crick and C. Koch, "The Problem of Consciousness," *Scientific American*, 267 (1992), 152-59; F. Crick, and C. Koch, "Are We Aware of Neural Activity in Primary Visual Cortex?" *Nature*, 375 (1995), 121-23; and S. Zeki and A. Bartels, "The Asynchrony of Consciousness," *Proceedings of the Royal Society of London, Series B— Biological Sciences*, 265 (1998), 1583-85.

14. The results of a recent PET study are fully consistent with this prediction; see A. R. McIntosh, M. N. Rajah, and N. J. Lobaugh, "Interactions of Prefrontal Cortex in Relation to Awareness in Sensory Learning," *Science*, 284 (1999), 1531-33. In this study, human subjects could be divided on the basis of whether they were aware that one tone predicted a visual event and another did not. It was observed that the correlations among the activities of brain regions that are functionally connected to the left prefrontal cortex (for example, the occipital and temporal regions) increased strongly at the time when awareness likely emerged. The authors concluded that awareness occurs through the

integration of distributed regions. Moreover, they noted that, depending on how the left prefrontal cortex interacts with other areas of the brain, the operations it performs (in this case, monitoring) may or may not contribute to awareness.

15. In line with the arrangement of cortical connectivity, however, the dynamic core is likely to be organized in a "radial" and hierarchical fashion. For example, cortical areas that deal with highly invariant aspects of perceived objects in *different* modalities (vision, hearing, touch, and so on) are more directly interconnected than are areas that deal with low-level aspects of the same objects. Thus, neuronal groups responding to faces and neuronal groups responding to voices may communicate directly, while neuronal groups responding to oriented bars and others responding to tones should not. Nevertheless, within the *same* modality, "high-level" and "low-level" neuronal groups are tightly linked. The functional interactions within the dynamic core, though constituting a single functional cluster, should reflect this organization (see also note 32, chapter 6).

16. It should be noted that many attentional effects can also be conceptualized as contextual effects in the evolution of the dynamic core, although the emergence of conscious states themselves should not be confounded with their attentional modulation.

17. M. H. Chase, "The Matriculating Brain," *Psychology Today*, 7 (1973), 82-87.

18. Tononi, Sporns, and Edelman, "Reentry and the Problem of Integrating Multiple Cortical Areas."

19. For references and a discussion of these estimates, see T. Nørretranders, *The User Illusion: Cutting Consciousness Down to Size* (New York: Viking, 1998). By comparison, TV has the capacity of millions of bits per sec. An estimate of the capacity of human sensory channels, if calculated this way, would also be around millions of bits per sec., while the capacity of our motor outputs, at the final stage, would be of ~40 bits per sec. See, for example, K. Küpfmüller, "Grundlage der Informationstheorie und Kybernetick," in *Physiologie des Menschen*, Vol. 10, eds. O. H. Grauer, K. Kramer, and R. Jung. (Munich: Urban & Schwarzenberg, 1971).

20. This crucial difference in the nature of information in consciousness also points out a difficulty with the metaphor of the "global workspace" used by B. J. Baars, *A Cognitive Theory of Consciousness* (New York: Cambridge University Press, 1988). In what is otherwise an excellent analysis of cognitive aspects of consciousness, Baars suggested that consciousness is like the stage of a theater or a TV broadcasting station. This view is centered on the notion of limited capacity: Only a few actors are under the spotlight at any given time (equivalent to a few chunks of information), but their message is widely distributed to the entire audience. Furthermore, people in the audience can, under certain conditions, go on stage and broadcast their messages publicly. Here, the idea is that information is in the message—that the information content of any conscious state is small (there is only one or at most a few messages at a time), but it is widely distributed. As we have seen, however, the information is not in the message, but in the number of system states that can be brought about by global interactions within the system itself. Thus, a better metaphor would not be that of a small stage with a wide audience, but of a riotous parliament trying to make a decision, signaled by its members raising their hands. Before the counting occurs, each member of the parliament is interacting with as many other members as possible not by persuasive rhetoric (there are no intrinsic meanings) but simply by pushing and pulling. Within 300 msec or so, a new vote is taken. How informed the decision turns out to be will depend on the number of diverse interactions within the parliament. In a totalitarian country, every member will vote the same; the information content of constant unanimity is zero. If there are two monolithic groups, left and right, such that the vote of each half is always the same, the information content

is only slightly higher. If nobody interacts with anyone, the voting will be purely random, and no information will be integrated within the system. Finally, if there are diverse interactions within the parliament, the final vote will be highly informed. The amount of information integrated by these interactions can be estimated using the complexity measure that we introduced in chapter 11.

21. H. Pashler, "Dual-Task Interference in Simple Tasks: Data and Theory," *Psychological Bulletin*, 116 (1994), 220-44.

22. Blumenthal, *The Process of Cognition*.

23. E. Vaadia, I. Haalman, M. Abeles, H. Bergman, Y. Prut, H. Slovin, and A. Aertsen, "Dynamics of Neuronal Interactions in Monkey Cortex in Relation to Behavioural Events," *Nature*, 373 (1995), 515-18.

24. E. Seidemann, I. Meilijson, M. Abeles, H. Bergman, and E. Vaadia, "Simultaneously Recorded Single Units in the Frontal Cortex Go Through Sequences of Discrete and Stable States in Monkeys Performing a Delayed Localization Task," *Journal of Neuroscience*, 16 (1996), 752-68.

CHAPTER THIRTEEN

1. This is the so-called inverted spectrum argument.

2. At the most general level, all the colors experienced by a person with normal color vision are described using just three parameters: hue, saturation, and lightness. Hue corresponds to the actual color, saturation to its purity, and lightness to how light or dark the color appears. For a detailed discussion of the psychophysics and neurophysiology of color vision, see A. Byrne and D. R. Hilbert, *Readings on Color* (Cambridge, Mass.: MIT Press, 1997); and K. R. Gegenfurtner and L. T. Sharpe, *Color Vision: From Genes to Perception* (Cambridge, England: Cambridge University Press, 1999).

3. There are also complementary neurons, such as those activated by green wavelengths and inhibited by red wavelengths. Moreover, there are neuronal groups responding to the same color for different positions of the visual field.

4. It is likely that a larger set of neuronal groups underlies the perception of color, including neurons responding to other color categories (for example, for green, yellow, orange, purple, and so on) and neurons responding to color in different spatial positions. It is also likely that neuronal groups in areas earlier than V4 and IT in the cortical hierarchy contribute certain aspects to the conscious perception of color, such as spatial detail and sensitivity to wavelength composition. We ignore these complications in the rest of our discussion.

5. Paul Churchland made the case that vector representations could be used by the brain to specify colors, odors, and faces economically. See P. M. Churchland, *The Engine of Reason, the Seat of the Soul: a Philosophical Journey into the Brain* (Cambridge, Mass.: MIT Press, 1995).

6. J. Wray and G. M. Edelman, "A Model of Color Vision Based on Cortical Reentry," *Cerebral Cortex*, 6 (1996), 701-16.

7. Such is the approach suggested by, for example, F. Crick and C. Koch "Are We Aware of Neural Activity in Primary Visual Cortex?" *Nature*, 375 (1995), 121-23; and even more explicitly by S. Zeki and A. Bartels, "The Asynchrony of Consciousness," *Proceedings of the Royal Society of London, Series B—Biological Sciences*, 265 (1998), 1583-85.

8. A classic way of evading the issue of qualia is the old idea of labeled lines (Müller's so-called law of specific nerve energies): The subjective feeling determining how the fir-

ing of this or that neuron feels is somehow specified in the sensory organs to which that neuron is connected. If that neuron is connected to the eye, it will give rise to a visual sensation; if it is connected to the skin, it will give rise to a tactile sensation. This is, of course, no explanation. For example, what about neurons sensitive to blood pressure that are connected to baroceptors in arterial walls? Why should they not be labeled like everything else and give rise to a quale of blood pressure?

9. Cf. the discussion of the "meaning" of neuronal firing in F. Crick and C. Koch, "Consciousness and Neuroscience," *Cerebral Cortex*, 8 (1998), 97-107.

10. A. Schopenhauer, *The World as Will and Representation*, trans. by E. F. J. Payne. (New York: Dover, 1966), § 7.

11. When a neurophysiologist records the activity of one or, at most, a few neurons at a time or when a psychophysicist examines some particular aspect of conscious experience, it is certainly acceptable to consider subspaces of less than N dimensions. However, on the basis of our discussion, one should be aware that most of the neural dimensions contributing to a given conscious state are being ignored and thus make sure that neural activity in the ignored dimensions stays at least relatively constant.

12. One may say that the quale of that discrimination is the same thing as its "meaning."

13. An exception is J. R. Searle, "How to Study Consciousness Scientifically," in *Consciousness and Human Identity*, ed. J. Cornwell (Oxford, England: Oxford University Press, 1998), 21-37.

14. Instead of identifying a different quale with a different conscious state, that is, with a discriminable point within the N-dimensional neural space corresponding to the dynamic core, another option would be to define *qualia* as corresponding to the N neural dimensions of the core. One could then say that the activity of a group of neurons corresponding to a particular dimension of the dynamic core determines how much that dimension contributes its quale to a given conscious state. Whichever definition one prefers, however, it should remain clear that identifying quale with a particular dimension of the core is meaningful only within the context of the entire dynamic core. In particular, the activity of a group of neurons would not generate any subjective feeling or quale by itself, but only to the extent that it defines discriminable points within the integrated N-dimensional space of the core. Furthermore, associating changes in a particular quale with changes in activity along a particular dimension of the core would be meaningful only to the extent that the activity of neuronal groups corresponding to the other dimensions of the core remain constant.

15. W. James, *The Principles of Psychology* (New York: Henry Holt, 1890), 224.

16. In particular, the actual distance between axes can be defined in terms of mutual information between subsets of axes using such techniques as hierarchical clustering. See B. Everitt, *Cluster Analysis* (London: Halsted Press, 1993). After we wrote this chapter, we became aware of a mathematical paper that discusses, in abstract terms, the properties of the phenomenological space defined by qualia; see R. P. Stanley, "Qualia Space," *Journal of Consciousness Studies*, 6 (1999), 49-60. Some aspects of this analysis, such as the consideration of the dimensionality, topology, metric, connectedness, linearity, orthogonality, and so forth of this space are along the lines of what we are suggesting here. However, this author considers an abstract qualia space associated with *all possible conscious experiences*. We consider instead the qualia space associated with all possible conscious states of *a single individual*, and we insist on its physical implementation, starting with the claim that its dimensions are given by the activity of actual groups of neurons belonging to the dynamic core.

17. Remember that voltage-dependent connections are those that can become activated by an excitatory input only if the voltage of the receiving neuron has been increased
by some other excitatory input.

18. Note that the possibility of achieving global effects based on local perturbations is
not, in itself, unique. For example, in certain physical systems, typically under far-from-
equilibrium conditions, one can observe dynamic regimes in which the "correlation
length" among the constituent elements is dramatically increased, meaning precisely that
any local perturbation has strong and rapid global effects. See G. Nicolis and
I. Prigogine, *Exploring Complexity: An Introduction* (San Francisco: W. H. Freeman, 1989).
Note that although such examples may convey the idea of global integration, which is a
prerequisite for making the dynamic core into a functional cluster, they typically lack its
complexity because the constituent elements are not functionally specialized to a high
degree.

19. Discussed by A. R. Damasio, "The Somatic Marker Hypothesis and the Possible
Functions of the Prefrontal Cortex," *Philosophical Transactions of the Royal Society of
London, Series B—Biological Sciences*, 351 (1996), 1413-20.

20. G. M. Edelman, *The Remembered Present: A Biological Theory of Consciousness* (New
York: Basic Books, 1989). In a recent book, *The Feeling of What Happens* (New York:
Harcourt Brace, 1999), A. R. Damasio extended the notion of self-nonself discrimination
underlying consciousness first discussed in G. M. Edelman, *Bright Air, Brilliant Fire: On
the Matter of the Mind* (New York: Basic Books, 1992), 117-33, 131-36.

CHAPTER FOURTEEN

1. See M. H. Chase, "The Matriculating Brain," *Psychology Today*, 7 (1973), 82-87.

2. For a review in a cognitive context, see B. J. Baars, *A Cognitive Theory of
Consciousness* (New York: Cambridge University Press, 1988).

3. We are not concerned here whether the ports out are in the primary motor cortex
or in some higher motor area or whether the connections with the motoneurons are
direct or go through several other synaptic steps in other motor structures, since the
thrust of the argument would not change.

4. Once again, we are not concerned here with the issue of how far the unconscious
sensory periphery normally extends into the central nervous system, for example, whether
the activity in the primary visual areas is "conscious" or not. This is an empirical issue
that could be resolved by applying the criteria prescribed by the dynamic-core hypothesis, but it does not affect our present argument.

5. M. V. Egger, *La Parole Intérieure* (Paris, 1881), quoted by W. James, *The Principles of
Psychology* (New York: Henry Holt, 1890), 280.

6. For the hippocampus, the situation is somewhat different. The anatomy would suggest that the outputs from the core to the hippocampus and the inputs from the hippocampus to the core are not restricted, as are the basal ganglia or cerebellum, to a small
number of ports out and ports in. Hippocampal circuits would be triggered by an entire
constellation of ports out being open, and the results of a hippocampal routine would hit
the core simultaneously at a large number of ports in. While a basal ganglion routine
may, for instance, find the right next word, hippocampal activity would be capable of
triggering the next right scene, as well as play a key role in allowing that scene to be
remembered. An interesting possibility is that the dynamic core may have privileged
access, thanks to the cooperative action of its many participating neuronal groups, to
triggering hippocampal activity. This possibility would be consistent with the fact that

consciousness is a prerequisite for episodic memory, which requires the hippocampus. But the hippocampus is not required for consciousness.

7. A. M. Graybiel, "Building Action Repertoires: Memory and Learning Functions of the Basal Ganglia," *Current Opinion in Neurobiology*, 5 (1995), 733-41; and A. Graybiel, "The Basal Ganglia," *Trends in Neurosciences*, 18 (1995), 60-62.

8. H. Bergman, A. Feingold, A. Nini, A. Raz, H. Slovin, M. Abeles, and E. Vaadia, "Physiological Aspects of Information Processing in the Basal Ganglia of Normal and Parkinsonian Primates," *Trends in Neurosciences*, 21 (1998), 32-38; and A. Nini, A. Feingold, H. Slovin, and H. Bergman, "Neurons in the Globus Pallidus Do Not Show Correlated Activity in the Normal Monkey, but Phase-Locked Oscillations Appear in the MPTP Model of Parkinsonism," *Journal of Neurophysiology*, 74 (1995), 1800-05.

9. An interesting possibility that is suggested by these considerations is that traditional associations (such as cat and mat, table and chair, and first and last name) may be mediated not by corticocortical connections, as is often assumed, but by segregated loops through the basal ganglia or other cortical appendages.

10. Graybiel, "Building Action Repertoires: Memory and Learning Functions of the Basal Ganglia"; and Graybiel, "The Basal Ganglia."

11. Graybiel, "The Basal Ganglia"; J. E. Hoover and P. L. Strick, "Multiple Output Channels in the Basal Ganglia," *Science*, 259 (1993), 819-21; and F. A. Middleton and P. L. Strick, "New Concepts About the Organization of Basal Ganglia Output," *Advances in Neurology*, 74 (1997), 57-68.

12. Before we conclude our brief examination of what kinds of neural processes remain unconscious and how they can nevertheless interact with the core, it may be worth considering one last issue. Empirically, it may not always be clear whether constraints or "rules" governing the contents of conscious states and the transitions among them are due to the connectivity among a set of neuronal groups or to the activity of another set. The transition from one conscious state to another is certainly governed, to a large extent, by the connectivity among a subset of active neuronal groups. The patterns of connectivity among neurons that form during evolution, development, and experience as a result of neural selection incorporate a large amount of knowledge about the environment that an organism has and will have encountered. A connectivity pattern expresses such knowledge as a disposition; it specifies that if such and such a pattern of activity were to occur in the dynamic core, for example, such and such patterns of activity would be more likely to follow than others. On the other hand, as we noted in the section on automatic behavior, there are many functionally insulated routines or inputs that go on unconsciously yet can influence the states of the core. It is an interesting but difficult question to establish in what proportion the transition from one conscious state to the next is mediated by the activation of automatic, functionally insulated unconscious routines occurring outside the subset of neuronal groups subserving conscious experience and to what extent it is due to the pattern of connections among these neuronal groups. In other words, when does the dynamic core change state because of internal constraints, and when does it do so by virtue of triggering functionally insulated routines that can, in turn, influence its next state? For instance, consider many "rules" that govern conscious experience, such as those of syntax. As demonstrated by studies of implicit versus explicit knowledge of artificial grammars, complex control problems, and sequence learning, we appear to know a large number of "rules," in the sense that they affect our performance, but we are not consciously aware of them. See A. S. Reber, *Implicit Learning and Tacit Knowledge: An Essay on the Cognitive Unconscious*, Oxford Psychology Series, No. 19

(New York: Oxford University Press, 1993); D. C. Berry, "Implicit Learning: Twenty-five Years on: A Tutorial," in *Attention and Performance 15: Conscious and Nonconscious Information Processing, Attention and Performance Series*, ed. M. M. Carlo Umilta (Cambridge, Mass.: MIT Press, 1994), 755-82. In many cases, the acquisition of such rules occurs implicitly, not in a conscious or deliberate way. At present, it is unclear whether such rules are incorporated in the patterns of connectivity among neuronal groups that contribute to conscious experience or whether they are the result of non-conscious processes that are carried out by other neuronal groups. These issues are further complicated by the inconsistent use of such terms as *implicit* and *explicit* in the literature. In connectionist approaches, the activity of neurons is often considered an *explicit* representation, as opposed to the connectivity, which is thought to represent *implicit* constraints on the neurons' interactions. In the psychological literature, *explicit* often stands for conscious and *implicit* for nonconscious. Finally, although con-nectivity may determine neural interactions, it is obvious that no interaction can occur in the absence of neural activity. To use a metaphor, the connectivity is like a network of paved roads that constrains where traffic can flow. If the traffic does not actually move, nobody gets anywhere. Similarly, no actual interactions among groups of neu-rons can take place unless neurons themselves are active and fire. In other words, one needs to distinguish between the actual occurrence of a dynamic process and the con-straints on how that process unfolds over space and time. This distinction holds whether such a process is associated with consciousness or not. The brainstem con-tains all the circuitry necessary for the coordination of locomotion. Nevertheless, no locomotion occurs if such circuits are not activated. Likewise, in a brain that has been turned off by deep anesthesia, no information is integrated in the thalamocortical sys-tem, and consciousness is lost. The knowledge of the environment that the thalamo-cortical system incorporated, however, has been preserved, as is apparent upon reawakening. To put it more tersely, like any other physical process, the rapid integra-tion of information underlying conscious experience requires the occurrence of an actual dynamic process with causal power.

13. See G. M. Edelman, *The Remembered Present: A Biological Theory of Consciousness* (New York: Basic Books, 1989), for illustrations of how such insulation may come about.

14. W. Schultz, P. Dayan, and P. M. Montague, "A Neural Substrate of Prediction and Reward," *Science*, 275 (1997), 1593-99.

15. Bergman et al., "Physiological Aspects of Information Processing in the Basal Ganglia of Normal and Parkinsonian Primates."

CHAPTER FIFTEEN

1. This is related to the so-called Baldwin effect. See G. G. Simpson, "The Baldwin Effect," *Evolution*, 7 (1952), 110–17.)

2. G. M. Edelman, *The Remembered Present: A Biological Theory Of Consciousness* (New York: Basic Books, 1989).

3. For an account of the expressive function of language, in contrast to the designative function, see C. Taylor, *Human Agency and Language*, Philosophical Papers, Vol. 1. (Cambridge, England: Cambridge University Press, 1985).

4. See, for example, M. Cavell, *The Psychoanalytic Mind: From Freud to Philosophy* (Cambridge, Mass.: Harvard University Press, 1993).

5. T. Nagel, "What Is It Like to Be a Bat?" in *Mortal Questions* (New York: Cambridge University Press, 1979).

CHAPTER SEVENTEEN

1. G. M. Edelman, *Neural Darwinism: The Theory of Neuronal Group Selection* (New York: Basic Books, 1987); and G. M. Edelman, *Bright Air, Brilliant Fire: On the Matter of the Mind* (New York: Basic Books, 1992).

2. Edelman, *Bright Air, Brilliant Fire.*

3. J. A. Wheeler, *At Home in the Universe* (New York: American Institute of Physics, 1994).

4. G. M. Edelman, *The Remembered Present: A Biological Theory of Consciousness* (New York: Basic Books, 1989).

5. W. V. Quine, "Epistemology Naturalized," in *Ontological Relativity and Other Essays* (New York: Columbia University Press, 1969); see also H. Kornblith, *Naturalizing Epistemology* (Cambridge, Mass.: MIT Press, 1994).

6. Notably Quine, "Epistemology Naturalized."

7. W. Köhler, *The Place of Value in a World of Fact* (New York: Liveright, 1938).

8. R. Penrose, *The Emperor's New Mind: Concerning Computers, Minds, and the Laws of Physics* (Oxford, England: Oxford University Press, 1989); and R. Penrose, *Shadows of the Mind: A Search for the Missing Science of Consciousness* (New York: Oxford University Press, 1994).

Bibliography

Almássy, N., Edelman, G. M., and Sporns, O. "Behavioral Constraints in the Development of Neuronal Properties: A Cortical Model Embedded in a Real-World Device." *Cerebral Cortex*, 8 (1998), 346-61.

Amassian, V. E., Cracco, R. Q., Maccabee, P. J., Cracco, J. B., Rudell, A. P., and Eberle, L. "Transcranial Magnetic Stimulation in Study of the Visual Pathway." *Journal of Clinical Neurophysiology*, 15 (1998), 288-304.

Baars, B. J. *A Cognitive Theory of Consciousness*. New York: Cambridge University Press, 1988.

———. *Inside the Theater of Consciousness: The Workspace of the Mind*. New York: Oxford University Press, 1997.

Baddeley, A. "The Fractionation of Working Memory." *Proceedings of the National Academy of Sciences of the United States of America*, 93 (1996), 13468-72.

Bateson, G. *Steps to an Ecology of Mind*. New York: Ballantine Books, 1972.

Bergman, H., Feingold, A., Nini, A., Raz, A., Slovin, H., Abeles, M., and Vaadia, E. "Physiological Aspects of Information Processing in the Basal Ganglia of Normal and Parkinsonian Primates." *Trends in Neurosciences*, 21 (1998), 32-38.

Berry, D. C. "Implicit Learning: Twenty-five Years on: A Tutorial." Pp. 755-82 in *Attention and Performance 15: Conscious and Nonconscious Information Processing, Attention and Performance Series*, ed. M. M. Carlo Umiltà. Cambridge, Mass.: MIT Press, 1994.

Biederman, I. "Perceiving Real-World Scenes." *Science* 177 (1972), 77-80.

Biederman, I., Mezzanotte, R. J., and Rabinowitz, J. C. "Scene Perception: Detecting and Judging Objects Undergoing Relational Violations." *Cognitive Psychology*, 14 (1982), 143-77.

Biederman, I., Rabinowitz, J. C., Glass, A. L., and Stacy, E. W. "On the Information Extracted from a Glance at a Scene." *Journal of Experimental Psychology*, 103 (1974), 597-600.

Bisiach, E., and Luzzatti, C. "Unilateral Neglect of Representational Space." *Cortex*, 14 (1978), 129-33.

Block, N. J., Flanagan, O. J., and Güzeldere, G. *The Nature of Consciousness: Philosophical Debates*. Cambridge, Mass.: MIT Press, 1997.

Blumenthal, A. L. *The Process of Cognition*. Englewood Cliffs, N.J.: Prentice-Hall, 1977.

Bogen, J. E. "On the Neurophysiology of Consciousness: I. An Overview." *Consciousness and Cognition*, 4 (1995), 52-62.

Braun, A. R., Balkin, T. J., Wesenten, N. J., Carson, R. E., Varga, M., Baldwin, P., Selbie, S., Belenky, G., and Herscovitch, P. "Regional Cerebral Blood Flow Throughout the Sleep-Wake Cycle: An H_2 ^{15}(O) PET Study." *Brain*, 120 (1997), 1173-97.

Bressler, S. L. "Large-Scale Cortical Networks and Cognition." *Brain Research—Brain Research Reviews*, 20 (1995), 288-304.

———. "Interareal Synchronization in the Visual Cortex." *Behavioural Brain Research*, 76 (1996), 37-49.

Bruner, J. S. *Beyond the Information Given: Studies in the Psychology of Knowing*. New York: W. W. Norton, 1973.

Buckner, R. L., Petersen, S. E., Ojemann, J. G., Miezin, F. M., Squire, L. R., and Raichle, M. E. "Functional Anatomical Studies of Explicit and Implicit Memory Retrieval Tasks." *Journal of Neuroscience*, 15 (1995), 12-29.

Burnet, F. M. *The Clonal Selection Theory of Acquired Immunity*. Nashville, Tenn.: Vanderbilt University Press, 1959.

Byrne, A., and Hilbert, D. R. *Readings on Color*. Cambridge, Mass.: MIT Press, 1997.

Cauller, L. "Layer I of Primary Sensory Neocortex: Where Top-Down Converges upon Bottom-Up." *Behavioural Brain Research*, 71 (1995), 163-70.

Cavell, M. *The Psychoanalytic Mind: From Freud to Philosophy*. Cambridge, Mass.: Harvard University Press, 1993.

Chalmers, D. J. "The Puzzle of Conscious Experience." *Scientific American*, 273 (1995), 80-86.

Chase, M. H. "The Matriculating Brain." *Psychology Today*, 7 (1973), 82-87.

Cheesman, J. M., and Merikle, P. M. "Priming with and without Awareness." *Perception & Psychophysics*, 36 (1984), 387-95.

———. "Distinguishing Conscious from Unconscious Perceptual Processes." *Canadian Journal of Psychology*, 40, (1986), 343-67.

Churchland, P. M. *The Engine of Reason, the Seat of the Soul: A Philosophical Journey into the Brain*. Cambridge, Mass.: MIT Press, 1995.

Cirelli, C., Pompeiano, M., and Tononi, G. "Neuronal Gene Expression in the Waking State: A Role for the Locus Coeruleus." *Science*, 274 (1996), 1211-15.

Cracco, R. Q., Cracco, J. B., Maccabee, P. J., and Amassian, V. E. "Cerebral Function Revealed by Transcranial Magnetic Stimulation." *Journal of Neuroscience Methods*, 86 (1999), 209-19.

Creutzfeldt, O. D. "Neurophysiological Mechanisms and Consciousness." *Ciba Foundation Symposium*, 69 (1979), 217-33.

Crick, F., and Koch, C. "Some Reflections on Visual Awareness." *Cold Spring Harbor Symposia on Quantitative Biology*, 55 (1990), 953-62.

———. "The Problem of Consciousness." *Scientific American*, 267 (1992), 152-59.

———. "Are We Aware of Neural Activity in Primary Visual Cortex?" *Nature*, 375 (1995), 121-23.

———. "Consciousness and Neuroscience." *Cerebral Cortex*, 8 (1998), 97-107.

Crick, F. H. C. *The Astonishing Hypothesis: The Scientific Search for the Soul*. New York: Charles Scribner's Sons, 1994.

Damasio, A. R. "Time-Locked Multiregional Retroactivation—A Systems-Level Proposal for the Neural Substrates of Recall and Recognition." *Cognition*, 33 (1989), 25-62.

———. *Decartes' Error: Emotion, Reason, and the Human Brain*. New York: G. P. Putnam's Sons, 1994.

———. "The Somatic Marker Hypothesis and the Possible Functions of the Prefrontal Cortex." *Philosophical Transactions of the Royal Society of London, Series B: Biological Sciences*, 351 (1996), 1413-20.

_____. *The Feeling of What Happens.* New York: Harcourt, Brace, 1999.

De Weerd, P., Gattass, R., Desimone, R., and Ungerleider, L. G. "Responses of Cells in Monkey Visual Cortex During Perceptual Filling-in of an Artificial Scotoma." *Nature,* 377 (1995), 731-34.

Dennett, D. C. *Consciousness Explained.* Boston: Little, Brown, 1991.

Descartes, R. *Meditationes de prima Philosophia* in *quibus Dei Existentia, & animae humanae à corpore distinctio, demonstrantur.* Amstelodami: Apud Danielem Elsevirium, 1642.

Desimone, R. "Neural Mechanisms for Visual Memory and Their Role in Attention." *Proceedings of the National Academy of Sciences of the United States of America,* 93 (1996), 13494-99.

Dewey, J. *Experience and Education.* New York: Simon & Schuster, 1997.

Diagnostic and Statistical Manual of Mental Disorders, Fourth Edition. Washington, D.C.: American Psychiatric Association, 1994.

Dixon, N. F. *Subliminal Perception: The Nature of a Controversy.* New York: McGraw-Hill, 1971.

_____. *Preconscious Processing.* New York: John Wiley & Sons, 1981.

Eccles, J. "A Unitary Hypothesis of Mind-Brain Interaction in the Cerebral Cortex." *Proceedings of the Royal Society of London, Series B: Biological Sciences,* 240 (1990), 433-51.

Edelman, G. M. "Origins and Mechanisms of Specificity in Clonal Selection." Pp. 1-37 in *Cellular Selection and Regulation in the Immune Response,* ed. G. M. Edelman. New York: Raven Press, 1974.

_____. *Neural Darwinism: The Theory of Neuronal Group Selection.* New York: Basic Books, 1987.

_____. *The Remembered Present: A Biological Theory of Consciousness.* New York: Basic Books, 1989.

_____. *Bright Air, Brilliant Fire: On the Matter of the Mind.* New York: Basic Books, 1992.

Edelman, G. M., and Mountcastle, V. B. *The Mindful Brain: Cortical Organization and the Group-Selective Theory of Higher Brain Function.* Cambridge, Mass.: MIT Press, 1978.

Edelman, G. M., Reeke, G. N. J., Gall, W. E., Tononi, G., Williams, D., and Sporns, O. "Synthetic Neural Modeling Applied to a Real-World Artifact." *Proceedings of the National Academy of Sciences of the United States of America,* 89 (1992), 7267-71.

Engel, A. K., Konig, P., Kreiter, A. K., and Singer, W. "Interhemispheric Synchronization of Oscillatory Neuronal Responses in Cat Visual Cortex." *Science,* 252 (1991), 1177-79.

Everitt, B. *Cluster Analysis.* London: Halsted Press, 1993.

Experimental and Theoretical Studies of Consciousness, Ciba Foundation Symposium, 174. Chichester, England: John Wiley & Sons, 1993.

Fabre-Thorpe, M., Richard, G., and Thorpe, S. J. "Rapid Categorization of Natural Images by Rhesus Monkeys." *Neuroreport,* 9 (1998), 303-08.

Finkel, L. H., and Edelman, G. M. "Integration of Distributed Cortical Systems by Reentry: A Computer Simulation of Interactive Functionally Segregated Visual Areas." *Journal of Neuroscience,* 9 (1989), 3188-208.

Flanagan, O. *Consciousness Reconsidered.* Cambridge, Mass.: MIT Press, 1992.

Foulkes, D. *Dreaming: A Cognitive-Psychological Analysis.* Hillsdale, N.J.: Lawrence Erlbaum Associates, 1985.

_____. "Dream Research: 1953-1993." *Sleep,* 19 (1996), 609-24.

Frackowiak, R. S. J., Friston, K. J., Frith, C. D., Dolan, R. J., and Mazziotta, J. C. *Human Brain Function.* San Diego, Calif.: Academic Press, 1997.

Freud, S., Strachey, J., and Freud, A. *The Psychopathology of Everyday Life*. London: Benn, 1966.

Friston, K. J. "Imaging Neuroscience: Principles or Maps?" *Proceedings of the National Academy of the United States of America*, 95 (1998), 796-802.

Friston, K. J., Tononi, G., Reeke, G. N. J., Sporns, O., and Edelman, G. M. "Value-dependent Selection in the Brain: Simulation in a Synthetic Neural Model." *Neuroscience*, 59, 229-43.

Friston, K. J., Tononi, G., Sporns, O., and Edelman, G. M. "Characterising the Complexity of Neuronal Interactions." *Human Brain Mapping*, 3 (1995), 302-14.

Fuster, J. M., Bauer, R. H., and Jervey, J. P. "Functional Interactions Between Inferotemporal and Prefrontal Cortex in a Cognitive Task." *Brain Research*, 330 (1985), 299-307.

Gasquoine, P. G. "Alien Hand Sign." *Journal of Clinical and Experimental Neuropsychology*, 15 (1993), 653-67.

Gazzaniga, M. S. *The Social Brain: Discovering the Networks of the Mind*. New York: Basic Books, 1985.

_____. "Principles of Human Brain Organization Derived from Split-Brain Studies." *Neuron*, 14 (1995), 217-28.

Gegenfurtner, K. R., and Sharpe, L. T. *Color Vision: From Genes to Perception*. Cambridge, England: Cambridge University Press, 1999.

Geschwind, D. H., Iacobini, M., Mega, M. S., Zaidel, D. W., Cloughesy, T., and Zaidel, E. "Alien Hand Syndrome: Interhemispheric Motor Disconnection Due to a Lesion in the Midbody of the Corpus Callosum." *Neurology*, 45 (1995), 802-08.

Geschwind, N. "Disconnexion Syndromes in Animals and Man." *Brain*, 88 (1965), 237-84, 585-644.

Gevins, A. "High-Resolution Electroencephalographic Studies of Cognition." *Advances in Neurology*, 66 (1995), 181-95.

Gevins, A., Smith, M. E., Le, J., Leong, H., Bennett, J., Martin, N., McEvoy, L., Du, R., and Whitfield, S. "High Resolution Evoked Potential Imaging of the Cortical Dynamics of Human Working Memory." *Electroencephalography & Clinical Neurophysiology*, 98 (1996), 327-48.

Goldman-Rakic, P. S., and Chafee, M. "Feedback Processing in Prefronto-Parietal Circuits During Memory-Guided Saccades." *Society for Neuroscience Abstracts*, 29 (1994), 808.

Graybiel, A. M. "The Basal Ganglia." *Trends in Neuroscience*, 18 (1995), 60-62.

_____. "Building Action Repertoires: Memory and Learning Functions of the Basal Ganglia." *Current Opinion in Neurobiology*, 5 (1995), 733-41.

Habeck, C. G., Edelman, G. M., and Tononi, G. "Dynamics of Sleep and Waking in a Large-Scale Model of the Cat Thalamocortical System." *Society for Neuroscience Abstracts*, 25 (1999), 361.

Haier, R. J., Siegel, B. V., Jr., MacLachlan, A., Soderling, E., Lottenberg, S., and Buchsbaum, M. S. "Regional Glucose Metabolic Changes after Learning a Complex Visuospatial/Motor Task: A Positron Emission Tomographic Study." *Brain Research*, 570 (1992), 134-43.

Halgren, E., and Chauvel, P. "Experimental Phenomena Evoked by Human Brain Electrical Stimulation." *Advances in Neurology*, 63 (1993), 123-40.

Haxby, J. V., Horwitz, B., Ungerleider, L. G., Maisog, J. M., Pietrini, P., and Grady, C. L. "The Functional Organization of Human Extrastriate Cortex: A PET-rCBF Study of Selective Attention to Faces and Locations." *Journal of Neuroscience*, 14 (1994), 6336-53.

He, S., Cavanagh, P., and Intriligator, J. "Attentional Resolution and the Locus of Visual Awareness." *Nature*, 383 (1996), 334-47.

He, S., Smallman, H. S., and MacLeod, D. I. A. "Neural and Cortical Limits on Visual Resolution." *Investigative Ophthalmology & Visual Science*, 36 (1995), S438.

Hilgard, E. R. *Divided Consciousness: Multiple Controls in Human Thought and Action.* New York: John Wiley & Sons, 1986.

Hobson, J. A., Stickgold, R., and Pace-Schott, E. F. "The Neuropsychology of REM Sleep Dreaming." *Neuroreport*, 9 (1998), R1-R14.

Holtzman, J. D., and Gazzaniga, M. S. "Enhanced Dual Task Performance Following Callosal Commissurotomy." *Neuropsychologia*, 23 (1985), 315-21.

Hoover, J. E., and Strick, P. L. "Multiple Output Channels in the Basal Ganglia." *Science*, 259 (1993), 819-21.

Humphrey, N. *A History of the Mind.* New York: Harper Perennial, 1993.

Huxley, T. H. *Methods and Results: Essays.* New York: D. Appleton, 1901.

Intraub, H. "Rapid Conceptual Identification of Sequentially Presented Pictures." *Journal of Experimental Psychology: Human Perception & Performance*, 7 (1981), 604-10.

Jackendoff, R. *Consciousness and the Computational Mind.* Cambridge, Mass.: MIT Press, 1987.

James, W. *The Principles of Psychology.* New York: Henry Holt, 1890.

Janet, P. *L'automatisme psychologique; essai de psychologie expérimentale sur les formes inférieures de l'activité humaine.* Paris: F. Alcan, 1930.

John, E. R. *Mechanisms of Memory.* New York: Academic Press, 1967.

John, E. R., and Killam, K. F. "Electrophysiological Correlates of Avoidance Conditioning in the Cat." *Journal of Pharmacological and Experimental Therapeutics*, 125 (1959), 252.

Joliot, M., Ribary, U., and Llinas, R. "Human Oscillatory Brain Activity Near 40 Hz Coexists with Cognitive Temporal Binding." *Proceedings of the National Academy of Sciences of the United States of America*, 91 (1994), 11748-51.

Jones, D. S. *Elementary Information Theory.* Oxford, England: Clarendon Press, 1979.

Kahn, D., Pace-Schott, E. F., and Hobson, J. A. "Consciousness in Waking and Dreaming: The Roles of Neuronal Oscillation and Neuromodulation in Determining Similarities and Differences." *Neuroscience*, 78 (1997), 13-38.

Karni, A., Meyer, G., Zessard, P., Adams, M. M., Turner, R., and Ungerleider, L. G. "Functional MRI Evidence for Adult Motor Cortex Plasticity During Motor Skill Learning." *Nature*, 377 (1995), 155-58.

Kihlstrom, J. F. "The Rediscovery of the Unconscious." Pp. 123-43 in *The Mind, the Brain, and Complex Adaptive Systems.* Santa Fe Institute Studies in the Sciences of Complexity, Vol. 22, ed. J. L. S. Harold Morowitz. Reading, Mass.: Addison-Wesley, 1994.

Kinney, H. C., and Samuels, M. A. "Neuropathology of the Persistent Vegetative State: A Review." *Journal of Neuropathology & Experimental Neurology*, 53 (1994), 548-58.

Kinsbourne, M. "Integrated Cortical Field Model of Consciousness." *Ciba Foundation Symposium*, 174 (1993), 43-50.

Knyazeva, M., Koeda, T., Njiokiktjien, C., Jonkman, E. J., Kurganskaya, M., de Sonneville, L., and Vildavsky, V. "EEG Coherence Changes During Finger Tapping in Acallosal and Normal Children: A Study of Inter- and Intrahemispheric Connectivity." *Behavioural Brain Research*, 89 (1997), 243-58.

Koch, C., and Braun, J. "Towards the Neuronal Correlate of Visual Awareness." *Current Opinion in Neurobiology*, 6 (1996), 158-64.

Köhler, W. *The Place of Value in a World of Fact.* New York: Liveright, 1938.

Kolbe, F. C., and Braun, J. "Blindsight in Normal Observers." *Nature,* 377 (1995), 336-38.

Kornblith, H. *Naturalizing Epistemology.* Cambridge, Mass.: MIT Press, 1994.

Kottler, M. J. "Charles Darwin and Alfred Russell Wallace: Two Decades of Debate over Natural Selection." Pp. 367-432 in *The Darwinian Heritage,* ed. D. Kohn. Princeton, N.J.: Princeton University Press, 1985.

Külpe, O., and Titchener, E. B. *Outlines of Psychology, Based upon the Results of Experimental Investigation.* New York: Macmillan, 1909.

Küpfmüller, K. "Grundlage der Informationstheorie und Kybernetick.: In *Physiologie des Menschen,* eds. O. H. Grauer, K. Kramer, and R. Jung. Munich: Urban & Schwarzenberg, 1971.

Leopold, D. A., and Logothetis, N. K. "Activity Changes in Early Visual Cortex Reflect Monkeys' Percepts During Binocular Rivalry." *Nature,* 379 (1996), 549-53.

Libet, B., Gleason, C. A., Wright, E. W., and Pearl, D. K. "Time of Conscious Intention to Act in Relation to Onset of Cerebral Activity (Readiness-Potential): The Unconscious Initiation of a Freely Voluntary Act." *Brain,* 106 (1983), 623-42.

Libet, B., Pearl, D. K., Morledge, D. E., Gleason, C. A., Hosobuchi, Y., and Barbaro, N. M. "Control of the Transition from Sensory Detection to Sensory Awareness in Man by the Duration of a Thalamic Stimulus: The Cerebral 'Time-on' Factor." *Brain,* 114 (1991), 1731-57.

Livingstone, M. S., and Hubel, D. H. "Effects of Sleep and Arousal on the Processing of Visual Information in the Cat." *Nature,* 291 (1981), 554-61.

Locke, J., Molyneux, W., Molyneux, T., and Limborch, P. V. *Familiar Letters Between Mr. John Locke, and Several of His Friends: In Which Are Explained His Notions in His Essay Concerning Human Understanding, and in Some of His Other Works.* London: F. Noble, 1742.

Locke, J., and Nidditch, P. H. *An Essay Concerning Human Understanding.* Oxford, England: Clarendon Press, 1975.

Logan, G. D. "Toward an Instance Theory of Automatization." *Psychological Review,* 95 (1988), 492-527.

Lonton, A. P. "The Characteristics of Patients with Encephaloceles." *Zeitschrift für Kinderchirurgie,* 45, Suppl. 1 (1990), 18-19.

Lumer, E. D., Edelman, G. M., and Tononi, G. "Neural Dynamics in a Model of the Thalamocortical System: 1. Layers, Loops and the Emergence of Fast Synchronous Rhythms." *Cerebral Cortex,* 7 (1997), 207-27.

———. "Neural Dynamics in a Model of the Thalamocortical System: 2. The Role of Neural Synchrony Tested Through Perturbations of Spike Timing." *Cerebral Cortex,* 7 (1997), 228-36.

MacKay, D. G., and Miller, M. D. "Semantic Blindness: Repeated Concepts Are Difficult to Encode and Recall Under Time Pressure." *Psychological Science,* 5 (1994), 52-55.

Macknik, S. L., and Livingstone, M. S. "Neuronal Correlates of Visibility and Invisibility in the Primate Visual System." *Nature Neuroscience,* 1 (1998), 144-49.

Maquet, P., Degueldre, C., Delfiore, G., Aerts, J., Péters, J. M., Luxen, A., and Franck, G. "Functional Neuroanatomy of Human Slow Wave Sleep." *Journal of Neuroscience,* 17 (1997), 2807-12.

Marcel, A. J. "Conscious and Unconscious Perception: An Approach to the Relations Between Phenomenal Experience and Perceptual Processes." *Cognitive Psychology,* 15 (1983), 238-300.

_____. "Conscious and Unconscious Perception: Experiments on Visual Masking and Word Recognition." *Cognitive Psychology*, 15 (1983), 197-237.

Marcel, A. J., and Bisiach, E. *Consciousness in Contemporary Science*. Oxford, England: Clarendon Press, 1988.

Maudsley, H. *The Physiology of Mind: Being the First Part of a 3d Ed., Rev., Enl., and in Great Part Rewritten, of "The Physiology and Pathology of Mind."* London: Macmillan, 1876.

Maunsell, J. H. "The Brain's Visual World: Representation of Visual Targets in Cerebral Cortex." *Science*, 270 (1995), 764-69.

McFie, J., and Zangwill, O. L. "Visual-Constructive Disabilities Associated with Lesions of the Left Cerebral Hemisphere." *Brain*, 83 (1960), 243-60.

McGinn, C. "Can We Solve the Mind-Body Problem?" *Mind*, 98 (1989), 349-66.

McIntosh, A. R. "Understanding Neural Interactions in Learning and Memory Using Functional Neuroimaging." *Annals of the New York Academy of Sciences*, 855 (1998), 556-71.

McIntosh, A. R., Rajah, M. N., and Lobaugh, N. J. "Interactions of Prefrontal Cortex in Relation to Awareness in Sensory Learning." *Science*, 284 (1999), 1531–33.

Meador, K. J., Ray, P. G., Day, L., Ghelani, H., and Loring, D. W. "Physiology of Somato-sensory Perception: Cerebral Lateralization and Extinction." *Neurology*, 51 (1998), 721-27.

Menon, V., Freeman, W. J., Cutillo, B. A. Desmond, J. E., Ward, M. F., Bressler, S. L., Laxer, K. D., Barbaro, N., and Gevins, A. S. "Spatio-Temporal Correlations in Human Gamma Band Electrocorticograms." *Electroencephalography & Clinical Neurophysiology*, 98 (1996), 89-102.

Merikle, P. M. "Perception Without Awareness: Critical Issues." *American Psychologist*, 47 (1992), 792-95.

Middleton, F. A., and Strick, P. L. "New Concepts About the Organization of Basal Ganglia Output." *Advances in Neurology*, 74 (1997), 57-68.

Mishkin, M. "Analogous Neural Models for Tactual and Visual Learning." *Neuropsychologia*, 17 (1979), 139-51.

Montplaisir, J., Nielsen, T., Côté, J., Boivin, D., Rouleau, I., and Lapierre, G. "Interhemispheric EEG Coherence Before and after Partial Callosotomy." *Clinical Electroencephalography*, 21 (1990), 42-47.

Morgan, M. J. *Molyneux's Question: Vision, Touch, and the Philosophy of Perception*. Cambridge, England: Cambridge University Press, 1977.

Moruzzi, G., and Magoun, H. W. "Brain Stem Reticular Formation and Activation of the EEG." *Electroencephaly and Clinical Neurophysiology*, 1 (1949), 455-73.

Mountcastle, V. B. "An Organizing Principle for Cerebral Function: The Unit Module and the Distributed System." Pp. 7-50 in *The Mindful Brain: Cortical Organization and the Group-Selective Theory of Higher Brain Function*, eds. G. M. Edelman and V. B. Mountcastle. Cambridge, Mass.: MIT Press, 1978.

Müller, F., Kunesch, E., Binkofski, F., and Freund, H. J. "Residual Sensorimotor Functions in a Patient After Right-Sided Hemispherectomy." *Neuropsychologia*, 29 (1991), 125-45.

Nagel, T. *Mortal Questions*. New York: Cambridge University Press, 1979.

Nakamura, R. K., and Mishkin, M. "Chronic 'Blindness' Following Lesions of Nonvisual Cortex in the Monkey." *Experimental Brain Research*, 63 (1986), 173-84.

Nakamura, R. K., Schein, S. J., and Desimone, R. "Visual Responses from Cells in Striate Cortex of Monkeys Rendered Chronically 'Blind' by Lesions of Nonvisual Cortex." *Experimental Brain Research*, 63 (1986),185-90.

Nehmiah, J. "Dissociation, Conversion, and Somatization." Pp. 248-60 in *American Psychiatric Press Review of Psychiatry*, eds. A. Tasman and S. M. Goldfinger. Washington, D.C.: American Psychiatric Press, 1991.

Newsome, W. T. S. C. D. "The Neuronal Basis of Motion Perception." *Ciba Foundation Symposium*, 174 (1993), 217-30.

Nicolis, G., and Prigogine, I. *Exploring Complexity: An Introduction*. San Francisco: W. H. Freeman, 1989.

Nielsen, T., Montplaisir, J., and Lassonde, M. "Decreased Interhemispheric EEG Coherence During Sleep in Agenesis of the Corpus Callosum." *European Neurology*, 33 (1993), 173-76.

Nini, A., Feingold, A., Slovin, H., and Bergman, H. "Neurons in the Globus Pallidus Do Not Show Correlated Activity in the Normal Monkey, but Phase-Locked Oscillations Appear in the MPTP Model of Parkinsonism." *Journal of Neurophysiology*, 74 (1995), 1800-05.

Norman, D. A., and Shallice, T. "Attention to Action: Willed and Automatic Control of Behavior." Pp. 1-18 in *Consciousness and Self-Regulation*, eds. R. J. Davidson, G. E. Schwartz, and D. Shapiro. New York: Plenum Press, 1986.

Nørretranders, T. *The User Illusion: Cutting Consciousness Down to Size*. New York: Viking Press, 1998.

Nyberg, L., McIntosh, A. R., Cabeza, R., Nilsson, L. G., Houle, S., Habib, R., and Tulving, E. "Network Analysis of Positron Emission Tomography Regional Cerebral Blood Flow Data: Ensemble Inhibition During Episodic Memory Retrieval." *Journal of Neuroscience*, 16 (1996), 3753-59.

Packard, V. O. *The Hidden Persuaders*. New York: D. McKay, 1957.

Papoulis, A. *Probability, Random Variables, and Stochastic Processes*. New York: McGraw-Hill, 1991.

Pashler, H. "Dual-Task Interference in Simple Tasks: Data and Theory." *Psychological Bulletin*, 116 (1994), 220-44.

Penfield, W. *The Excitable Cortex in Conscious Man*. Springfield, Ill.: Charles C Thomas, 1958.

_____. *The Mystery of the Mind: A Critical Study of Consciousness and the Human Brain*. Princeton, N.J.: Princeton University Press, 1975.

Penrose, R. *The Emperor's New Mind: Concerning Computers, Minds, and the Laws of Physics*. New York: Oxford University Press, 1989.

_____. *Shadows of the Mind: A Search for the Missing Science of Consciousness*. New York: Oxford University Press, 1994.

Petersen, S. E., vanMier, H., Fiez, J. A., and Raichle, M. E. "The Effects of Practice on the Functional Anatomy of Task Performance." *Proceedings of the National Academy of Sciences of the United States of America*, 95 (1998), 853-60.

Picton, T. W., and Stuss, D. T. "Neurobiology of Conscious Experience." *Current Opinion in Neurobiology*, 4 (1994), 256-65.

Pigarev, I. N., Nothdurft, H. C., and Kastner, S. "Evidence for Asynchronous Development of Sleep in Cortical Areas." *Neuroreport*, 8 (1997), 2557-60.

Plum, F. "Coma and Related Global Disturbances of the Human Conscious State." Pp. 359-425 in *Normal and Altered States of Function*, eds. A. Peters and E. G. Jones. New York: Plenum Press, 1991.

Posner, M. I. "Attention: The Mechanisms of Consciousness." *Proceedings of the National Academy of Sciences of the United States of America*, 91 (1994), 7398-403.

Posner, M. I., and Raichle, M. E. *Images of Mind*. New York: Scientific American Library, 1994.

Posner, M. I., and Snyder, C. R. R. "Attention and Cognitive Control." Pp. 55-85 in *Information Processing and Cognition: The Loyola Symposium*, ed. R. L. Solso. Hillsdale, N.J.: Lawrence Erlbaum Associates, 1975.

Rager, G., and Singer, W. "The Response of Cat Visual Cortex to Flicker Stimuli of Variable Frequency." *European Journal of Neuroscience*, 10 (1998), 1856-77.

Ramachandran, V. S., and Gregory, R. I. "Perceptual Filling in of Artificially Induced Scotomas in Human Vision." *Nature*, 350 (1991), 699-702.

Reason, J. T., and Mycielska, K. *Absent-minded? The Psychology of Mental Lapses and Everyday Errors.* Englewood Cliffs, N.J.: Prentice Hall, 1982.

Reber, A. S. *Implicit Learning and Tacit Knowledge: An Essay on the Cognitive Unconscious.* Oxford Psychology Series No. 19. New York: Oxford University Press, 1993.

Rechtschaffen, A. "The Single-Mindedness and Isolation of Dreams." *Sleep*, 1 (1978), 97-109.

Rieke, F., Warland D., de Ruyter van Steveninck, B., and Bialek, W. *Spikes: Exploring the Neural Code.* Cambridge, Mass.: MIT Press, 1997.

Rodriguez, E., George, N., Lachaux, J. P., Martinerie, J., Renault, B., and Varela, F. J. "Perception's Shadow: Long-distance Synchronization of Human Brain Activity." *Nature*, 397 (1999), 430-33.

Roland, P. E. *Brain Activation.* New York: Wiley-Liss, 1993.

Rucci, M., Tononi, G., and Edelman, G. M. "Registration of Neural Maps Through Value-Dependent Learning: Modeling the Alignment of Auditory and Visual Maps in the Barn Owl's Optic Tectum." *Journal of Neuroscience*, 17 (1997), 334-52.

Ryle, G. *The Concept of Mind.* London: Hutchinson, 1949.

Sastre, J. P., and Jouvet, M. "Oneiric Behavior in Cats." *Physiology and Behavior*, 22 (1979), 979-89.

Schacter, D. L. "Implicit Knowledge: New Perspectives on Unconscious Processes." *Proceedings of the National Academy of Sciences of the United States of America*, 89 (1992), 11113-17.

Scheibel, A. B. "Anatomical and Physiological Substrates of Arousal: A View from the Bridge." Pp. 55-66 in *The Reticular Formation Revisited*, eds. J. A. Hobson and M. A. B. Brazier. New York: Raven Press, 1980.

Schenck, C. H., Bundlie, S. R., Ettinger, M. G., and Mahowald, M. W. "Chronic Behavioral Disorders of Human REM Sleep: A New Category of Parasomnia." *Sleep*, 9 (1986), 293-308.

Schneider, W., and Shiffrin, R. M. "Controlled and Automatic Human Information Processing: I. Detection, Search, and Attention." *Psychological Review*, 84 (1977), 1-66.

Schultz, W., Dayan, P., and Montague, P. R. "A Neural Substrate of Prediction and Reward." *Science*, 275 (1997), 1593-99.

Schuster, H. G. *Deterministic Chaos: An Introduction*, 2nd rev. ed. New York: VCH, 1988.

Searle, J. R. *The Rediscovery of the Mind.* Cambridge, Mass.: MIT Press, 1992.

_____. "How to Study Consciousness Scientifically." Pp. 21-37 in *Consciousness and Human Identity*, ed. J. Cornwell. Oxford, England: Oxford University Press, 1998.

Seidemann, E., Meilijson, I., Abeles, M., Bergman, H., and Vaadia, E. "Simultaneously Recorded Single Units in the Frontal Cortex Go Through Sequences of Discrete and Stable States in Monkeys Performing a Delayed Localization Task." *Journal of Neuroscience*, 16 (1996), 752-68.

Shannon, C. E., and Weaver, W. *The Mathematical Theory of Communication.* Urbana: University of Illinois Press, 1963.

Shear, J. *Explaining Consciousness: The "Hard Problem."* Cambridge, Mass.: MIT Press, 1997.

Shenberg, D. L., and Logothetis, N. K. "The Role of Temporal Cortical Areas in Perceptual Organization." *Proceedings of the National Academy of Sciences of the United States of America*, 94 (1997), 3408-13.

Shiffrin, R. M., and Schneider, W. "Controlled and Automatic Human Information Processing: II. Perceptual Learning, Automatic Attending and a General Theory." *Psychological Review*, 84 (1977), 127-90.

Simons, D. J., and Levin, D. T. "Change Blindness." *Trends in Cognitive Sciences*, 1 (1997), 261-67.

Simpson, G. G. "The Baldwin Effect." *Evolution*, 7 (1952), 110-17.

Singer, W. "Bilateral EEG Synchronization and Interhemispheric Transfer of Somato-Sensory and Visual Evoked Potentials in Chronic and Acute Split-Brain Preparations of Cat." *Electroencephalography & Clinical Neurophysiology*, 26 (1969), 434.

Singer, W., and Gray, C. M. "Visual Feature Integration and the Temporal Correlation Hypothesis." *Annual Review of Neuroscience*, 18 (1995), 555-86.

Solms, M. *The Neuropsychology of Dreams: A Clinico-Anatomical Study*. Mahwah, N.J.: Lawrence Erlbaum Associates, 1997.

Spencer, H. *First Principles*. New York: D. Appleton, 1920.

Sperling, G. "The Information Available in Brief Visual Presentations" (doctoral diss.). Washington, D.C.: American Psychological Association, 1960.

Sperry, R. W. "Brain Bisection and Consciousness." Pp. 298-313 in *Brain and Conscious Experience*, ed. J. C. Eccles. New York: Springer Verlag, 1966.

_____. "Lateral Specialization in the Surgically Separated Hemispheres." In *Neurosciences: Third Study Program*, eds. F. O. Schmitt and F. G. Worden. Cambridge, Mass.: MIT Press, 1974.

Sporns, O., and Tononi, G. "Selectionism and the Brain." In *International Review of Neurobiology*. San Diego, Calif.: Academic Press, 1994.

Sporns, O., Tononi, G., and Edelman, G. M. "Theoretical Neuroanatomy: Relating Anatomical and Functional Connectivity in Graphs and Cortical Connection Matrices." *Cerebral Cortex*, 10 (2000), 127–41.

_____. "Modeling Perceptual Grouping and Figure-Ground Segregation by Means of Active Reentrant Connections." *Proceedings of the National Academy of Sciences of the United States of America*, 88 (1991), 129-33.

Srinivasan, R., Russell, D. P., Edelman, G. M., and Tononi, G. "Increased Synchronization of Magnetic Responses During Conscious Perception." *Journal of Neuroscience*, 19 (1999), 5435-48.

Stanley, R. P. "Qualia Space." *Journal of Consciousness Studies*, 6 (1999), 49-60.

Steriade, M., and Hobson, J. "Neuronal Activity During the Sleep-Waking Cycle." *Progress in Neurobiology*, 6 (1976), 155-376.

Steriade, M., and McCarley, R. W. *Brainstem Control of Wakefulness and Sleep*. New York: Plenum Press, 1990.

Steriade, M., McCormick, D. A., and Sejnowski, T. J. "Thalamocortical Oscillations in the Sleeping and Aroused Brain." *Science*, 262 (1993), 679-85.

Stroop, J. R. "Studies of Interference in Serial Verbal Reactions." *Journal of Experimental Psychology*, 18 (1935), 643-62.

Taylor, C. *Human Agency and Language*. Philosophical Papers, Vol. 1. Cambridge, England: Cambridge University Press, 1985.

TenHouten, W. D., Walter, D. O., Hoppe, K. D., and Bogen, J. E. "Alexithymia and the Split Brain: V. EEG Alpha-Band Interhemispheric Coherence Analysis." *Psychotherapy and Psychosomatics*, 47 (1987), 1-10.

Titchener, E. B. *An Outline of Psychology*. New York: Macmillan, 1901.

Tononi, G. "Reentry and the Problem of Cortical Integration." *International Review of Neurobiology*, 37 (1994), 127-52.

Tononi, G., Cirelli, C., and Pompeiano, M. "Changes in Gene Expression During the Sleep-Waking Cycle: A New View of Activating Systems." *Archives Italiennes de Biologie,* 134 (1995), 21-37.

Tononi, G., and Edelman, G. M. "Information: In the Stimulus or in the Context?" *Behavioral and Brain Sciences,* 20 (1997), 698-700.

_____. "Consciousness and Complexity." *Science,* 282 (1998), 1846-51.

_____. "Consciousness and the Integration of Information in the Brain." Pp. 245-80 in *Consciousness,* eds. H. H. Jasper, L. Descarries, V. F. Castellucci, and S. Rossignol. New York: Plenum Press, 1998.

_____. "Schizophrenia and the Mechanisms of Conscious Integration." *Brain Research Reviews,* in press.

Tononi, G., Edelman, G. M., and Sporns, O. "Complexity and the Integration of Information in the Brain." *Trends in Cognitive Science,* 2 (1998), 44-52.

Tononi, G., McIntosh, A. R., Russell, D. P., and Edelman, G. M. "Functional Clustering: Identifying Strongly Interactive Brain Regions in Neuroimaging Data." *Neuroimage,* 7 (1998), 133-49.

Tononi, G., Sporns, O., and Edelman, G. M. "Reentry and the Problem of Integrating Multiple Cortical Areas: Simulation of Dynamic Integration in the Visual System." *Cerebral Cortex,* 2 (1992), 310-35.

_____. "A Measure for Brain Complexity: Relating Functional Segregation and Integration in the Nervous System." *Proceedings of the National Academy of Sciences of the United States of America,* 91 (1994), 5033-37.

_____. "A Complexity Measure for Selective Matching of Signals by the Brain." *Proceedings of the National Academy of Sciences of the United States of America,* 93 (1996), 3422-27.

_____. "Measures of Degeneracy and Redundancy in Biological Networks." *Proceedings of the National Academy of Sciences of the United States of America,* 96 (1999), 3257-62.

Tononi, G., Srinivasan, R., Russell, D. P., and Edelman, G. M. "Investigating Neural Correlates of Conscious Perception by Frequency-Tagged Neuromagnetic Responses." *Proceedings of the National Academy of Sciences of the United States of America,* 95 (1998), 3198-203.

Treisman, A., and Schmidt, H. "Illusory Conjunctions in the Perception of Objects." *Cognitive Psychology,* 14 (1982), 107-41.

Trevarthen, C., and Sperry, R. W. "Perceptual Unity of the Ambient Visual Field in Human Commissurotomy Patients." *Brain,* 96 (1973), 547-70.

Vaadia, E., Haalman, I., Abeles, M., Bergman, H., Prut, Y., Slovin, H., and Aertsen, A. "Dynamics of Neuronal Interactions in Monkey Cortex in Relation to Behavioural Events." *Nature,* 373 (1995), 515-18.

Velmans, M. *The Science of Consciousness: Psychological, Neuropsychological and Clinical Reviews.* London: Routledge, 1996.

Vining, E. P., Freeman, J. M., Pillas, D. J., Uematsu, S., Carson, B. S., Brandt, J., Boatman, D., Pulsifer, M. B., and Zuckerberg, A. "Why Would You Remove Half a Brain? The Outcome of 58 Children After Hemispherectomy—The Johns Hopkins Experience: 1968 to 1996." *Pediatrics,* 100 (1997), 163-71.

Warner, R., and Szubka, T. *The Mind-Body Problem: A Guide to the Current Debate.* Cambridge, Mass.: Blackwell, 1994.

Weiskrantz, L. *Consciousness Lost and Found: A Neuropsychological Exploration.* New York: Oxford University Press, 1997.

Wheeler, J. A. *At Home in the Universe.* New York: American Institute of Physics, 1994.

Wray, J., and Edelman, G. M. "A Model of Color Vision Based on Cortical Reentry." *Cerebral Cortex*, 6 (1996), 701-16.

Young, G. B., Ropper, A. H., and Bolton, C. F. *Coma and Impaired Consciousness: A Clinical Perspective*. New York: McGraw-Hill, 1998.

Zeki, S. *A Vision of the Brain*. Boston: Blackwell, 1993.

Zeki, S., and Bartels, A. "The Asynchrony of Consciousness." *Proceedings of the Royal Society of London, Series B—Biological Sciences*, 265 (1998), 1583-85.

Ziemann, U., Steinhoff, B. J., Tergau, F., and Paulus, W. "Transcranial Magnetic Stimulation: Its Current Role in Epilepsy Research." *Epilepsy Research*, 30 (1998), 11-30.

Zurek, W. H. *Complexity, Entropy, and the Physics of Information: The Proceedings of the 1988 Workshop on Complexity, Entropy, and the Physics of Information, Held May-June, 1989, in Santa Fe, New Mexico*. Redwood City, Calif.: Addison-Wesley, 1990.

Credits

Frontispiece. Composite from a detail of Michelangelo's *Creation of Adam*, Sistine Chapel, Rome, and from *Saggio sopra la vera struttura del cervello dell' uomo e degli animali e sopra le funzioni del sistema nervoso*, con figure in rame disegnate ed incise dall' autore, Sassari, Nella Stamperia da S.S.R.M. Privilegiata, 1809, fig. 1, by Luigi Rolando. Biblioteca Nazionale Universitaria, Turin, M.V.G. 321. Figure 1.1. From: *De homine figuris et latinitate donatus*, a Florentio Schuyl, Lugduni Batavorum, apud Franciscum Moyardum & Petrum Leffen, 1662, fig. 34, Biblioteca Comunale dell' Archiginnasio, Bologna: 9F.IV.4. Figure 2.1. "A skeleton contemplates a skull." Permission granted by Octavo Corporation (1999). All right reserved. Figure 2.2. William James, pfMS Am 1092: Pach C–1, by permission of the Houghton Library, Harvard University. Figure 3.1. Henri Rousseau, *Virgin Forest with Setting Sun*. Permission granted by Öffentliche Kunstsammlung Basel, Kunstmuseum. Photo: Öffentliche Kunstsammlung Basel, Martin B,hler. Figure 3.2. "Egyptian-Eyezed Tête-à-Tête" from *Mind Sights*, by Robert Shepard. Permission granted by Roger Shepard. Figure 3.3. From: J.C. Marshall and P.W. Halligan, "Visuo-Spatial Neglect: A New Copying Test to Assess Perceptual Parsing." *Journal of Neurology* 240:37–40, 1993. Permission granted by Springer Verlag. Figure 3.4. Permission granted by David A. Cook, Film Studies Program. Figure 4.1. Modified from: *Fundamental Neuroanatomy*, by Nauta and Feirtag © 1986 by W.H. Freeman and Company. Used with permission. Figure 4.2. From: *Histology of the Nervous System*, 2 Volume Set, by Santiago Ramon y Cajal, translated by Larry Swanson & Neely Swanson, translation copyright © 1995 by Oxford University Press, Inc. Used by permission of Oxford University Press, Inc. Figure 4.3. Modified from: *The Central Nervous System*, by P. Brodal, Oxford University Press, New York, 1992. Permission granted by Tano Ascheoug Publishing, Oslo, Norway. Figures 5.1 and 6. 3. From: R. Srinivasan, D. P. Russell, G. M. Edelman, and G. Tononi, "Increased Synchronization of Magnetic Responses During Conscious Perception." *Journal of Neuroscience*. 19:5435–48 (1999). Permission granted by The Society for Neuroscience. Figure 6.1. From the atlas of Louis Achille Foville's *Traité complet* (1844), Plate VII, Fig. 1; artist E. Beau; engraver F. Bion. Figure 6.2. Bertha Pappenheim. Permission granted by the Institut für Stadtgeschichte, Frankfurt am Main. Figure 7.1. Photograph of Charles Darwin, aged 40 by T. H.

Maguire, 1849. Permission granted by The British Museum. Figure 7.3. Modified from: *Neuroscience*, by M. F. Bear, B. W. Connors, and M. A. Paradiso, Williams & Wilkins, 1996. Permission granted by Williams and Wilkins. Figure 7.4. From: G. M. Edelman, G. N. J. Reeke, W. E. Gall, G. Tononi , D. Williams, and O. Sporns (1992). "Synthetic Neural Modeling Applied to a Real-World Artifact." *Proceedings of the National Academy of Sciences of the United States of America* 89 (15):7267–71. Figure 8.2. Originally published in *National Geographic Magazine*, June 1951, p. 835 (photo by Don C. Knudson). Figure 10.1. From J.W. Scammell, and M. P. Young (1993). "The Connectional Organization of Neural Systems in the Cat Cerebral Cortex." *Current Biology*, 3: 191–200. Figures 10.2. and 10.3. From: G. Tononi, O. Sporns, and G. M. Edelman (1992). "Reentry and the Problem of Integrating Multiple Cortical Areas: Simulation of Dynamic Integration in the Visual System." *Cerebral Cortex* 2 (4):310–35. Permission granted by Oxford University Press. Figure 12.1. Permission granted by Anglo-Australian Observatory. Photography by David Malin. Figure 17.1. From: G. M. Edelman, *Bright Air, Brilliant Fire: On the Matter of the Mind*, New York: Basic Books, 1992. Permission granted by Perseus Books. Figure 17.2. From: *Eve and the Apple, with Counterpart*, by Arcimboldo. Private Collection, Basel, photograph by Peter Hamen.

Index